No. 467
$12.95

# BROADCAST STATION OPERATING GUIDE

By Sol Robinson

TAB BOOKS
BLUE RIDGE SUMMIT, PA. 17214

FIRST EDITION

FIRST PRINTING — JANUARY 1969


Copyright © 1968 by TAB BOOKS



Printed in the United States
of America

Library of Congress Card Number: 68-8649

# Contents

# Foreword

In July of 1967 I was asked to submit an article for publication in BM/E. The subject: Define the most essential factors for successful station operation in small to medium size markets, and explain how these factors can be evolved into operating practices which will improve the station profit picture. Although I was happy to provide the article, it became obvious that a thorough coverage of the subject could only be given in a full length book.

It is not my intention to present a history of the broadcast industry from its early days. This book is mainly for those now involved in the operation of radio stations in small to medium sized markets and for those who might desire to become active in the industry. I do not, however, want to create the impression that those in large markets or population centers do not have many of the same problems of the smaller stations. To the contrary, their problems are similar, and with some embellishment of the methods employed by the so-called "small station operator" many of their problems can be solved.

At the close of World War II the broadcasting industry began to evolve from infancy to adolescence. By that time the pioneers of broadcasting had long since disappeared from the scene or were involved only in large community or network operations. The industry began to expand, with a station literally springing up in practically every area and community of the United States. This so-called second generation, or as I like to refer to them, the adolescent generation of broadcasters, came mainly from the heart of the industry itself. It was the Station Manager, the Radio Engineer, the

Sales Manager, the Program Director and the Announcer who began applying for construction permits and building the radio stations. By sheer numbers they began to dominate the industry. On January 1, 1945 there were 884 AM and 46 FM licensed commercial stations. On January 1, 1950 there were 2051 AM and 733 FM licensed commercial stations. Unfortunately too many of them were idealists, undercapitalized, with little or no knowledge of commercial practices and the concept of broadcasting as a business. Thus, they found themselves in dire straights and had to either close or sell their facilities. Other factors contributing to such failings were the competition of the networks who were still in their hey day and had not yet begun concentrating on the then new medium of television; the "listening loyalty" of the public accustomed to the sound and appeal of the older established stations; the wane of advertising dollars from war-time sponsors who were no longer spending in order to decrease their excess profit taxes; the solid entrenchment of the printed media; the increased competition of the mushrooming industry; and the control by the FCC, through its 1946 "Blue Book," as to the amount of advertising that the medium could accept.

Out of what seemed a debacle, the radio broadcasting industry grew to its maturity. New faces and forces gave industry a potent blood transfusion, introducing many new concepts. The broadcaster developed new attitudes. He became more socially and community oriented. He certainly became more businesslike in his attitude. He was less interested in the so-called glamour of the medium and more interested in dollars and profits. Out of necessity, he had to concern himself with producing quality programming in order to obtain quantity listenership. He began to inquire into the "why's and wherefore's" and made more and more use of the researcher. Showmanship gave way to scientific, proven methods; "hit and miss" programming gave way to "format programming"; the 15-minute, half-hour and full-hour shows gave way to "block programming" and the creation of the "disc jockey"; the three-times-a-day "news report" gave way to the short newscast on the hour and the half hour; the big name comedian to the "personality"; the singer to the "interviewer" and aloofness to a growing consciousness of social problems and involvement in community affairs.

Radio broadcasting did indeed mature. With its maturity,

contrary to the prophets of doom who were proclaiming its impending demise because of the growth of television, it did not become volatile but a voluble, potent, and viable force. Its economic growth now began to draw the attention of the investor. More and more money became available for the construction of new outlets, for purchasing old established financially successful stations as well as new stations that were having financial difficulties. The "sharpies" and the "frequency traders" began to invade the industry. The "29% down" deal became the trader's password and passport. The practice became so acute that the FCC had to promulgate regulations forbidding "trafficking in licenses" and making it mandatory that a licensee operate a facility for a minimum of three years before applying for permission to transfer a license or sell a facility.

Much credit must be given to the FCC for the present sound and stable position of the radio broadcasting industry. There are now more radio receivers and listeners than ever before. The number of radio broadcasting facilities, both AM and FM, is now at an all-time high. The quality of programming and the "catering to the public need" has reached a high degree of excellence. The number of "profit making" stations far exceeds the number of stations in financial difficulty. Where once there was only the "owned and operated" station controlled by the professional, there are now a preponderance of stations operated by the professional but owned by the Investor—the absentee owner who provides the dollars but lets his hired personnel plan and operate the facility. We now have a predominance of individuals in broadcasting who are mainly interested in profits. . .dollars returned in relationship to dollars invested.

Though radio broadcasting facilities are licensed to operate "in the public interest," this does not mean that a broadcaster is forbidden to earn a profit on his investment. Actually the amount of profit he can earn is <u>unlimited</u>! With this in mind I have written this book. . .not as a panacea or catholicon for the problems that plague the industry. . .but rather as a guide or series of suggestions that might prove valuable to the investor, owner, manager, and personnel of radio stations. For those who seek to enter the challenging and rewarding field of radio broadcasting, whether as investors or participants, I hope that they too will find the content interesting, enlightening, and helpful.

Sol Robinson

Danbury, Conn.

## ACKNOWLEDGMENT

In writing this book I have gathered information from innumerable sources in addition to my personal experience as a sales manager, station manager, and owner of several broadcast facilities.

To the researchers, authors of articles in numerous publications, authors on many of the specialized fields in which broadcasting is involved, and to all those who have made it possible for me to accumulate my knowledge of the broadcasting industry I am beholden.

It is an impossibility for me to name or list all the men and women in the broadcasting industry, advertising agencies, professional and business community who through their research, writing, and counselling have aided me in compiling this data. It is only through the combined efforts of all these devoted men and women that the broadcast industry has been able to attain its present stature.

Grateful acknowledgment is herewith offered to all who may find in this book some personal contribution to the vast font of broadcast knowledge.

# CHAPTER 1

# Market Studies

The first step in planning a radio station is a study of the prospective market. There are four principal factors to consider:

1. Market size
2. Audience
3. Availability and distribution of advertising dollars
4. Availability and use of present advertising media

To have a financially successful operation it is necessary that you have a complete understanding of each factor and know how to apply this knowledge to your individual situation.

## Market Size

One of the most important considerations in evaluating the potential success of any new radio station is the size of the market. The only thing a radio station can offer its advertisers is listeners. It is purely academic that if no one is listening, your advertiser's message cannot produce any customers for him. Likewise, it follows that the greater the population the better the possibility to produce a large audience and the better the opportunity for your station to create customer traffic and a greater number of purchasers.

Without a complete knowledge of the likes, dislikes, interests, and activities of your potential audience, it is impossible to intelligently establish a program format for your station. It also follows, that to be financially successful in your undertaking you should know how much money is available in your area for advertising purposes; how much is actually spent; how it is being used; and, how much of this available money you can realistically expect to be spent on your station. To arrive at any reasonably accurate conclusions you must acquaint yourself with all advertising media in the area; how and to what extent they are being used; and, how you can divert an ample share of the available advertising dollars from these media to your station.

## Determining Population

The National Association of Broadcasters, in preparing statistics to be used as a broad yardstick in evaluating and comparing operations in similar markets, uses two categories in defining "market size"—one is population, the other is revenue. They divide total market population into nine categories:

1. 2.5 million or more
2. 1 to 2.5 million
3. 500,000 to 1 million
4. 250,000 to 500,000
5. 100,000 to 250,000
6. 50,000 to 100,000
7. 25,000 to 50,000
8. 10,000 to 25,000
9. Less than 10,000

Once your consulting engineer has furnished you with a "coverage map," indicating the areas served by your primary signal, secondary signal, and intermittent signal, you can begin your survey as to the total population you will serve.

Most states issue a yearly "Register and Manual" in which they give the latest population figures for each county, city, and town. In addition to this, or should such a publication not be available, you should make extensive use of the latest edition of the "United States Census of Population by States," available at most city halls, town halls, libraries, or through the U.S. Department of Labor, Bureau of the Census. If your station is located in any one of the New England States an excellent reference is Sales Management's annual "Survey of Buying Power." I strongly recommend that you make a careful study of census bureau statistics, for in this work much of the demographic breakdown of your potential audience is available.

## Revenue Potential

The second category in the NAB statistics breaks down market revenue potentials into ten categories:

1. $750,000 or more
2. $500,000 to $750,000
3. $300,000 to $500,000
4. $200,000 to $300,000
5. $150,000 to $200,000
6. $125,000 to $150,000
7. $100,000 to $125,000
8. $ 75,000 to $100,000
9. $ 50,000 to $ 75,000
10. less than $50,000

It does not necessarily follow that if your population is small your revenue will be small also. Quite the contrary. There are many stations located in heavily populated markets whose revenue is small; likewise, there are many stations collecting a fairly high revenue in spite of a much smaller population. Market revenue figures should be of great interest, especially when evaluating or comparing your station with others in markets with the same revenue potential. They do not, however, influence an agency time buyer nor do they have much effect in developing local sales.

As a radio station operator you undoubtedly will be seeking financial gain by steadily increasing your revenue. There are many factors and methods to be considered in achieving this goal. They are discussed throughout this book; but, usually, you will find that it is the audience your station can deliver to a sponsor that will be the determining factor in revenue development. The much used cliche says that "everyone loves a winner." Though the financially successful operator receives greater respect than an unsuccessful operator, the advertiser wants but one thing from your station—a large audience that will listen to his message and buy his product or service. He, too, wants to be a "winner," and the amount he spends on radio will depend upon what your station can do to help him attain his goals. First and foremost you must be able to reach an audience in his behalf.

## Audience Demographics

Webster defines an audience as an assembly of hearers.

Yet, an audience is people, and people fall into many categories. They are of different sizes, sex, and ages; single, married, divorced, or widowed; educational levels vary; they work at different occupations and are engaged in various professions; earn different amounts of money and spend it in different ways; people differ as to their likes and dislikes; have different religious and political leanings, and they differ in their awareness to the social needs of their communities and the amount of volunteer service they offer to meet these needs.

Both the advertiser and programmer are no longer interested in reaching the broad mass of people; rather, they go after that very special segment who are potential listeners and customers and have a particular desire for their program, product, or service.

The American Research Bureau, a research and rating service highly respected by the broadcast industry, in their "Radio Circulation Report" segments the audience as to (1) total men; (2) total women; and, (3) teens 12 - 17. But to intelligently program your station and to develop as large an audience as possible you must know more than the demographic measures of age, sex, and income. You must consider desires and preferences. The audience for popular music differs from the audience for classical music, obviously; there are those who prefer news as opposed to music; a certain segment of your audience would rather hear sports broadcasts; and so it goes. Of course, there are overlaps—those preferring a little of each. Though educational levels differ within an audience, do not lose sight of the fact that the gap is slowly but surely diminishing. Today those with only a high school education comprise about 10% of our population; in the not too distant future some 30% or more will have had some exposure to a college education. The Vocational Service Department of B'nai B'rith, the largest Jewish service organization in the world, reports that of the eligible Jewish youth, both male and female, 85% are now enrolled and attending a college or university. This is not unique for this ethnic group alone. The ever increasing college enrollment bears more than mute evidence as to the speed in which the educational gap is closing. By now it must be quite apparent as to why you as a radio station operator must know the differences in the makeup of the population you serve—to determine and intelligently plan your programming schedule to attract the largest possible audience.

## Conducting Audience Surveys

To help in reaching a market feasibility decision you also should seek the following information:

1. The number of <u>households</u> in the area. (Two-family homes are two households; an apartment house has many households.)
2. The <u>number</u> of persons in each household.
3. The number of <u>males</u> and <u>females</u> of all ages.
4. An age breakdown in the following groupings: (a) under 12; (b) 12 - 17; (c) 17 - 25; (d) 25 - 40; (e) 40 - 55; (f) 55 - 68; (g) over 68.
5. A <u>marital</u> <u>status</u> breakdown in the following categories: (a) single; (b) married; (c) divorced or separated; (d) widowed.
6. Annual <u>family</u> <u>income</u> in the following groupings: (a) under $4000; (b) $4000 - $6000; (c) $6000 - $8000; (d) $8000 - $10,000; (e) over $10,000.
7. <u>Educational</u> <u>background</u> in these categories: (a) non-graduates of elementary school; (b) elementary school graduates but no high school exposure; (c) some high school exposure; (d) high school graduates but no college exposure; (e) some college exposure; (f) college graduates.
8. <u>Occupations.</u> If you can ascertain also the working schedules it will be of great help to your program department and enable your sales department in determining the traffic hours. Many advertisers of nationally sold services and products are interested only in having their commercials broadcast during the traffic hours.
9. <u>Professions.</u>
10. <u>Religious</u> <u>preferences.</u>
11. <u>Reading habits</u>: (a) newspapers; (b) books; (c)magazines and periodicals.
12. <u>Radio listening</u> <u>habits</u> broken down as to the time spent listening to the radio per day: (a) less than one hour; (b) 1 - 3 hours; (c) 3 - 5 hours; (d) more than 5 hours. Type of programs listened to: (a) by women; (b) by men; (c) 12 - 17 year age group.

In gathering your information as to the program types preferred you might use these broad categories: (a) newscasts; (b) audience participation; (c) music: popular, standards, religious, orchestra, show tunes, semi-classical, classical, folk, country and western, band, etc.; (d) sports broadcasts; (e) talk shows; (f) discussion programs; (g) religious services or devotionals; (h) dramas, either serialized or complete.

There are many ways to gather this information. In addition to the references previously mentioned you can secure valuable information from the chamber of commerce, school departments, and city directories published by Price and Lee. If your facility is to be located in a large population area you may use the services of many reliable research firms such as C. E. Hooper, Pulse, American Research Bureau, A. C. Nielson, etc. Many of the stations in large population markets have employed noted researchers and sociologists in making specialized studies. The American Broadcasting Company in media surveys for its radio network employed Daniel Yankelovich, Incorporated, who prepared one of the finest reports aimed at giving the advertiser more information about radio and its uses. Radio Station WMCA (New York City), in researching the New York radio audience as to its characteristics, habits, motivations, and tastes, covering New York radio listeners in general and the WMCA listener in particular, had one of the most complete reports presented by the Marketing and Social Research Division of the Psychological Corporation of New York City.

Of course such studies are expensive and I do not suggest that you spend such large sums in making preliminary surveys. Ingenuity is the keyword in saving time and expense. In small markets you can undertake market surveys by creating cooperative programs with area colleges. Such studies generally interest classes in statistics, communications, sociology, psychology, business administration, and political science. Your study should be soundly conceived, carefully executed, and honestly reported. I recommend that you utilize either of the following two methods—the personal interview or the telephone survey, with preference given to the personal interview method.

The personal interview results in a more accurate report, inasmuch as every person in a household may be questioned.

Usually, the interviewer can spend more time with the person and obtain more information. Among the disadvantages ...the expenses involved and the slowness in receiving and compiling the reports. In addition, this method requires a large corps of interviewers. Extreme care must be observed in selecting interviewers and in the preparation of the questionnaire they use.

The telephone survey technique is very popular because of its flexibility and lower cost. Telephone directories are always available and in small market areas telephone charges are relatively low. On the minus side, the interview must be rather brief, and where a lengthy questionnaire is involved this method may be inefficient. It also becomes virtually impossible to interview every member of the household.

In hiring interviewers be sure to advise them that you have no preconceived ideas or prejudices and expect of them an open-minded approach free of previously conceived convictions. Impress upon them the fact that you are seeking only reliable information suitable for the purpose of the survey. There is no doubt that it will be impossible to make a thorough survey in which every household and person will be visited and interviewed. You will have to create a "sample design" and project your findings. Remember, no one has yet created the "one sample," in either size or character, which will give answers to all the questions desired. The size of your sample will have to depend on the various categories you want to explore, the type and scope of the desired information, and the survey technique to be used. By all means make full use of the U.S. Census Bureau reports. They come closest to being the one single reference source that will supply you with the greatest amount of desired information.

## Availability and Distribution of Advertising Dollars

Just as we recommend wide use of census bureau reports for the demographic breakdown, we highly recommend Sales Management's "Survey of Buying Power" when determining the availability and use of advertising dollars. The "Top Ten" markets listed by this publication in June, 1966 are:

      1.  New York, New York
      2.  Chicago, Illinois

3. Los Angeles, California
4. Philadelphia, Pennsylvania
5. Detroit, Michigan
6. Houston, Texas
7. Baltimore, Maryland
8. Cleveland, Ohio
9. Dallas, Texas
10. Washington, D.C.

Strangely enough, perhaps, not only are these the top ten in population but also the top ten in retail sales. The retail sales figure for New York City for the year 1965 was $11,574,028,000. In Chicago it was $6,496,882,000. In Los Angeles the figure was $4,927,805,000. The tenth city, Washington, D.C., had retail sales of $1,618,338,000. New York City had 4.11% of all retail sales in the United States. Chicago had 2.31%.

The availability of advertising dollars in an area depends entirely upon retail sales and the number of retail outlets. Retailers generally allocate advertising dollars in proportion to the amount of their sales revenue, not to the amount of profit, and this percentage varies with retail categories. Food stores generally do not spend more than 2% of their gross revenue on advertising. Department stores do not spend more than 4%, while some credit jewelers and furniture stores spend as high as 10%. There is no set percentage figure for each and every retail category. Most certified public accountants frown upon advertising expenditures exceeding 4% of their client's gross retail sales. They do this regardless of their client's retail category, or the amount or degree of the competition faced by their client. It is very difficult to advise any retailer as to how much he should spend on advertising, since no one has ever been able to exactly measure the return or sales potential of any advertising campaign. The individual who can come up with this yardstick can open a two-by-four office on Madison Avenue (New York's "advertising" district) and reap a huge fortune.

As a potential radio station operator it is incumbent upon you to know the exact number of outlets in each retail category within the area, as well as the total retail sales per category and individual outlet. Most economists use the following broad retail categories:

1. Food stores and markets.
2. Eating and drinking establishments.
3. Department stores (includes 5 & 10¢ stores).
4. Apparel stores: (a) men; (b) women; (c) teenagers (12 - 17); (d) children.
5. Furniture stores.
6. Household appliance stores.
7. Automobile: (a) new; (b) used.
8. Gas stations.
9. Building trades: (a) lumber; (b) hardware; (c) masonry, including concrete.
10. Drug: (a) pharmacies; (b) cosmetic stores.
11. Mail order concerns serving the area.

The figures in each category should be obtainable from the local chamber of commerce, advertising agency executives, the Census Bureau, and from Sales Management's "Survey of Buying Power." Another good source is the city or state's sales tax department, if your facility is to be located in a city or state which levies such a tax; however, these figures may not be accurate, inasmuch as certain items and/or age groups are usually excluded from such taxes.

The reason I suggest knowing the exact number of outlets per category becomes more apparent as you examine each category. Though total retail sales reported by food stores and markets is high, should your station be located in an area where there are few "supermarkets" and a proliferation of small independent neighborhood grocery stores and vegetable markets, it is almost impossible to obtain much advertising revenue from this category. The same theory applies to eating and drinking establishments. Here, again, if there is a large number of neighborhood "bars and grills," the advertising dollar potential is practically nil; however, the greater the number of bars in an area the greater the retail sales reported for beer. (This figure should be used to get the beer distributor and brewery to spend national advertising dollars on your station.) Department stores are very good prospects;

they usually spend up to 4% of their sales revenue for advertising. Five and dime stores on the other hand spend much more for what is called "A-one locations" than on advertising. If they do advertise, it is usually on a periodic basis with emphasis on the big-dollar items.

Apparel stores are an excellent source for advertising dollars, with women's specialty shops as prime customers. These advertisers, like the department store, are steady customers, with additional expenditures during special periods ...like Easter, Mother's Day, and Christmas. Do not overlook the teenage market. Studies indicate that this segment of the population has surprisingly large sums of money at their disposal, and more and more department stores are creating "teen shops" and concentrating on this market.

Furniture stores are a great source of advertising revenue. Many—especially those who specialize in installment buying— spend up to 10% of their sales revenue for advertising. Most retailers work on a 33 1/3% markup, but there doesn't seem to be a set markup in the furniture trade (many work on a 50% markup, approximately). Household appliance stores should be one of the main revenue sources. They deal in a high-dollar items and usually are recipients of cooperative advertising programs in which the distributor and manufacturer reimburse them at a rate from 50% to as high as 75% of their advertising costs. With few exceptions drug stores do not spend much for advertising purposes; however, cosmetic and cut rate drug stores do advertise frequently, especially before St. Valentine's Day, Mother's Day, and Christmas.

Most automobile dealers advertise to create a market for used cars. Among automobile dealers there is an axiom that 80% of new car buyers always buy new cars, and 90% of used car buyers never buy new cars. Auto dealers concentrate on new car sales during two periods of the year—when the new car is introduced and at the close of the year to move their new car inventory prior to the introduction of the next year's models. Even during these concentrated periods they usually prepare their advertising message to include used cars. Such reasoning is quite logical from an economic standpoint— seldom does a new car dealer just sell a new car, nor does he make a profit on the sale of a new car until after the third sale of the transaction. It goes as follows: When he sells a new car a used car is generally taken in trade, along with some cash; when he sells this first used car he usually takes another used car in trade (along with cash); it is only when he sells the second used car (for which he generally gets all cash) that he is through with the transaction and able to assess his profit. Therefore, the bulk of automobile dealer advertising must be concentrated on used cars on a year-around basis. A word of caution regarding the automotive trade. Most surveys indicating retail sales include all automotive parts such as tires, batteries, spark plugs, etc. With the exception of tires, very few dollars are spent by retailers to advertise the other products. In making your calculations be sure to take this into consideration. In fact, it is a good idea to set up a sub-title of "tires" in this category. Tire dealers can be another source of advertising revenue, especially during the period preceding the need for snow tires and in the spring of the year.

Gas station operators are one of the poorest revenue sources. They rely entirely ypon distributor advertising. Most gasoline stations are independently owned and operated, and very few return more than a living wage to their owners. The local gas station operator strives to build up a following in his area by the quality of individual service he can furnish. If located on a main thoroughfare he relies upon the brand of gasoline he is selling to attract the traveler. For this "plus" he looks to the distributor for advertising assistance—"credit cards," displays, giveaways, and the use of all available advertising media. Unless your radio station is located in a top market it will take a unique situation for you to receive any of this money.

Do not overlook the building trades industry as a source of advertising dollars. Lumber yards and dealers are finding it more and more profitable to advertise, especially since the advent of "do-it-yourselfer." Hardware stores are becoming better advertisers, not only for the same reason, but because they are attempting to reach wider markets—household appliances and kitchenware, including china and glassware. Very little advertising dollars can be expected from masonry and concrete establishments. Whatever they do spend will be for specialized services such as paving and repairing driveways. However, they can be a good source of "institutional advertising" revenue.

You may be wondering why I have included so many categories which traditionally spend very little on advertising. Your revenue from advertising will come not only from the retailer, but also (I hope) from the advertiser of nationally sold products and services. In order to interest manufacturers and distributors it is necessary for you to show that large sums are spent for these products and services in your area. If large potential markets exist the national advertiser will use local media with three views in mind: (1) to advise his potential customers of the product or service; (2) to keep his present customers from switching to another brand; and, (3) lure users of other brands over to his product or service. Of course, he will not advertise in any area where he doesn't have distribution, but if enough retail sales are reported for a given product or service he will attempt to establish such distribution.

Mail order sales, in many areas, are important for several reasons. Not only are high volume mail order firms an excellent prospect for advertising revenue, but also another source of sales figures. An explanation as to your interest in these figures should bring cooperation. Mail order firms usually specialize in the sale of brand name or nationally advertised items. These figures added to those already compiled should enhance your image in the eyes of brand name manufacturers and distributors. Several business categories usually not included in retail sales reports also are great potentials for advertising revenues. These can be called the "service" groups with an annual volume running into the billions. Considerable sums are spent in advertising their services through various local media.

Banking institutions, both commercial and savings banks, spend far more advertising their services today than ever dreamed of in the days when a banker considered himself the sole guardian of the community's wealth. Just like every industry which began essentially with one type of product or service, the banking business has become quite diversified. Banks were originally formed to safeguard gold, money, and other valuables. From that they progressed to lending, then to various types of savings, loans, and all the myriad services they now perform. To a banker today advertising is his lifeline for increased deposits, enabling him to offer his many services that result in increased profits. Also in this category are the investment banking and stock brokerage houses who also are spending large sums of money in advertising their services.

While on the subject of loans, do not overlook the "small" loan and auto loan companies. Such operations have changed during the last few years. In the past these companies, working on the assumption that people didn't want to be seen entering or leaving their places of business, generally rented space on the second floor of office buildings or in stores located off the main thoroughfare. To offset the consequence of secondary area locations they spent large sums in advertising. Today, realizing that practically everyone is borrowing in one form or another, and that no stigma is placed upon a person who does business with them, small loan companies are now locating in what is called "prime locations." To offset the higher rental expenditures many companies cut back on advertising outlays. But with the added effort inaugurated by commercial and savings banks to increase their small loan business most finance companies have returned to the policy of mass media advertising. They now look upon their prime location as an added service to their customers.

Those businesses engaged in what is referred to as the "entertainment field" are also a good source of advertising revenues. The neighborhood movie theatre generally changes its feature at least once a week and the theatre operator has turned more and more to radio to advertise his current and upcoming attractions. He finds it to be one of the cheapest "dollar per thousand" expenditures. In making your projections do not overlook the following recreational facilities: bowling alleys, billiard parlors, riding academies, and theatres and theatrical groups catering to the drama and musical connoisseur. We might also include in this category the various schools offering instruction in singing, dancing, art, musical instruments, as well as artists, art galleries, and dealers in antiques; also, country clubs whose golf course, swimming pool, and other facilities are open to the public.

The entire area of services dealing with repairs and renovations should be included in your survey, too. Among these are the following: air conditioning and heating servicemen, radio, hi-fi, and TV repairmen, shoe repair and hat renovating establishments, auto repair services (body shops, towing, wreckers, etc.), furniture repair shops and upholsterers, chimney cleaning and repair, contractors who specialize in home and office repairs and renovation, painters and decorators, landscape gardeners and lawn care specialists, piano tuners and repairmen, plumbers, electricians, roof repairers, window cleaners, exterminators, snow and garbage removal servcies, and silversmiths. All of these firms offer valuable and needed services which stand to benefit from radio as an advertising medium. Likewise, don't overlook travel agencies, the aviation services in your area that offer air freight, charter flight, and courses in flying and aerial photography, marinas and other related services to the boating fraternity, transportation facilities such as bus lines and railroad companies, auto and truck rental agencies, and taxi and limousine services.

Among frequent advertisers in the service field are: hearing aid firms, diaper servcies, morticians (funeral homes), privately owned convalescent homes and hospitals, ambulance services, day camps and day nurseries, kennels, and the myriad of services connected with the boarding, grooming, and care of pets, opticians, photographers, and hotels and motels. Barber shops as a rule seldom make use of any advertising media. However, many beauty salons and massage parlors advertise their services extensively, as do dry cleaning establishments, tailors who specialize in repairs and remodeling, costume and formal wear rental shops, florists, "second-hand" stores, pawn brokers, carpet and rug cleaners, coin and stamp dealers, food freezer plan operators, employment agencies, and wholesale printers and stationers, especially those selling business machines like typewriters, adding machines, office furniture, etc.

The following three categories have been saved to conclude this section because they deserve special consideration—moving and storage services, real estate operators and developers, and insurance agencies. More and more today we find that the independent local moving and storage company is becoming a thing of the past. Practically every local firm is now or will soon be affiliated with an interstate group. This group can be an excellent source of revenue, but it requires an educated and knowledgeable approach. Most moving and storage companies advertise heavily in the "yellow pages" of the telephone directory. They will tell you that 90 to 95% of the time the homeowner will tell them, in answer to their inquiry as to how they came to call their particular firm, that they "got them out of the yellow pages." This undoubtedly is true. To overcome this I suggest the following approach.

Open the telephone directory to his advertisement. Point out to your client the vast number of competitors who are likewise listed there. Ask him why the customer chose his ad from among the many, not only in this section of the directory but on the same page. Point out to him that, in all likelihood, his company was chosen at the recommendation of a satisfied customer. People who are about to move generally seek the advice of those who have recently moved or know that a particular firm moved a friend, and his survey should reflect this information. In other words, his query should not stop with the "yellow pages" response; at best, probably, the yellow pages ad merely served as a reminder and supplied the telephone number. Also, at one time or another, the customer must have seen his vans with the company name emblazoned on both sides. If not, why waste money in painting the van. They also at one time or another have seen his or his affiliate's ad in the newspaper or heard it on radio or seen it on TV. Very few people move constantly, and they do not save moving company ads or write down the telephone number of moving concerns. When they are ready to move they go to the directory and while perusing the ads the name rings a bell—they saw his van, remembered that he had moved a friend who was satisfied with the service, they were told by a friend that this is a reliable concern, they had used him once before. Therefore the only real thing his telephone directory ad did was to provide the motivation in the choice.

When it comes to the real estate operator, do not overestimate the amount of revenue you can get from this group, unless they are development operators. Though the real estate operator, or the realtor as he likes to be called, usually has more than one house for sale, his advertisements generally list but one house. The person in the market for a house is interested only in buying one house, so a good real estate ad will list all of the pertinent information and stress the features of a particular house. People do not listen that closely to radio commercials as to be able to absorb all this information. House buyers also have become "shoppers" and want to see several houses before they make a decision. It is much simpler for them to turn to the real estate section of the newspaper and read and compare offerings before they contact the realtor for an appointment. It would be impossible for a radio station to give this kind of service. The messages would necessarily have to be given very slowly and the repetition of one offering after another would only confuse the listener. In addition, you would lose many listeners who are not interested in buying a house. They will listen to a one-minute commercial in which they are not interested, but fifteen or more such commercials bunched together, one after the other, would seem an eternity. You would lose this listener not only for this segment of your program time but most likely for the balance of the day, should he become engrossed in listening to another station. Remember, you owe it to all your advertisers to deliver as large a listening audience as possible.

However, when it comes to a real estate developer the picture changes radically. The realtor or builder who is opening a new development will find that radio advertising is his best media. He can deliver his message in one minute. He has more than one house to sell in one area. He is interested in mass response, not only in buyers but also in "lookers." A series of twenty one-minute announcements in a day will bring him a greater response than a full page ad in a newspaper, because radio reaches the out-of-town prospect who doesn't read the local paper. Don't discount the worker who commutes to his job and would like to locate near his place of employment. He generally doesn't read the local paper but does listen to the local radio station while traveling to and from work, so he is a real prime target for the developer and can best be reached by radio at the lowest cost. But don't be misled into thinking that you can derive a large amount of advertising dollars from this group. First of all the number of real estate developments are very few and when they do occur they are well spaced out. Secondly, the developer will advertise only during the initial phases of the development. When the largest proportion of his development is sold he then will resort to using the classified section or real estate section of the newspaper to dispose of the "left overs" on an individual house basis.

Insurance agencies are a good source of radio advertising revenue. Just like banking institutions and other businesses which began essentially with one type of service, the insurance industry also has become greatly segmented. Every personal activity from birth to death can be covered by insurance. This coverage pertains to everyone whether they are active in business, retired, young, or adult. In every community, no matter how small, there is a segment of the business population dealing in insurance. Some of these firms specialize only in life insurance, but on the whole you will find that today's insurance agent can provide any and all types of coverage. There is, of course, life insurance, insurance against multiple births, health, accident, hospitalization, income, retirement, fire, theft, casualty, auto, home and mortgage, rain, education, and many, many more. I list these activities to indicate the complexity and the challenges you face when you secure an insurance account. It is most foolish indeed to try to sell all of these services in any one commercial, unless perhaps it is an institutional type of advertisement. Insurance costs and premiums vary with such things as age, location, hazards, etc., so it becomes impossible to advertise prices. Once you can intelligently explain this to a prospective insurance advertiser and get him to accept the fact that in each of his ads he should concentrate on one phase of his operations, the better his results and the larger his advertising expenditures. So in making your survey as to the advertising dollars available in a community be sure to include the revenue that can be derived from this source.

## Availability and Use of Present Advertising Media

To round out your survey you must become acquainted with the various advertising media available in the community, how they are being utilized, and what inroads you can expect to make. Depending on the population and size of the community, these are the prime media generally used by advertisers:

1. Newspapers
2. Periodicals
3. Directories
4. Billboards
5. Transportation (bus cards, taxis, etc.)
6. Direct Mail
7. TV
8. Radio

The above list is not intended to reflect popularity or importance, since they will vary from community to community due to many factors such as: longevity in the community, advertiser orientation, results obtained, available service, the ingenuity of the medium sales staff, etc. Each medium offers the advertiser specific advantages, depending on his individual need.

Advertising falls into two main categories—institutional and merchandising. I mention this now because too often one finds that advertisers are using the wrong medium and a knowledgeable radio time salesman can divert some of those mis-spent funds to his station.

Institutional advertising promotes the overall image of a firm or one of its specific activities or products. Its purpose is to create goodwill, prestige, and recognition, rather than to produce immediate sales. Many times a more dignified approach is taken instead of the strong "commercial" sound. Institutional advertising seldom quotes prices of articles and should not try to explain in detail the product or service that is being offered.

Merchandising advertising is exactly what its name implies, for merchandise is defined as things, goods, commodities, and wares that are bought and sold. In addition to being used to acquaint prospective customers with an advertiser's product or service, his name and location, it must quote prices, explain the product or service in detail, and create immediate and increased sales. By means of such "merchandising" advertisements one can also create prestige, goodwill, and a reputation for his establishment.

There are very few literate people who do not read at least one newspaper a day. Although we are fast approaching (and many say we have arrived at) the age of the "one newspaper city," those newspapers now being published are being read. A recent study made in New York City indicates that only about 13% of the people do not read a newspaper printed in the English language. (This group is strongly dependent upon radio and television as their source of news.) Not only do today's newspapers enjoy large paid circulations but they also are the recipient of billions of dollars in advertising revenue. The Los Angeles _Times_ says it published 101,414,589 lines of advertising in 1965. This is equivalent to 41,000 full pages! The Chicago _Tribune_ lists its 1965 advertising revenue at $85,000,000. Airline advertising alone accounted for $2,463,000. _Parade_, a Sunday newspaper supplement, claims that they reach 12,600,000 families through 75 newspapers each week. The Scripps-Howard newspaper chain claims a paid weekly circulation of 9,941,089 homes representing an income of 23 billion dollars.

Every newspaper today woos the advertiser on both the local and national level. Their advertising departments constantly research their area along the same lines suggested in this chapter and use this information to obtain advertising. The Philadelphia _Inquirer_ has a special department within its advertising department that offers to supply any advertiser with audience demographics to match his marketing objectives. They offer to provide comparable figures for newspapers, magazines, and radio and television audiences covering their circulation area. I mention all of this because radio station operators must be alerted, if they are not now aware of it, that in any given area the number one competition for the advertising dollar is the newspaper. This is especially true in small or medium markets served by a local daily newspaper.

You must, if you want to be financially successful, know everything about all newspapers in the area you have selected for your radio station. What is their daily circulation? How much advertising lineage do they print daily, weekly, and monthly? What are their rates? What is their total advertising revenue from local advertisers? What is their advertising revenue from national advertisers? In what categories do these advertisers fall? How much of this advertising can you divert from newspaper to radio? Don't forget to include any weekly shopping guides. From 80% to 90% of their space is devoted to advertising. By adding up the advertising lineage and multiplying this figure by the charges as listed on the newspaper's rate card you can easily arrive at the advertising revenue figure. It is suggested, however, that you add up only the lineage of those accounts that you feel reasonably sure are potential advertisers for your planned radio station.

One category that you should pay particular attention to is the advertiser who is using the newspaper for institutional advertising. The newspaper is primarily a merchandising medium, and to use a newspaper for institutional advertising in most cases is a very costly practice. Therefore, those advertisers are very good prospects for radio. Also check on the number of national advertisers. If the newspaper is carrying any national advertising you can be sure he has distribution in your area. The knowledge of the retail sales volume in this category and the number of outlets dispensing his product or service will be of great help to you in diverting some of this revenue from the newspaper to your station.

Notwithstanding the demise of many periodicals due to the great popularity of television and the curtailment of advertising revenues, people in large numbers do read magazines. The W. R. Simmons and Associates Research, Incorporated, reports that of those people earning $15,000 a year or more 16% read Time; 20.4% read Newsweek; 25.5% read Fortune; and, 48.2% read Business Week. Life magazine claims 32,000,000 readers and gives the following demographics: 42.1% of the households have incomes of $8,000 per year, 27.7% of the households have incomes of $10,000 per year or over, 34.6% of the heads of households have had some exposure to college, 30.9% of the household heads are in a professional or managerial profession, 36.6% of its adult readers are in the 18 - 34 age group, and 33.4% of its adult readers are in the 35 - 49 age group. U.S. News and World Report states in their promotional material that they have over 1,400,000 subscribers and boast of never having sold door-to-door subscriptions.

The <u>Ladies</u> <u>Home</u> <u>Journal</u> claims a circulation of 6,700,000 as of July, 1966, with tremendous increases in advertising lineage and revenue; the <u>Farm</u> <u>Journal</u> lists a circulation of 3,000,000. The <u>National</u> <u>Geographic</u> magazine estimated that their circulation base would reach to over 5 million in 1966. They claim that one in every three families in the U.S. with incomes of $25,000 or more per year read their publication. <u>Woman's</u> <u>Day</u> claimed a circulation of 7,000,000 in 1966 and states that 77.5% of their readers are married, 52% earn $8,000 or more per year, and 72.4% are high school graduates. Add to these such magazines as <u>Look</u>, the <u>Saturday</u> <u>Evening</u> <u>Post</u>, the <u>Readers</u> <u>Digest</u>, <u>Good</u> <u>Housekeeping</u>, <u>The</u> <u>New</u> <u>Yorker</u> and many, many others too numerous to list, and you can readily see that people do and still are reading magazines. In fact, a recent survey in New York City produced the startling statistic that out of 1800 people asked, some 36% of them had read a magazine that day!

With very rare exceptions advertisers use magazines as an institutional advertising medium. You seldom see prices quoted. Advertisements usually try to acquaint prospective customers with a product or service and where it can be obtained. The ads are used primarily to gain prestige and goodwill with the hope that over a period of time there will be an increase in sales. Again, with a view toward projecting national advertising revenue, you should acquaint yourself with the advertisers using the magazines read by the poeple in your area. If the retail sales survey indicates these products have distribution in your area you should be able to funnel some of those advertising dollars into radio. Often, though, you find items and services advertised in magazines <u>with</u> circulation in your area that do not have any distribution in your area.

Directory advertising is a popular medium, with the telephone company directory "yellow pages" the largest in this group. In addition, the directories published by Price and Lee for the various cities and towns carries a great deal of advertising lineage. Directories as an advertising medium should be used only for institutional advertising. By the very nature of the medium one can understand why an intelligent advertiser would not try to use a directory for merchandising purposes. However, you should be able to make good use of the directory in compiling a list of prospective clients.

Billboards, bus cards, and placards should also interest you. Though all three were designed for and used only for institutional advertising they readily give you an insight into what products and services have distribution in your area. Unlike magazines and some directories they are located in your local area to attract the attention of local people. They are sometimes referred to as "point-of-sale" advertising. Remember, they cannot use these media for merchandising advertising but every institutional type of advertiser is a potential merchandising type of advertiser if properly approached and intelligently sold.

"Direct mail" is one of the most misused and misunderstood forms of advertising. The cost per thousand prospects is very high, in many instances much higher than any other media. Persons who have devoted their lifetime to making a study of the advertising field often state that no one should employ this advertising technique if there is a merchandising medium available to them. These experts say that direct mail advertising, if it is necessary, should be used only with the following three thoughts in mind:

1. To contact presently active customers and acquaint them with some special event or with a product or service you plan to offer at a saving or reduced price.

2. To contact former customers who for some reason have not patronized your establishment recently. The special sale, with emphasis on prices and savings, is the hoped for tool to re-establish them as customers.

3. To contact prospective customers who have never had any business dealings with you, and to acquaint them with your location and the products or services you can make available to them at prices less than those being offered by your competitors.

It is common practice for people who regard direct mail advertising as "trash mail" to discard it without ever opening or reading it, especially if they don't know you, haven't heard about you, or ever done business with you. A person who is at present a customer of yours will in most instances open and read your mail. A person who at one time was a customer but is now in your dormant file also will in most instances open a piece of direct mail. Their curiosity will be aroused as to why you are contacting them. But seldom, if ever, will those who have had no contact with you open a piece of direct mail advertising.

Other disadvantages accompany direct mail advertising, too. The advertising "piece" will come to the attention of your competitor, allowing him to merchandise the same product or service at a lower price, thus creating the image that you are a "high-priced establishment." And as direct mail is used for future events it will also alert your competition. The time that must be spent in developing and sending the mailing piece, as well as the cost of printing and postage, can be prohibitive; and, last but not least is the proven small return for the dollar spent. A survey as to those who use direct mail and the amount they spend should give the radio station operator an idea as to the amount of revenue he might be able to acquire by making a merchandising medium available to this group of advertisers.

Of all advertising media available television is by far the best and finest. It combines the oral and visual medium and lends itself to both institutional and merchandising advertising. Because of its visual aspects TV can overcome language and literacy problems, and with the large number of TV sets now in use it can deliver a very large audience. As an industry it receives the largest amount of the available advertising dollar. If there is a local television station in your radio area every effort should be made to ascertain its advertising revenue and to obtain a list of advertisers using the station. Those who advertise on TV generally buy advertising in the other media as a "back-up."

Although its cost per thousand may be small its cost per message is rather high, especially when one considers the cost of producing the commercial, talent fees, and production costs if the advertiser is sponsoring a program. The medium is generally used by the more affluent merchants in the area, and they seldom "put their eggs in one basket." They are excellent prospects for advertising revenue for every advertising media. Those national sponsors on local TV should be approached in the same manner using the same technique that we discussed above. If there is no local TV station, you should survey the TV outlets watched by residents in your market; the national advertisers on these stations are all very good prospects for your station if there is distribution in your area and the retail sales for the product or service is high.

Radio, like TV, lends itself to both institutional and merchandising advertising. Because of its oral aspects it easily overcomes any literacy problems. And with at least 3 to 4 radio sets in practically every home it can deliver the largest audience possible. In addition, there are the millions of radio sets in automobiles, plus the millions of battery-operated portable receivers that allow listening in every part of the house, the street, the beach, the boat, the airplane, etc. It is listened to by people of all ages, income levels, educational achievements, occupations, or professions. Its cost per thousand makes it one of the least expensive of all advertising media.

If there is a radio station now operating in the area, every effort must be made to ascertain its advertising revenue and to obtain a list of sponsors. You should also try to ascertain what percentage of the area advertising dollar is being spent on that station. Is it getting its fair and full share of the advertising dollar? What are its rates? Are they too high or too low? Is the station accepted by both the listening public and the business community? Has the station reached its full capacity or is it growing? Will you be able to financially compete with the existing station, or will the introduction of another station mean financial chaos for both of you? Does anticipated area growth indicate that both of you can expect to be financially successful? What is the number and quality of his staff?

The economic survey cannot be completed unless prime consideration is given to any radio station competition. Unfortunately, though, you cannot base a survey on the business of an existing radio station. You must complete the study in its entirety before you begin a survey of an existing radio station, otherwise you will not have any facts on which to base your answers to the questions just posed regarding competition from such a station. Of course, if no radio station is operating in your area you will be spared this part of the survey.

# CHAPTER 2

# Programming and the FCC

In preparing a program schedule there are three criteria a radio station operator must consider:

1.  The individual station's audience survey.
2.  A complete understanding of all FCC programming requirements.
3.  The programming intentions stated in the original license application or renewal application.

People listen to radio for many and varied reasons—personal enjoyment, information, music, sports, news, and information to satisfy psychological and sociological motives, and for the creation of a mood. It is impossible for any radio station, or for that matter any communications medium, to satisfy the needs and desires of all the people all the time. However, by knowing and understanding the varying needs of your potential audience you can create a program schedule emphasising those areas of greatest appeal and minimize those areas of the weakest appeal, thereby insuring the largest possible audience for your station.

If the people in your area are characteristic of the average radio listener you will discover the following listening habits. In the morning prior to 9 AM your audience will include teenagers, adult men and women, and older adults; from 9 AM to 12 noon it will be composed of adult women and older adult men and women; from 12 noon to 2 PM it will consist of young adult men and women and older adults; from 2 to 5 PM primarily teenagers and young adults, and in the evening hours the audience is generally made up of teenagers and adult males. To achieve the status of the "ideal" radio station with the largest possible audience, your programming must be enjoyable and cater to the individual's different interests and tastes for music, news, sports, discussions, and interviews in the field of art, literature, and science. Obtrusiveness and offensiveness must be avoided at all costs. Remember the old adage "you can catch more flies with sugar than with vinegar."

## Formulating a Program Schedule

Inasmuch as the FCC is charged with the licensing and supervision of broadcast operations it is most important that a station operator be fully informed as to all the FCC requirements, rules, and regulations, especially as they pertain to programming. The FCC by law is not permitted to act as a censor. The Commission stated in its "1960 Report and Statement of Policy" that its pronouncements "have never been intended as a rigid mold or fixed formula for station operation. The ascertainment of the needed program elements for the audience he is obligated to serve remains primarily the function of the licensee. The Commission further stated that "any other course would tend to substitute the judgment of the Commission for that of the licensee."

In planning a program schedule the Commission desires that the licensee: (a) consider the taste, needs, and desires of the public he is licensed to serve, (b) exercise conscientious efforts not only to ascertain them but also to carry them out as well as he reasonably can, (c) reasonably attempt to meet all such needs and interests on an equitable basis, (d) take the necessary steps to inform himself of the real needs and interests of the areas he serves and to provide programming to meet these needs and interests, and provide: (1) opportunity for the development and use of local talent, (2) programs for children, religious groups, educational institutions and political candidates, (3) programs that cover the following categories: local self expression, public affairs, editorials, agriculture, news, weather and market reports, sports, service to minority groups, and entertainment.

The FCC defines various program types as follows:

Agricultural Programs: Information specifically addressed, or primarily of interest, to the agricultural population, including market reports and farming information.

Entertainment Programs: All programs intended primarily as entertainment, such as music, drama, variety, comedy, quiz, etc.

News Programs: Reports dealing with current local, national, and international events, including weather and stock market reports, and when an integral part of a news program, commentary, analysis and sports news.

Public Affairs Programs: Talks, commentaries, discussions, speeches, editorials, political programs, documentaries, forums, panels, round tables, and similar programs primarily concerning local, national, and international public affairs.

Religious Programs: Sermons or devotionals, religious news, and music, drama and other types of programs designed primarily for religious purposes.

Instructional Programs: Programs (other than those classified under agricultural, news, public affairs, religious or sports) involving the discussion of, or primarily designed to further an appreciation or understanding of literature, music, fine arts, history, geography, and the natural and social sciences: programs devoted to occupational and vocational instruction, instruction with respect to hobbies, and similar programs intended primarily to instruct.

Sports Programs: Includes play-by-play and pre- or post-game related activities, and separate programs of sports instructions, news or information (e.g., fishing opportunities, golfing instructions, etc.)

Other Programs: All programs not falling within the previous definitions.

Editorials: Programs presented for the purpose of stating opinions of the licensee.

Political Programs: Those which present candidates for public office or which give expression (other than in station editorials) to views on such candidates or on issues subject to public ballot.

Educational Institution Programs: Any programs prepared by, in behalf of, or in cooperation with, educational institutions, educational organizations, libraries, museums, PTAs or similar organizations. Sports programs shall not be included.

The FCC defines various program sources as follows:

Local Program: Any program orginated or produced by the station, or for the production of which the station is substantially responsible, and employing live talent more than 50% of the time. Such a program, taped, recorded, or filmed for later broadcast shall be classified by the station as local. A local program fed to a network shall be classified by the originating station as local. All non-network news programs may be classified as local. Programs primarily featuring syndicated or feature films or other non-locally recorded programs shall be classified as "recorded" even though a station personality appears in connection with such material. However, identifiable units of such programs which are live and separately logged as such may be classified as local (e.g., if during the course of a film program, a non-network 2-minute news report is given and logged as a news program, the report may be classified as local).

Network Program: Any program furnished to the station by a network (national, regional, or special). Delayed broadcasts of programs originated by networks are classified as network.

Recorded Program: Any program not defined above, including without limitation, syndicated programs, taped or transcribed programs, and feature films.

The FCC defines "commercial matter"—commercial continuity (network and non-network) and commercial announcement (network and non-network) as follows:

Commercial continuity is the advertising message of a program sponsor.

Commercial announcements are any other advertising messages for which a charge is made or other consideration is received. Included are (1) "bonus spots," (2) trade-out spots, and (3) promotional announcements of a future program where consideration is received for such an announcement or where such announcement identifies the sponsor of a future program beyond mention of the sponsor's name as an integral part of the program; (e.g., where the agreement for the sale of time provides that the sponsor will receive promotional announcements, or when the promotional announcements contain a statement such as "LISTEN TOMORROW FOR THE (name of program) BROUGHT TO YOU BY (sponsor's name)." Other announcements including (but not limited to) the following are not commercial announcements: (1) Promotional announcements, except as heretofore defined above; (2) station identification announcements for which no charge is made; (3) mechanical reproduction announcements; (4) public service announcements: (5) announcements that materials or services have been furnished as an inducement to broadcast a political program or a program involving the discussion of a controversial public issue; (6) announcements made pursuant to the local notice requirements of "pre-grant" and "designation for hearing."

The FCC defines a public service announcement as a message for which no charge is made and which promotes programs, activities, or services of federal, state or local governments (e.g., recruiting, bond sales, etc.) or the programs, activities, or services of non-profit organizations (e.g., Red Cross, community chest, etc), and other announcements regarded as serving community interests, excluding time signals, routine weather announcements, and promotional announcements.

The FCC also defines the method of computing commercial time so that the duration of commercial matter shall be as close an approximation to the time consumed as possible. The amount of commercial time scheduled will usually be sufficient. It is not necessary, for example, to correct an entry of a "one-minute" commercial to accommodate varying reading speeds even though the actual time consumed might be a few seconds more or less than the scheduled time. However, it is incumbent upon the licensee to ensure that the entry represents as close an approximation of the time actually consumed as possible. In scheduling commercial programs and announcements a broadcaster should be aware of the fact that although the FCC has not promulgated any rules or regutions as to the amount of commercial matter or time a radio station may program, it has taken a firm stand regarding over-commercialization. As a general rule the FCC will accept a maximum of 18 minutes in any one hour with a maximum average of fourteen minutes per hour for the broadcast day. In fact, at the time a radio station files for a renewal of its license it has to report all hours in which commercial matter exceeded 18 minutes and explain why this excess time was scheduled.

The FCC also requires "station identification"—letters and location. The statement "This is station (call letters)" is insufficient. The announcement must be "This is station (call letters, name of city in which the station is licensed to broadcast)." Broadcasters may add other statements to this announcement such as "your community station"; "your station for news", etc., but the call letters together with the "location" must be given. Station identification announcements must be made at the beginning and at the end of each day's operation. In addition, during the day's operation they must be made on the hour, either on the half hour or quarter hour following the hour and at the quarter hour preceding the next hour (e.g., 9:30; 10; 10:30; or, 10:15; 10:45; 11:15; 11:45, etc.). There are certain exceptions to the above: (1) When the announcement would interrupt a single consecutive speech, play, religious service, symphony concert, or operatic production of longer duration than 30 minutes (station identification in above cases should be made at the beginning of the program, at the first interruption of the entertainment continuity, and at the end of the program); in cases of variety shows, baseball games, or similar programs of longer duration than 30 minutes, the announcement should be made within 5 minutes of the hour and the times referred to previously.

The FCC also requires broadcasters to advise their audience of any program, over one minute in length, that is mechanically reproduced in which the element of time is of special significance or in which the element of time would create, either intentionally or otherwise, the impression or belief on the part of the listening audience that the event or the program being broadcast is occurring simultaneously with the broadcast. Such an announcement must be made either at the beginning or end of the program. Broadcasters are also required to make such announcements in order not to create the impression that a mechanically reproduced program consists of live talent. The exact language of this announcement is not prescribed, but the language must be clear and in terms commonly used and understood. Some radio stations use the following language: (1) the following (or this) program was previously recorded for presentation at this time; (2) portions of the following (or preceding) program were previously recorded for presentation at this time; etc.

In following chapters we will discuss the necessity of planning your programming before you begin any action in connection with filing your application for a "construction permit." This is necessary because the Commission requires that you state, in percentages, the amount of time you plan to devote to each program category. At the time a licensee files an application for license renewal he must furnish the Commission a complete report of a typical broadcast week and indicate percentages for the various types of programs. The Commission will then compare the latter set of figures with his original or previously submitted figures to determine whether or not the licensee has performed according to his promises and obligations. This does not mean, however, that a licensee cannot change his program format or the "percentages" during the lifetime of the license. If for any valid reason the broadcaster desires to make any change that will affect his previously reported intentions, he can do so by applying to the FCC, setting forth the reasons for the changes. The Commission does not act in a capricious or arbitrary manner and will at all times cooperate with any licensee, providing it is in the best interest to the public the licensee is serving.

## Past Programming Data

Inasmuch as your attorney will advise you in completing your application for a new broadcast station (FCC Form 302), and inasmuch as the program sections in that application are similar to the application for renewal of a broadcast station license (Form 303), we will consider the information required in the renewal application, especially Section IV-A which deals with the "Statement of Program Service of Broadcast Applicant." Part I deals with the "Ascertainment of Program Needs." The licensee is required to furnish exhibits or narratives to show the following:

● The methods used by the applicant to ascertain the needs and interests of the public served by the station. Such information shall include (1) identification of representative groups, interests, and organizations which were consulted, and (2) the major communities or principal areas which the applicant undertakes to serve.

● The significant needs and interests of the public which the applicant believes his station will serve during the coming license period, including those with respect to national and international matters.

● A list of typical and illustrative programs or program series (excluding entertainment and news) that the applicant plans to broadcast during the coming license period.

Regarding the above the FCC requires that all radio stations keep on file a sufficient record to support claims made in the application. The file must be available and open for inspection by the Commission, and it must be kept for a minimum of three years and is not subject to public scrutiny.

In order not to be deluged with all license renewal applications at one time, those stations up for renewal each year are assigned filing dates according to states or regions, thus maintaining a more uniform flow through processing channels. For instance, all stations in Connecticut must file at the same time (the last date was December 31, 1965). To determine programming performance during the license period, the Commission calls for program logs based on a "composite" week, a log for each of seven days during the past three years, chosen by the Commission. For example, the following "composite" week was chosen by the FCC for a specific area: Sunday, March 7, 1965; Monday, January 18, 1965; Tuesday, October 20, 1964; Wednesday, June 16, 1965; Thursday, April 29, 1965; Friday, September 3, 1965; and Saturday, February 20, 1965.

In Part II (Section IV-A) the renewal application must include the following "past programming" information, using computations based on the composite week:

●A statement of the total number of hours of operation during the composite week, together with the originals or exact copies of the program logs for each day of the composite week. If for any reason the station was not operating during any day of the composite week the Commission will substitute another day.

●The amount of time in hours and minutes and the percentage of total time programmed in the following categories: (a) news (b) public affairs, and (c) all other programs exclusive of entertainment and sports. If for any reason the licensee feels that the composite week does not adequately represent the station's programming during its current license period, the applicant may file additional figures using a full month's logs in making his computations, but he must so notify the Commission, giving the exact dates of the logs used.

●List those typical and illustrative programs or program series (excluding entertainment and news) broadcast during the year preceding the filing date which served public needs and interests, with special emphasis on those programs that were designed to inform the public on local, national, or international problems. These programs must be listed by title, source (network, non-network, rebroadcast, etc.), with a brief description and the time and duration of the broadcast and how often broadcast. I would suggest that the program director keep a diary in which he records all such programs as they are broadcast, thus saving a great amount of time and negating the necessity of perusing a full year's program logs.

●Information concerning the station's news programs detailing the staff, news gathering facilities, newswire services, and other sources utilized. In addition, the applicant must furnish an estimate of the percentage of news program time devoted to local and regional news.

● A statement of station policy in making time available for the discussion of public issues and the methods employed in the selection of subjects and participants. This should be an honest and true statement of policy and operation. Many stations answer this part of the application by stating "It is the policy of the applicant to make adequate and suitable time available for the discussion of public issues and to see that equal opportunity is afforded at all times to opposing viewpoints with the best informed persons available being sought out and presented."

● A brief description of the applicant's program format during the past 12 months and the approximate percentage of time per week devoted to each format element. If your basic format is "Music-News-Sports" you would list music (type such as standards, pops, classical, etc.) and the percentage, news and the percentage, and sports and the percentage.

● A statement as to how and to what extent your station contributed to the overall diversity of program services available in the area you serve during the current license period. In order to complete this part of the application it is necessary to know the programming of all stations serving your area.

●If you were affiliated with any national, regional, or special radio network during the current license period you have to furnish the FCC with the names of every network.

● The total number of public service announcements broadcast during the composite week—note the number, regardless of their length, of all non-commercial public service announcements (not programs).

● A statement that all of the above information adequately reflects the station's programming during the current license period. If for any reason it does not, you may supply such additional information as you deem necessary. If for any reason your programming practices varied from those stated in your last license application you should submit a statement explaining the variations and the reasons for such variations.

## Proposed Programming

Part III (Section IV-A) of the application deals with the proposed programming for the ensuing license period, which at the present time is three years. In this part of the application you will have to state the following:

● The proposed total hours of operation during a typical week. It is suggested that you base this reply on the same composite week used in Part II of the application. The reason for this suggestion is that unless you plan to radically change your format, the comparisons between the proposed program schedule and the composite week report should be about equal and the figures practically the same.

● A statement as to the minimum time you propose to devote each week to (a) news, (b) public affairs, and (c) all other programs exclusive of entertainment and sports. This will have to be in the form of how many hours and minutes and the respective percentages of the total time on the air.

● Information concerning your proposed news programs. In this statement the applicant must indicate (a) the staff, (b) news gathering facilities, (c) news services to be used and contracted for, (d) all other sources to be utilized, and (e) an estimate of the percentages of news program time to be devoted to local and regional news.

● A statement of public affairs programming policy—making time available for the discussion of public issues and the method of selecting subjects and participants.

● A description of the applicant's proposed programming format and the percentage of time per week to be devoted to such format. (To answer this section refer to the preceding discussion.)

● A statement indicating the intention to contribute to the overall diversity of program services available in the community the station serves.

● A statement of the minimum number of public service announcements the applicant proposes to present during a typical week. This estimate should be as accurate as possible.

● If the station is affiliated with any network, either national, regional, or specialized, the applicant must furnish the names of all such networks.

## Past Commercial Practices

In Part IV the licensee must report on his past commercial practices, showing the total hours of operation during the composite week and the hours between 6 AM and 6 PM. It must be remembered that some stations operate only during daytime hours and do not sign on at 6 AM; therefore, it is possible that the two figures will be different. The following must be shown:

• Time devoted to commercial matter for all hours and from 6 AM to 6 PM; the actual amount of commercial time in hours and minutes.

• The percentages of commercial time for all hours and for the period from 6 AM to 6 PM.

• A statement by the licensee as to whether or not the information supplied adequately reflects station commercial practices. In this section the applicant may explain any variations from his previous presentations.

• A report of the number of 60-minute segments of the composite week containing the following amounts of commercial matter:

    a. up to and including 10 minutes
    b. over 10 and up to and including 14 minutes
    c. over 14 and up to and including 18 minutes
    d. over 18 minutes. If any are reported, each segment must be listed, specifying the amount of commercial time and the day and time broadcast. In regard to this you should remember that the FCC by law cannot restrict the amount of commercial matter a station broadcasts, but inasmuch as this information will be compared with your original license proposal, or your last license renewal application, the FCC will take particular note if there is a case of overcommercialization. A good rule of thumb to follow is not to have more than 18 minutes of commercial matter in any one hour, with an average of 14 minutes per hour for the broadcast day.

## Proposed Commercial Practices

Part V of the application relates to proposed commercial practices. The applicant must furnish the following:

●A statement of the maximum percentage of commercial matter the applicant proposes to allow during all hours and for the period from 6 AM to 6 PM. It is suggested that the applicant not request more than 30% for either of those periods.

●A statement of the maximum commercial matter to be allowed in any 60-minute segment. It is suggested that you request no more than 18 minutes. In this section you also are permitted to state under what circumstances and how often you will exceed this requested time.

## General Policy and Procedures

Part VI of the application refers to general station policies and procedures. In this section the following information must be supplied:

●The names and positions of all persons who determine the day-to-day programming decisions and direct the operation of the station covered by the application, and whether or not such persons are employed full-time.

●The established policies of the station with respect to programming and advertising standards. Many stations belong to and subscribe to the National Association of Broadcasters and their advertising code. Such stations need only to state such membership. All others have to submit a full statement.

●A statement of the methods by which the applicant keeps informed of the requirements of the Communications Act and FCC Rules and Regulations, and a description of the procedures established to acquaint station personnel with such requirements to ensure their compliance. In answering this section do not hesitate to be as explicit as possible. Some of the methods you may employ and state are:

—Retaining the services of a qualified FCC attorney who from time to time furnishes you with memorandum, letters, and advice.

—Subscribing to the Government Printing office service regarding Parts I and III of the FCC rules.
—Membership in any of the trade organizations such as the National Association of Broadcasters, State Broadcasting Associations, etc.
—Attendance at broadcasting trade conventions.
—Subscribing to various trade publications who report on FCC activities.
—Circulating memoranda to the staff.
—Staff meetings.
—Posting instructional material.
—Periodic review and spot checking by the supervisory staff.

● A statement of the number of employees on the staff. If more than 10, the information must indicate the number of full-time and part-time employees in programming, sales, technical, and general and administrative departments.

Part VII concerns other matters and certification. The applicant may submit a statement of additional information which, in its judgment, is necessary to adequately describe or to present fairly its services and operations in relation to the public interest. It would be well to submit such a statement indicating the citations and awards the radio station has received during the past license period, as well as a report on letters of commendation from church, school, fraternal, civic, and social welfare agencies. Wherever possible the applicant should list all community and trade organizations in which any staff member holds office.

## Categorical Program Breakdown

Section IV of FCC Form 303, the renewal application, concerns itself with the percentages for each program category both as to past and proposed operation. The Commission desires to know the exact percentage of the composite week devoted to and proposed for the following categories: (1) entertainment, (2) religious programming, (3) agricultural programs, (4) educational programming, (5) news, (6) discussion, and (7) talks. The following is a breakdown approved by the FCC for a radio station operating in a small market since 1947:

- Entertainment    70. 6%
- Religious         6. 0%
- Agricultural       .3%
- Educational        .3%
- News             13. 0%
- Discussion        1. 5%
- Talks             8. 3%

This particular station is located in the northeast section of the country in a city of less than 50,000 but serves an area with a population of 100,000.   It is mainly an industrial area with some dairy farming.  The educational level would not be classified as high.  In fact,  of those in the core city who are older than 23 only 23% are high school graduates.  Outside the core area the educational level is much higher with a goodly percentage having had some exposure to college.   Ethnically it is quite diversified and supports a great number of churches of many demoninations.

Part III of Section IV calls for a report on the number of commercial announcements broadcast in 15-minute periods. The following breakdown is requested:

1.  Number of 15-minute periods with no commercial announcements.
2.  Number of 15-minute periods with one commercial announcement.
3.  Number of 15-minute periods with two commercial announcements.
4.  Number of 15-minute periods with three commercial announcements.
5.  Number of 15-minute periods with four commercial announcements.
6.  Number of 15-minute periods with five or more commercial announcements.

Also required is the number of commercial announcements which exceeded one minute in length and a statement of station practice with respect to the number and length of commercial announcements that will be allowed in a given period. A suggested statement is "applicant's policy is to limit spot announcements to 60 seconds in length and that no more than 18 minutes of commercial continuity and spot announcements will be allowed within any one hour."

Part 4 of Section IV requires an analysis of the program logs for the composite week and a statement of the percentage of time devoted to and proposed for each program class during specific hours of the broadcast day. The time categories are 8AM-6PM, 6PM-11PM, all other hours, and the total programming is broken down into the following classifications and the percentage of each listed under the appropriate time category:

- Network commercial
- Network sustaining
- Recorded commercial
- Recorded sustaining
- Wire commercial
- Wire sustaining
- Live commercial
- Live sustaining
- Total commercial
- Total sustaining
- Complete total
- Actual broadcast hours (per week)
- Number of spot announcements (per week)
- Number of non-commercial spot announcements (per week)

Do not become alarmed if the figures in the "total" column differ. They should differ. A suggestion to be followed, should your totals for commercial time be rather on the small side, is to attach a statement that every effort is being made to increase the commercial percentages. This will be of great help as you increase your revenue during the license period. As to the number of non-commercial spot announcements to be broadcast, a fair rule of thumb is to schedule one announcement for every seven commercial announcements.

## Sponsor Identification

The FCC requires clear and unmistakable identification of all "sponsors"; i.e., where money, services, or valuable consideration is either directly or indirectly paid or promised for any broadcast matter, including spot announcements, an announcement identifying the sponsor must accompany such matter. The Commission is most adamant in enforcing this regulation and many radio stations have received stiff fines for its violation. The reasoning behind this rule is to ensure that the listening public will always know with whom he will be dealing if persuaded to act by the announcement or program commercial. Many stations carry "commercials" for record albums and Christmas trees or toys and suggest that the listener order these items by addressing a card or letter to "Records" c/o the station; or "Toys," "Trees," etc. Unless the name of the firm offering these products is included in the announcement at the time the offer is made, it is in violation of the rules and subject to a fine for every violation. The announcement must fully and fairly disclose the true identity of the person or persons by whom or in whose behalf such services or other valuable consideration is received.

At the time of broadcast appropriate identification must be made also of any political program sponsor or any program involving the discussion of any controversial issue for which any films, records, transcriptions, talent, scripts, or other material or service of any kind furnished without charge or at a nominal charge, directly or indirectly, as an inducement to the broadcast of such a program. The entire matter of sponsor identification became so complex that the 86th Congress issued a report which was incorporated as part of the Commission's rules, citing 27 illustrations in an attempt to demonstrate when sponsorship identification announcements were not required. This helped to distinguish "payola" from the "free record" situation. (We will discuss "payola" in detail later). All payola "deals" require a sponsor identification announcement, whereas the Commission does not require announcements where stations receive free records without performance guarantees or any other consideration.

Illustrative Example 17 as furnished by the Congress indicates the distinction. "An automobile manufacturer furnishes his identifiable current model car for use in a mystery program, and it is used by a detective to chase a villain. No announcement is required. If it is understood, however, that the producer may keep the car for his personal use, an announcement would be required. Similarly, an announcement is required if the car is loaned in exchange for a mention on the program beyond that reasonably related to its use, such as the villain saying: "If you hadn't had that speedy Chrysler, you never would have caught me." In regard to "free records" no announcement is required when a record distributor or manufacturer supplies a station or its personnel with copies of records for broadcast purposes. Announcements would be required if the record distributor or manufacturer supplied the station with 25 to 50 copies of the same release as "give aways," with the implied or expressed agreement that the radio station will play this record; or if the record is supplied on the condition that the disc jockey make a special mention of the artist or record in any manner other than that which he usually uses on his program, or where the disc jockey receives any service or renumeration for playing the record on his program. A good yardstick to follow, so as not to run afoul of the law, is to make announcements whenever you are in doubt, especially where payment in any form is made to the station or to anyone engaged in the selection or broadcast of program matter.

No announcements are required in the following instances where: (1) free books or theatre tickets are furnished to the station's dramatic critic or book reviewer; (2) news releases are furnished by government, business, labor, and civic organizations, and private persons, with respect to their activities; (3) air transportation is furnished news personnel by the government to accompany government officials and foreign dignitaries on their travels throughout the country; (4) street signs and disposal containers are supplied by a municipality for use as props on a program; (5) a hotel grants permission to originate a program on the hotel's premises (providing no agreement was made to mention the hotel's name in a manner not reasonably related to the use made of the hotel's facilities); (6) a refrigerator is furnished as a prop in a kitchen scene; (7) a soft drink distributor furnishes a dispenser for use as a prop; (8) a private zoo furnishes animals for use on a program; (9) a university makes one of its professors available to give lectures in an educational series; (10) a well-known performer appears as a guest artist at a fee lower than which he ordinarily commands, because he likes the show; (11) a promoter permits broadcasts of athletic events (provided no payment or agreement is made to identify the promoter or event in a manner not reasonably related to the broadcast of the event; (12) service or property is furnished free for use on or in connection with a program (unless there is an expressed or implied agreement that identification beyond mere use of the service or property on the program); (13) prizes for programs furnished for "give-away" programs with the understanding that a brand identification and description will be made at the time of the award; (14) an airplane manufacturer furnishes free transportation to a cast on a new jet plane to a remote site, and the arrival of the cast at the site is shown as part of the program. The name of the manufacturer is identifiable on the fuselage of the plane (no announcement is required because in this instance such identification is reasonably related to the use of the service on the program); (15) a bus company prepares a scenic travel film which it furnishes free to broadcast stations, provided no mention is made in the film of the company or its buses; (16) a manufacturer furnishes a grand piano for use on a concert program (unless the manufacturer insists that the enlarged insignia of its brand name be affixed over the normal insignia on the piano); (17) an automobile manufacturer or dealer furnishes a number of automobiles to be used on programs and for other purposes in connection with the production of the program, such as transportation for the crew, cast, equipment, and supplies from location to location and where there is no understanding that there will be any identification of the automobiles used beyond that which is reasonably related to the use of the automobiles on the program and where no other consideration is involved; and (18) a hotel permits a program to originate from its premises and furnishes hotel services, such as room and board for cast, production, and technical staff, free of charge, with no other consideration.

So remember, all commercial matter must contain an explicit identification of the advertiser or the generally known trade or brand name of the goods advertised. Here are some examples where stations fail to abide by the rules and become liable for citation and subject to a fine: (1) Announcements or programs, soliciting mail orders from listeners, where the sponsor is referred to in the announcement or program and in the address as "Seeds," "Flowers," "Records," etc. Such an identification is insufficient and the FCC does not consider it in compliance with the sponsor identification rules, since it is limited to a description of the product and not the name of the manufacturer or seller of the goods. (2) "Teaser" announcements using catch words, slogans, etc., aimed at arousing the curiosity of the listener that something is "coming soon." Even if it is the intention of the station and the seller or manufacturer to identify the sponsor at a later date, the use of the "teaser" without full disclosure of the sponsor is prohibited. (3) Announcements or programs on behalf of political candidates, or opponents or proponents of any public controversial issue, must fully and fairly disclose the true identity of the person or persons by whom or in whose behalf payment was made. The statement that "the preceding was a paid political announcement" will not suffice.

## "Payola"

In regard to "payola," the law requires that any station employee who accepts or agrees to accept from any person (other than the radio station by which he is employed), or any person who pays or agrees to pay such employee, any money, service, or other valuable consideration for the broadcast of any matter over such station, shall, in advance of such broadcast, disclose the fact of such acceptance or agreement to the station management. Any person who violates any provision of this section of the rules and regulations shall for each such violation be fined not more than $10,000 or imprisoned not more than one year, or both. This means that any person who, in connection with the preparation or production of any program or announcement intended for broadcast on any radio station, accepts or agrees to accept, or pays or agrees to pay, any money, service, or other valuable consideration for the inclusion of any matter as a part of such program, must, in advance of the broadcast of the program, disclose the fact of such acceptance or payment or agreement to the payee's employer, or to the person for whom such program is being produced, or to the licensee of the station over which the program is to be broadcast.

While this particular regulation appears to apply to station personnel it is the duty of the station licensee to take reasonable and dilligent steps to obtain from his personnel all information concerning sponsorship identification announcements. Any failure on the licensee's part to exercise such measures could result in disciplinary action. The term "service or other valuable consideration" does not include any service or property furnished without charge or at a nominal cost for use, or in connection with, a broadcast, or for use on a program which is intended for broadcasting, unless the required identification or mention related to such use, service, or property is beyond the usual related reference as used by the station.

One of the problems confronting station management is the appearance of disc jockies at "record hops." This is generally good publicity for the station and it increases the audience of the DJ's program. There should be no objection to such participation from management, especially if the radio station sells regular commercial announcements to the organization which is promoting the record hop. When such announcements are broadcast they are logged as regular commercial spots. The problem is the plug or casual mention of the record hop on the air where the station or the employee is receiving remuneration and that fact is not made known to the public. To overcome this problem some stations have taken the drastic step of prohibiting any DJ from mentioning directly or indirectly their appearance at record hops or other affairs for which they or the station will receive any remuneration. It should be remembered that whether the record hop or affair is a charitable event or a commercial venture the public must be advised that the station personality is appearing for pay. It also should be remembered that if the DJ distributes recordings at these affairs (which were received free from the distributor or manufacturer) he must also comment that the records that will be distributed were donated by the distributor or manufacturer.

To safeguard itself one radio station issued the following directive to all its employees:

"The FCC requires that at periods not to extend beyond six months, each employee must file, in writing, a complete questionnaire which sets forth any and all past (6 months), present, and future outside employment or business, either regular or sporadic. It is important that you file with me, at once, a statement listing all your outside employment activities, full- or part-time, for the past six months, any in which you are now engaged in, or any plans you may have for the future. You should also make a statement in your own language that you have never, nor are now, receiving any remuneration, either in cash or gifts from anyone in order to plug or announce their product or place of business. These statements should be notorized and in my hands no later than (date). Failure to do this may lead to your suspension as an employee."

(Signed - Manager)

Another manager issued the following directive to station personnel.

"The FCC requests that all radio stations furnish certain information with respect to compensation, other than that paid by the station, which has been received by anyone connected with the station. The Commission's rules require, in essence, that the public know whether the station is receiving compensation for any matter broadcast by it. In order to comply with the spirit and interest of the rule, we are setting forth below our policies on the matter:

1. Unless it is obvious from the nature of the commercial copy in a program or announcement that the station receives remuneration for the broadcast, the announcer shall make specific reference to the fact that the program or announcement is paid for and by whom.

2. No person associated with this station will be permitted to accept any remuneration, directly or indirectly, from any person other than the station management for broadcasting any matter over the air. In other words, you may not accept any sums or services other than your compensation for that work which you perform at this station.

3. If you are approached by any person offering such remuneration, you are to notify the station manager immediately.

4. As used above, the term "remuneration" includes the acceptance of gifts or substantial services. We do not mean to preclude you from accepting normal hospitality such as a luncheon, dinner, or a drink from people with whom we do business. However, you are not to accept any other type of hospitality without the specific approval in writing from the sta-

tion manager. This would include "junkets" that are occasionally offered by companies in order to acquaint broadcast personnel with new projects in which they are interested. Where such "junkets" have a direct relationship to our broadcasting activity, the station management will consider the specific project and advise you.

5. You are not permitted to have any interest of any kind in any company which is related to broadcasting in any manner, without first receiving the approval in writing from management.

6. Any violation of the foregoing instructions will cause your dismissal.

We do not mean to be unduly harsh in issuing these instructions, but feel that there are no alternatives to the procedures described above."

(Signed - Station Manager)

## Lotteries

Section 1304 of the Federal Criminal Code concerning the broadcast of lottery information reads as follows: "Whoever broadcasts by means of any radio station for which a license is required by any law of the United States, or whoever, operating any such station, knowingly permits the broadcast of any advertisement of or information concerning any lottery, gift enterprise, or similar scheme offering prizes dependent in whole or in part upon lot or chance, or any list of the prizes drawn or awarded by means of any such lottery, gift enterprise or scheme, whether said list contains any part or all of such prizes, shall be fined not more than $1,000, or imprisoned not more than one year, or both."

FCC rules and regulations state that no construction permit, license, license renewal, or any other authorization for the operation of a broadcast station, will be granted where the applicant proposes to follow or continue to follow a policy or practice of broadcasting or permitting the broadcasting of any advertisement of or information concerning any lottery, gift enterprise, or similar scheme, offering prizes dependent in whole or in part upon lot or chance, or any list of the prizes drawn or awarded by means of any such lottery, gift enterprise, or scheme, whether said list contains any part or all of such prizes. The FCC considers any program to come within this provision if it offers or refers to a prize consisting of money or things of value to be awarded to any person whose selection is dependent in whole or in part upon lot or chance, if as a condition of winning or competing for such prize, such winner or winners are required to furnish any money or things of value or are required to have in their possession any product sold, manufactured, furnished or distributed by a sponsor of a program broadcast on the station.

Broadcasters must remember that it is the federal law and not the local law which determines what consitutes a lottery. The Supreme Court of the United States has made it clear that the statutory provisions apply only to those "schemes" which are, in fact, lotteries. The court in effect labeled the words "gift enterprise or similar schemes" as surplusage. Thus, even though bingo games may not be a lottery under local laws, radio stations may not broadcast information concerning bingo games because they are lotteries under federal laws. The same prohibition applies to broadcasts concerning the Irish Sweepstakes, the New York State Lottery, the New Hampshire State Lottery, or the various games in Nevada. It is important to note that a radio station cannot broadcast any advertisement or information concerning a lottery even though the contest is not being conducted over the air.

For a contest to be considered a lottery it must have three essential characteristics: (1) prize, (2) chance, and (3) considerations. Many attorneys state that all three elements must be present to classify a contest as a lottery and that the absence of any one of these elements removes the contest from the lottery category. The first two elements—prize and chance— are relatively simple and generally understood. It is the third element—consideration—that poses the major problems. Federal courts have ruled that the following do not constitute "consideration": (1) the requirement of listening to a radio station; (2) the requirement that a participant visit the promoter's place of business in order to register or receive a card. The same courts have ruled that "consideration" exists when the participant is required to purchase something, produce evidence of a purchase, or where the amount of the prize is increased if a purchase has been made.

Inasmuch as radio stations are licensed to operate in the public interest, and that it is to the public benefit that a station's news coverage be as wide as possible, it is some attorneys' view that a station would not be in jeopardy if it broadcast important news concerning a lottery, providing it is important news. It is not sufficient that the information be news. It must be unusual news which may have only an incidental effect in the promotion of the lottery. It is an impossibility to describe or define the many situations which can arise in connection with contests. When in doubt it is best to consult with your attorney or to abstain altogether. Violations of the lottery law, and the FCC rules and regulations concerning lotteries, can lead to criminal penalties and to large fines and/or the revocation of the station license.

## Rebroadcast

Many stations, especially those operating in remote areas and small markets, and who are not affiliated with any network, sometimes rebroadcast programs originated at other stations. The FCC rules and regulations define such rebroadcasts as "reception by radio of the programs of a radio station and the simultaneous or subsequent retransmission of such programs by a broadcast station." This means any program, in full or in part. However, if the station receives the program from the originating station by means of telephone facilities it is not considered a "rebroadcast."

The Commission permits such rebroadcasts providing that it is notified and permission is obtained from the originating station. At the time such notification is sent to the FCC the call letters of the originating station and its location must be furnished to the Commission. Notification must be sent within three days of the rebroadcast. If arrangements are made between stations for rebroadcasts over a period of time or for several times within a license period, notice and certification of consent must be given for the ensuing license period at the time the station applies for license renewal or at the beginning of the agreement period if the agreement is made during a license period. When such agreements are made it is not necessary to notify the FCC of each and every rebroadcast.

There are several exceptions to the rebroadcast rule: (1)

The rebroadcast of a non-commercial program on a non-commercial basis (programs of a U.S. International Broadcasting station); (2) the rebroadcast of a program relayed by a remote pickup broadcast station; (3) the rebroadcast of Defense Network Programs (blanket authorizations have been filed with the FCC by all Defense Network Stations); (4) In cases where the program will be rebroadcast by several stations, the originating station will file for all the stations involved. For example, space shots, inauguration ceremonies of the president of the U.S. or governor of a state, state funerals, convention proceedings, etc.

### Networks

All contracts with networks, whether national, regional, or special services, must be filed with the Commission. It must be noted that the FCC will not grant a license to a station which is party to any contract, arrangement, or understanding, express or implied, with a network that provides, by original term, provisions for renewal or otherwise for the affiliation of the station with the network for a period longer than two years. A contract may be made, however, within six months prior to the commencement of the two-year period. The FCC shall also refuse to license a station who contracts with a network on an exclusive basis where the station is prevented, hindered from or penalized for, broadcasting programs of other networks. Likewise, the station cannot forbid, prevent, or hinder the network in making its services available to other stations, even if those stations serve substantionally the same area. Contracts for "first call" in the station's primary service area are permitted.

The FCC divides the broadcast day, in considering network program option time, into four categories—8 AM to 1 PM, 1 PM to 6 PM, 6 PM to 11 PM, and 11 PM to 8 AM. Option time is not permitted if it is subject to call on less than 56 days notice, or if more time than a total of 3 hours within each of the four above mentioned segments is called for. Such option time may not be exclusive as against other networks and the network cannot prevent or hinder the station from selling any or all of the time covered by the option to any other network. The FCC defines such option time as a contract, arrangement, or understanding, expressed or implied, between a station and a network which prevents or hinders the station from scheduling programs before the network agrees· to utilize the time during which such programs are scheduled, or which requires the station to clear time already scheduled where the network seeks to utilize the time.

Network contracts may not prohibit a station from rejecting any network program that the station reasonably believes to be unsatisfactory, unsuitable, contrary to the public interest, or from substituting a program of outstanding local or national importance. The Commission also forbids networks to control the station's rates for time sales or to insist that the station agree to the continuation of the affiliation in case of a sale or transfer of control.

## Political Programs

In scheduling political programs and broadcasts it is mandatory that all broadcasters thoroughly know section 315 of the Communications Act. In simple terms it makes it mandatory that all stations who permit any legally qualified candidate to use their facilities must afford all other legally qualified candidates for the same office an equal opportunity to use the same facilities. It also states that any charges made must not exceed those charges for a comparable use of the station's facilities for other purposes. All discounts offered to commercial advertisers must also be offered to the candidates. Rebates by any means or manner, direct or indirect, are specifically forbidden.

The Act does not force or make it mandatory that a radio station make its facilities available for political broadcasts or programs. Stations have the right to deny their facilities to all candidates for political office, but if they deny it to one candidate they must deny it to all. If one candidate is permitted to use the station's facilities, all candidates for the same office must be given the same permission. The Act was amended in 1959 to exempt from the equal time provision all news programs, news interviews, and other news coverage programs on which political candidates appear. Extreme care should be taken that these programs are "bona fide" news programs. Radio stations do not have the right or power to censor any material broadcast by a political candidate. Stations do have the power and right to censor any material broadcast by others in behalf of any candidate. Federal laws and many state laws have exempted radio stations from libel prosecution because of this regulation.

The FCC defines "a legally qualified candidate" as a person who has publicly announced that he is a candidate for nomination by a convention of a political party or for nomination or election in a primary, special, or general election, municipal, county, state, or national, and who meets the qualifications prescribed by the applicable laws to hold the office for which he is a candidate, so that he may be voted for by the electorate directly or by means of delegates or electors; and who: (1) has qualified for a place on the ballot; or (2) is eligible by law to be voted for by sticker or written ballot or "write-in"; and (3) has been duly nominated by a commonly known or regarded political party; or (4) makes a substantial showing that he is a bona fide candidate for nomination or office, as the case may be. Any candidate's request for equal time must be submitted to the licensee within one week of the day on which the prior use occurred. All candidates who request time, or equal time, or who complain to the FCC of non-compliance on the part of the station, have the burden of proving that they are legally qualified candidates for public office. The Commission requires that all radio stations maintain a file for a period of two years, which shall be open to public inspection, containing a complete record of all requests received from or made on behalf of candidates for public office. Appropriate notations must be made upon all such requests indicating the disposition made, and if granted, the charges made for use of the facility.

We will be discussing the "fairness doctrine" later in this chapter, but there are certain aspects of the "fairness doctrine" that apply to political candidates that are not covered by Sec. 315 of the Communications Act that need to be mentioned at this time. It is important to note that when a program deals with a controversial issue involving a personal attack upon an individual or an organization, the FCC requires that the station send the text of the broadcast to the individual or organization attacked and make a specific offer of the station's facilities for an adequate response. Likewise, when a station's commentator or any other person, other than a candidate, takes a partisan position on issues involved in a political contest, or attacks a candidate, or supports a candidate, a transcript of the program must be sent to each candidate or group concerned, accompanied by an offer of adequate time to answer. This holds true when a radio station permits broadcasts for the presentation of views regarding an issue of current public importance. The station must seek out and offer to spokesmen for other responsible groups within the community similar opportunities for the expression of contrasting viewpoints.

A radio station licensee must bear in mind that although he has no right or power to censor the programs of a legally qualified candidate, he does have the right and power to censor all other programs. To avoid a proliferation of demands for equal time and the possibility of law suits for libel, the station's management and program director should take all necessary and adequate steps to carefully read and censor all programs that may be of a controversial nature. The salient point of Sec. 315 of the Communications Act is that the law refers only to qualified political candidates. It does not confer rights upon a political party or organization as such, nor upon spokesmen speaking in behalf of qualified political candidates, neither does this section of the law apply in support of or in opposition to any public question to be voted on in a referendum or election.

Another point that must be thoroughly understood is that the use of station facilities by any legally qualified candidate, no matter in what manner or capacity, requires that equal time be offered to that candidate's legally qualified opponents. For instance, if a legally qualified candidate uses the station's broadcast facilities for other than a discussion directly related to his candidacy; if a congressman or senator or other elected official reports to his constituency while he is an announced candidate for re-election; if a legally qualified candidate appears on any program even for a brief bow or statement; if a legally qualified candidate appears on a station for a speech in connection with a ceremonial activity or other public service such as opening a bridge, etc.; if the legally qualified candidate delivers a non-political lecture on a regularly scheduled series; if a legally qualified candidate is attacked by a third party and is granted the opportunity for reply; or if any of the station's personnel appear in any capacity after having qualified as a candidate for public office. The law does not apply when a legally qualified candidate's broadcasts originate and are limited to a foreign station, even though those signals can be and are received in the U.S. Section 315 applies only to stations that are licensed by the FCC. Also, the law does not apply to acceptance speeches made by candidates as the FCC has held that such a speech falls within the broadcasting of "bona fide" news.

The actual determination as to who is a legally qualified candidate must be determined by the existing laws in each individual state where the election is being held. A good rule of thumb is that a candidate is legally qualified if he can be voted for in the state or district in which the election is being held, and, if elected, is eligible to serve in that office. The fact that a person's name does not appear on the ballot does not mean that he is not "legally qualified." If that person makes a true and real race for the office, and if by law his name can be written in by the voters, he is "legally qualified." The mere fact alone that his name can be written in does not make him "legally qualified." He must be a truly bona fide candidate actively seeking the office. Radio stations may not refuse equal time to any qualified candidate as described above, even if in the opinion of the licensee that candidate has absolutely no possibility of being elected. On the other hand should any state or government official having jurisdiction over a candidate's legal qualifications rule that such a person is not a legally qualified candidate under local election laws a station can refuse its facilities to that person. Remember, Section 315 refers only to equal opportunities for "opposing" candidates. A station can make its facilities available to candidates for a particular office and refuse its facilities to candidates for all other offices. Likewise, in primaries the provisions of the law apply only to candidates for the same nomination from the same party.

The term "equal opportunities" in Section 315 means that no station shall make any discrimination in charges, practices, regulations, facilities, or services rendered to candidates for a particular office. It can adopt a policy of selling time, or of giving time to candidates free of charge, or a combination of both. But whatever policy it adopts in one case, all candidates for the same office must be treated alike. A station is not allowed or required to give free time to one candidate where it has sold time to his opponent. Unlike the "fairness doctrine," where it is the station's responsibility to seek out opposing views, licensees are not required to seek out and inform candidates or political parties and advise them what their opponents are doing. However, all stations must keep a public record of all requests for political time and must make them available if they are requested.

Stations may refuse to sell candidates a specific time segment, and stations are not required to sell candidates a time segment unlimited in total and length. This does not preclude a station from selling more time to one candidate than his opponent, providing the opponent does not wish to purchase an equal amount of time. In all instances radio stations should try to afford candidates time segments that are comparable as to desirability. This does not mean that a station must make available the exact same time periods, nor the time period any candidate requests; on the other hand, if candidates are permitted to appear without cost to themselves on programs sponsored by commercial advertisers, opposing candidates are entitled to receive comparable time also at no cost.

One of the biggest problems in adhering to the full meaning of Section 315 is the scheduling of "debates" between candidates. Many stations, as a public service, try to set up programs for a face-to-face confrontation between candidates. If a station schedules a program on which the details are determined solely by the station and invites all candidates for a particular office to appear, should one candidate reject the offer while the others appear, the station must, by law, honor the equal time request of the candidate who refused to appear on the program, if such request is made within the period specified by the FCC. The Commission has ruled that the obligations under Section 315 can not be avoided by unilateral action in choosing a program format and offering it on a "take it or leave it" basis. The thrust of the Commission's ruling is that Section 315 bestows upon the candidate the right to choose the format or other similar aspects of the broadcast material with no right on the part of the station to "censorship." As stated earlier, Section 315 does not allow or permit a station to censor a candidate's remarks or programs. The Supreme Court of the U.S. has upheld this section of the law and at the same time absolved radio stations from any libel liabilites. However, the same immunity does not apply is cases where non-candidates, no matter what position they may or may not hold in political parties, broadcast speeches in behalf of a candidate and libel the candidate's opponent. Such speeches do not fall under the provisions of Section 315 and are subject to censorship by the station.

Candidates themselves may say whatever they wish—they do not have to speak about a subject directly related to their candidacy. This, however, does not mean that a candidate's opponent must limit himself to the same subject when he is granted equal time. All candidates may use the facilities granted as they deem best in their own interest without any censorship on the part of a licensee. Radio stations, although not permitted to censor a candidate's speech, may adopt a policy of requiring candidates to submit their speeches in advance of the broadcast; providing the same policy is uniform for all candidates.

There are two additional responsibilities to which stations are obligated: (1) to maintain records concerning equal time requests, and (2) the necessity to announce that political programs or programs involving discussions of controversial issues are sponsored if the station receives any consideration whatsoever for such programs. Number one was discussed previously. However, regarding number two, it is insufficent to say "the preceding was a paid political announcement." If the program is more than 5 minutes an announcement must be made at the beginning and end of the program identifying the person or group who actually paid for the program. If the program is 5 minutes or less, only one announcement at the end of the program must be made. However, regardless of program length, the announcement must identify the person or group who paid for the program. If the program or announcement in behalf of a candidate is paid for, or prepared, etc., by a corporation, committee, association, or other group, the sponsorship announcement must disclose the name of that corporation, committee, group, etc. In addition, the station must have in its possession a list of the chief executive officers or members of the executive committee or of the board of directors of the corporation, committee, etc., and the list of such personnel must be available for public inspection. A type of announcement acceptable by the FCC is: "This announcement was paid for and furnished by "Citizens for (candidate)." In addition to the records referred to above, the station must make a direct notation on the program log of the name and political affiliation of every political candidate who appears on the air, even if that speech is only a one-minute or shorter spot announcement.

During the past few years the FCC and Congress have requested detailed information from stations concerning political broadcasts. The questionnaire generally requires a considerable amount of record keeping and work. It involves the tabulation of: (1) All program times and announcements purchased by candidates or supporters for either party, (2) the sustaining program time made available by the station, (3) the number of political broadcasts carried in designated hours, (4) information with reference to editorials on candidates or issues, (5) free time offered by the station on its own initiative to candidates or supporters, and (6) if a network affiliate, the extent to which the station carried the political programs offered by the network, either on a sustaining or a non-sustaining basis.

## Editorializing

In June 1949 the FCC stated that radio stations have the right to editorialize, provided that those stations who did editorialize would diligently seek out and present the opposing point of view. This raised many questions on the part of management and program directors. Though it has not been specific, the Commission by implication has redefined and re-evaluated the obligations placed upon stations who have an editorial policy. From recent action it appears that if the editorial content relates to a broad or general subject, such as safety on the highways, fire prevention, purchase of U.S. savings and defense bonds, conservation of natural resources, etc., it is not necessary for a station to seek out and present the other side. However, if the editorial deals with a specific controversial national or international subject, such as admission of Red China into the U.N., " an increase in benefits under Medicare, " etc., spokesman for the other side should be sought out, advised of the editorial, and afforded the opportunity for reply.

Stations that editorialize must be sure that should the editorial make a specific attack upon an individual or a group, it is given the opportunity to reply. In addition to seeking out the individual or group, the radio station must supply the person or group with a copy of the editorial either before or at the time it is presented on the air. By the offer of time for reply the station will have discharged its responsibility under the regulation. It is not necessary for the station to pursue the matter and force the individual or group to reply. As stated under "political programming," radio stations who editorialize on behalf of a political candidate must, prior to the time the editorial is broadcast, supply the candidate's opponents with a copy of the editorial and afford the opponents an opportunity for reply.

There are no hard and fast rules governing the question of "seeking out and affording the other side an opportunity for reply"; each situation stands on its own and must be separately evaluated. However, the following guidelines may be of benefit:

1. If the editorial is about a specific controversial issue, the opponents should be advised of the editorial and given the opportunity for reply.

2. If the editorial attacks a specific person of local, state, or national prominence, that person must be given a copy of the editorial as soon as possible and afforded the opportunity to reply.

3. If the editorial deals with a specific national issue, responsible spokesmen for the "other side" should be sought out, and if available, afforded the opportunity to reply.

4. If the editorial deals with subjects of a general or broad national or international nature there is no obligation to seek out the opponents; however, if a responsible spokesman representing the opposing point of view demands the opportunity to reply, it would be in the station's interest to grant the demand.

### The "Fairness Doctrine"

It is quite possible that by the time you read this the entire matter concerning the FCC and its "fairness doctrine" will be moot, as the U.S. Supreme Court has agreed to hear arguments and to decide upon its constitutionality. The fairness doctrine stipulates that a licensee has an affirmative obligation to afford reasonable opportunity for the presentation of contrasting viewpoints on any controversial issue which he chooses to cover. In July 1963 the FCC, instead of a primer defining the licensee's responsibilities, issued a public notice establishing the following basic guidelines:

1. When a controversial program involves a personal attack upon an individual or organization, the licensee must transmit the text of the broadcast to the person or group attacked, wherever located, either prior to or at the time of the broadcast, with a specific offer of his station's facilities for an adequate response.

2. When a licensee permits the use of his facilities by a commentator or any person other than a candidate to take a partisan position on the issues involved in a contest for political office or to attack one candidate or support another by direct or indirect identification, he must immediately send a transcript of the pertinent continuity to each candidate concerned and offer a comparable opportunity to answer the broadcast, either himself or through a designated spokesman.

3. When a licensee permits the use of his facilities for the presentation of views regarding an issue of current importance such as racial segregation, integration, or discrimination, or any other issue of public importance, he must offer spokesmen for other responsible groups within the community similar opportunities for the expression of contrasting viewpoints.

In its determination as to what constitutes compliance with the fairness doctrine, the Commission looks to substance rather than to label or form. The station operator must realize that to the Commission it is quite immaterial whether a program or viewpoint is presented under the label of "Americanism," "anti-communism" or states' rights"; or whether it is in the form of a paid announcement, official speech, editorial, or religious broadcast. Regardless of label, type, or form, the Commission is adamant that if one viewpoint of a controversial issue is presented, the broadcaster is obligated to make a reasonable effort to present the other opposing viewpoint.

# CHAPTER 3

# Programming Concepts and Formats

Psychologists tell us that the so-called "mass" audience is composed of many small groups, totally heterogeneous. A broadcaster delivers a program without knowing how each small group in his total audience reacts to it. He can only hope that each program will find favor with the greater majority of each group. Further compounding the programmer's problem today is the listener's preoccupation with other things such as housework, shopping, shaving, driving, reading, etc.

In planning any particular program fare the broadcaster must realize that he seldom has a "ready-made" audience. What he should attempt to accomplish is to attract as many listeners as possible, thus creating his audience. To achieve this elusive goal the broadcaster must arrange a program schedule tailored to the majority interest. He must eliminate personal or staff programming preferences if they do not parallel the interests of a sufficiently large audience segment. Of course, it is absolutely impossible to create or schedule a program that meets the tastes and desires of an entire community. And he must be aware of the fact that he cannot afford to cater to a highly specialized audience, because those with special interests in a particular problem or those seeking a special type of entertainment generally will not turn to radio to satisfy that interest or desire. Instead, they attend lectures, concerts, movies, the theatre, etc. Of course, a broadcaster can create and schedule special programs for selected audience segments, such as broadcasts of symphonies, operas, football games, baseball games, etc., and often meet with success in creating a specialized audience of large numbers—if there are enough potential listeners. In fact, that must be the criterion in all program considerations—are there enough potential listeners?

In planning particular programs, especially news commentaries, discussions, etc., it is important to realize that radio audiences place a high degree of credibility on everything they hear broadcast. This is ever truer today even when radio listeners have become more demanding in regard to the reliability of information. Elmo Roper, in a public opinion survey to determine media least believable, (conducted in 1961) discovered that of those interviewed only 9% listed radio, whereas 25% listed magazines and 28% listed newspapers.

## The Importance of Audience Demographics

In preparing a program schedule I cannot stress too strongly the need to know the demographics of your potential audience. At the same time you must realize that it is unrealistic to expect that any iron-clad formula can be applied to attain the ultimate in programming. Listening habits do not remain static and a program director must always be flexible and in a position to change the station's programming as listening habits change. One of the most appropriate guidelines for a program director is a statement by Robert Landry, a former director of the New York University Summer Radio Workshop. Mr. Landry said, "The aim of radio programming is to devise divertisements capable of attracting and beguiling mass audiences. Circulation is the be-all and end-all of commercial radio."

Living in the past is risky business for any individual, and certainly an attitude to be shunned in planning—or maintaining —a program schedule. To be sure, it is much easier to rely solely on past experience, or to duplicate as nearly as possible what others are doing, but in modern radio a program director must forget all that has happened before and plan his programming solely on his knowledge of the present and what he thinks the future will require. We know that everyone has a nostalgia for the familiar and that "imitation is the sincerest form of flattery"; however, in today's race to achieve larger and larger radio audiences a program director cannot afford to stifle his creative ability by relying too heavily on what went on before, nor can he stand pat by programming the familiar. He must experiment; he must constantly reach out for the new, the novel, the original, and the untried. At the same time all of his plans must rest on a proven and sound foundation, considering any and all pertinent information.

There are many surveys, based on rather extensive research, which purport to expose the listening habits of the "radio audience." Nearly all researchers agree that age, sex, and income level are accurate indicators of program preference. Surveys show that:

• Men prefer 1. news, 2. sports, 3. familiar music, and 4. public issue discussions, in that order. Psychologists tell us that men operate by rationalizations and are most influenced by facts.

• Women prefer 1. serials (soap operas), 2. news and talk programs, 3. audience participation programs, 4. popular music, and 5. programs offering "homemaker" ideas. The greater proportion of female listeners are housewives with fewer opportunities for outside diversion or amusement. Psychologists feel that housewives get a mental release from radio which combats loneliness, anxiety, and worry.

• Adults prefer 1. news, 2. music, 3. public issue discussions, 4. quiz programs, and 5. religious programs. Adult audiences are the most difficult to retain. They are more selective in choosing their programs, a habit often called "dial switching."

• Children (up to age 14) prefer 1. adventure drama such as "Superman," "Batman," etc., 2. music, 3. comedy and variety shows, and 4. some sports. Television and radio are their most popular entertainment media. In fact, psychologists report that both television and radio have a tremendous emotional impact upon this age group.

• Teenagers spend more time listening to radio than any other form of entertainment, including television. They prefer 1. music for dancing with vocals featuring the current "hit" singer(s), 2. sports, 3. adventure stories, 4. emotional

70

romantic programs, 5. news about abilities. This age group is the "constant listener." Once they decide upon a radio station they will keep their dial "set" to that station; they're not known as "dial switchers."

Do not overlook or minimize the importance of the teenager in your program plans. Presently they comprise 12% of our population and by 1985 over 19% of our population will be in the 15- to 19-year-age group. Of the families in the U.S. 26% have at least one teenager in the household, and these teenagers exert an influence on how 10% of all consumer dollars are spent. Furthermore, it may be a great surprise to learn that the 1966 annual teenage income amounted to more than twelve billion dollars (little wonder many advertisers go after the teenage market!). Obviously, teenagers represent a rather potent economic force. To illustrate here are some statistics showing their influence in several areas:

- Auto ownership—20%
- New car sales—9%
- Radio receiver sales—39%
- Record sales—43%
- Movie attendance—53%
- Candy bar consumption—15%
- Women's clothing sales—20%
- Cosmetics—23%

"Teenagers" represent all that is new and different in our present complex society. They supply the impetus that influences changes in styles, preferences, and social behavior. Program directors would be wise to listen to their opinions and to cater to their desires. Remember, when teenagers listen to the radio they play it "loud"—loud enough for everyone in the household to hear!

The researchers also report on radio listening habits during the 6 AM to 6 PM time period. Here is how they break it down:

- 6 to 7 AM: Very good weekdays, fair on Saturday, very poor on Sunday. Of the total audience 66% are in the lower income group.

- 7 to 9 AM: Peak listening hours; very good weekdays and Saturday, fair on Sunday. More than 50% belong to the middle and upper income groups.

- 9 to noon: Excellent time to reach housewives and older adults.

- Noon to 1 PM: Peak listening period.

- 1 to 3 PM: Excellent for housewives and older adults.

- 3 to 6 PM: Peak listening especially children and the working force.

## Listening Habits and Program Blocks

Radio listening habits have changed radically since television assumed the role as the primary means of home entertainment, providing drama, comedy, etc. Today's audience uses radio as an adjunct to their daily routine, as a companion while pursuing other interests. Radio programs fill different needs for and is used differently by each listener, while driving a car, for example, or while engaged in housework, walking the streets or sitting on the beach (portable radios), reading, shaving, and a host of many other occupations. It has a tremendous influence upon the listener, for radio is the only medium that can keep changing with the mood of the listener and the time of the day. Radio serves as a "background," for entertainment, and relaxation, and offers listening flexibility in terms of time and place. Unlike other media it offers the immediacy and availability of information at a moment's notice and is more personal and selective.

Because today's radio listener seldom switches from station to station, that is, stop whatever he is doing to "tune-in" a special program on a particular station and then "tune-in" another program on another station, most program directors have adopted the "block programming" technique. They schedule particular or compatible types of programs for long periods or segments of the broadcast day. Radio stations no longer schedule the one-hour or half-hour show, because they have discovered that it tends to decrease rather than increase the total constant audience. As a result, sales personnel have difficulty selling such programs. Also, a one-hour or half-hour program is unpopular with local sponsors because they are the most expensive in terms of cost per minute of commercial time.

The 15-minute program is, however, very popular with local sponsors. The cost per minute of commercial time is quite comparable with the "spot announcement" rate, inasmuch as three minutes of commercial matter accompany each program. Program directors, however, should be wary about scheduling 15-minute programs in a haphazard fashion. They should be compatible with the program matter preceding and following. It is always the best policy to schedule a 15-minute program as part of a larger program. The 5-minute program is the most popular and most often used by local sponsors. It is the least expensive in terms of cost per commercial minute with about a minute and a half of commercial matter within the program. It is used extensively for news programs, sport shows, and vignettes, and a 5-minute program is easy to integrate in the program schedule without running the risk of losing audience interest.

After the above conditions are satisfied, and only then, should the program director authorize a writer to begin script production. It is the program director's duty to communicate to the writer the purpose and basic program idea. Without such information, the best writer is at a loss to produce effective material.

## Program Formats

In radio programming today everything is format, labels, or general terms used in the broadcast industry to describe the basic station sound and program structure. Such labels are useful to national advertisers and their agencies, since distance and time limitations prohibit a thorough analysis of each station; therefore, time buyers (personnel responsible for ordering broadcast advertising) must rely on labels if they are to reach the desired audience. In spite of the overlap due to format variations, a time buyer knows that he can reach a specific audience by purchasing the appropriate format.

Most stations adhere to one of four basic formats: (1) "all music" with various segmentations of (a) "middle-of-the-road," (b) "rock and roll," and (c) "classical"; (2) "music-news-and-sports"; (3) "all talk"; and (4) "all news."

Purposely not included in the above list is a broad and difficult to define "format" called "middle of the road" by many. "Middle of the road" <u>music</u> (mentioned above) is a more specific definition than that used by many program directors in describing a <u>station</u> format. A middle-of-the-road format is probably the most misunderstood and difficult to describe term in radio jargon. Every program director who states that his format is "middle of the road" has a slightly different description of his programming. Most MOR (middle of the road) program directors will agree, however, that what their format attempts to do is to provide the largest segment of the potential listening audience with what that segment wants to hear. If a station's programming is geared to the general audience, rather than to any one particular demographic segment of the audience, it is probable that its program format is called "middle of the road." In other words, if it is not "all news," "all talk," or "all music," or if it doesn't concentrate the greater portion of its programming schedule on any of the above, it is thought of as an MOR station. It is generally agreed, too, that the type of music programmed also determines whether or not that station is MOR.

## The "All-Music" Format

All music stations appeal either to the devotee of a certain type of music or to a more general audience segment. Some cater to teenagers, others to specific ethnic groups, while some attempt to reach a broader demographic spectrum. All-music stations follow one of several basic formats:

"<u>Middle of the Road</u>": To many people an MOR musical format must feature nothing but familiar or "standard" music of the past. I personally disagree with them. To me an MOR format should have a smattering of every kind of music rather than feature any specific type. To achieve balance a typical format hour should include some semi-classical, some familiar or standard tunes, some folk music, some country and western, and some rock and roll. But all types must be well integrated to avoid offending any listener, while attempting to hold the listener throughout the entire day. With about 10 to 12 recordings played during a typical hour a "middle-of-the-road" music format would most likely have one rock and roll, one folk or country and western, one semi-classical, two musical comedy or show tunes and the standards or familiar. Of course, the selections need not follow that categorical order or the same order from hour to hour and they should alternate on the basis of an instrumental, a male vocalist, an instrumental, a female vocalist, etc., for example, rather than invite monotony by the lack of planning. Of course, during those segments of the broadcast day when the station wishes to appeal to a particular demographic segment, the music types included each hour will differ, as will the ratio of instrumental selections to vocal selections differ.

"Rock and Roll": For our purposes here, this category includes various types of "popular" music other than "classical," "semi-classical," "show tunes," etc. If a station programs mostly "rock and roll" music I refer to it as a "rock" station. If it features "folk tunes" and "country and western" music I refer to it as a "C & W" station. If it follows a playlist comprising the "top 40" records, as determined by the various music survey charts, regardless of the category of the music, I consider it as a "Top 40" station. None of these categories need to be explained. They are too well known and do not pose any differences in definition or interpretation. Many stations who have adopted any one of these particular music formats have watched audience ratings soar and their financial picture brighten considerably. The major problem with this type of programming is the availability of personalities to host or "mc" the programs. They must be well versed with the type of music chosen, the artists, and the composers. They must have an unusual style of delivery and must be excellent "ad libbers." Whether or not this type of program succeeds depends equally on the music and the ability of the announcer or disc jockey to befriend the audience.

Classical: This category includes "show tunes," semi-classical," or classical music, or a combination of several types. Though most people will state that "they love the show tunes and the semi-classics," and a fair percentage will admit "loving the classics," stations who have adopted this type of music format rarely are financial successes. The few exceptions are those stations that are located in very large markets. Many stations have tried to compete in multi-station markets by programming to the audience segment who appreciates this type of music, often referred to as "background music," have met with financial failure. And this has happened not only in smaller markets but in cities like Boston, Massachusetts and Philadelphia, Pennsylvania. All one has to do is examine the existing music formats to discover the almost complete absence of such stations. Today many FM stations, who for many years were the only source for this type of music, also have abandoned the format and adopted another.

A "classical" station must choose its announcers with extreme care. They must have mature voices denoting a degree of culture and education. They must be fully, and I mean fully, acquainted with the music, the artists, and the composers, and above all they must be experts in the pronunciation of musical titles, artists' and composers' names. No group of people are more apt and ready to critize an announcer.

## The "Middle-of-the Road" Format

Many stations use the signature: "Your station for Music, News, and Sports." Regardless of format or music policy, practically all stations feature news programs and some programs with "sports" content. Generally speaking a radio station programming 70% music, 10% news, 5% sports, and 15% in all other categories would qualify as a "Music, News, and Sports" format operation. Most stations in small to medium markets adopt this program format. Music is usually of the "middle-of-the-road" type, news programs are presented at specified times throughout the day, and the schedule includes at least one 15-minute program for reporting on sports or athletic events. Due to variety of programming, the announcing staff of a "music, news, and sports" station must be very versatile and interchangeable. Many of the top flight announcers of today began at this type of radio station.

## Value of News

To successfully implement this type of format a program

director must be aware of the fact that "news" is one of the most important facets in developing a large and loyal listening audience. Listeners will stay tuned to a particular station if they are convinced that they will receive the news as soon as it happens and with the greatest degree of accuracy. If your radio station is located in a small to medium market chances are there is no daily newspaper. Or if there is a "daily" newspaper, it probably is an afternoon edition, and practically all afternoon newspapers "go to bed" at 12 noon or earlier. With more and more cities becoming a "one newspaper town," people rely on radio and television for news, especially for the events that are happening in their local community. Radio stations have a decided advantage over both the newspaper and the television industries when it comes to reporting immediate news and in broadcasting events directly from the scene of action.

To keep up to date on the news, people no longer rely entirely on a newspaper. They look to the local radio station, especially for those events occuring between newspaper editions. Listeners do not expect "in depth" news coverage from radio—newspaper and magazines provide that. What they want from radio is "news as it is happening" and radio stations, obviously, are in the best position to meet this demand. By concentrating on "local" news a station can develop the largest possible listening audience; in fact, local news is a vital ingredient in achieving a financially successful operation. As stated previously the size of your news staff and the variety and type of equipment employed is strictly an individual choice, depending entirely on the type of operation you desire. However, if there is any common denominator among broadcasters they all agree that their present success and future growth can be predicated almost entirely upon a successful news department.

## News Schedules and Formats

A variety of news schedules and formats are in use today. Here are several of the most popular schedules:

- A 5-minute newscast every 30 minutes, with 15-minute newscasts at 8 AM, 12 noon, 6 PM and 11 PM.

- A 5-minute newscast every 30 minutes before 8 AM with 5-

minute newscasts thereafter on the hour, supplemented with 15-minute newscasts at 8 AM, 12 noon, 6 PM, and 11 PM.

● A 5-minute newscast every hour on the hour with 15-minute "news in depth" reports at 8 AM, 12 noon, 6 PM, and 11 PM. In many stations this schedule is supplemented by one-minute "news headline" reports on the half hour.

Newscast formats differ from station to station. Here are some successful 5- and 15-minute formats:

5-minute newscasts:

OPENING: "Today is (day of week and date) and here is the (time) news brought to you by (name of sponsor). Here are the headlines": (give three headlines), "The details in a minute."

(One-Minute Commercial)
(Three minutes of News)

CLOSE: "You have just heard the (time) news, brought to you by (sponsor). This news was prepared and edited by the news department of (call letters). Be sure to listen at (time) for our next newscast. Bulletins are always given at once.

A 15-minute newscast with one sponsor:

OPENING: "The time is (time) and (sponsor) brings you the latest local, national, and international news. In the headlines": (give five headlines) "The details in one minute."

(One-minute commercial)
(Five minutes of local news)

"More news follows in 60 seconds."

(One-minute commercial)
(Five minutes state, national, and international news)

"The weather and sports report after this message"

(One-minute commercial)
(Weather and sports report)

CLOSE: "This has been the (time) news brought to you by (sponsor). This newscast was prepared and edited by the news department of (station's call letters). Be sure to listen at (time) for our next news reports. Important bulletins are broadcast as received".

A 15-minute newscast with multiple sponsors:

OPENING: "It is (day and date) and here is the (time) news. In the headlines at this moment": (give five headlines) "The details in a moment."

(First Commercial)
(Five minutes of local news)

"More news after this message"
(Second Commercial)
(Five minutes of state, national, and international news)
"I'll have the weather and sports report in 60 seconds."
(Third Commercial)
Weather and sports report.

CLOSE: "This has been the (time) news as received over the wires of (name of wire service) and prepared and edited by the (station call letters)'s news department. Be sure to listen at (time) for our next news report. Your announcer has been (name)."

There are many, many variations of the news formats suggested above. The responsibility of preparing the format belongs to the program director; the wording of the format is the responsibility of the continuity writer. The news stories, other than those read verbatum from the wire service, should be prepared by the news department and read by an announcer specifically assigned to that task. Wherever possible every effort should be made to give the announcer sufficient time to pre-read the news so that he can check on the correct pronunciation of proper names and places.

United Press International recently issued a report on 27 selected stations who have achieved remarkable success in developing and increasing audiences and revenues by properly programming news. These stations operate in markets ranging from 6,000 to 2,500,000 population. They represent 20 states and every section of the country and include both network affiliates and independent operators. Some are "daytime only" stations; others are 24-hour "around the clock" operations. Staff sizes vary from elaborate to small. Some have an abundance of equipment; others have very little. And program formats cover the full spectrum from "rock and roll" to "classical" to "all talk." However, each and every station operator is aware that his audience demands this type of service.

## Equipping a News Department

Equipping a news department is strictly an individual matter. News directors never seem to have enough equipment, and such equipment is costly and seems to be in constant need of repairs. But there is one piece of equipment you need, whether your market is small, medium, or large—the news "ticker." Most stations affiliate with either the Associated Press or United Press International. Some radio stations enter into a contract with both news-wire services, while others prefer one over the other. Here, again, it is strictly a matter of individual choice, as the cost of either wire service is about the same. In deciding whether to affiliate with UPI or AP, it would be well to determine which wire service is now being used by other stations and the "local" newspaper now serving your area. Wire services are available to all radio stations on a contract basis. It is illegal for any wire service to grant monopolies. In communities where there are several radio stations it is not rare to find that many use the same wire service. The cost of the service varies with the location of the facility and the type of service and equipment a station desires. Most wire service contracts are for a 5-year period. (There is a possibility that this contract term may be lowered to 3 years. As of this writing the FCC is examining the matter but as yet has made no determination.)

In addition to a news-wire service, some stations maintain some or all of the following equipment:

1. Telephones equipped with "beepers" for recording or broadcasting phone conversations.
2. Tape recorders of all sizes (mostly portable)
3. Two-way radio systems
4. Walkie-talkies
5. Mobile Units
6. Radio News Cars
7. Permanent "remote" setups in such places as hospitals, police and fire headquarters, mayor's office, etc.
8. Radio receivers with police monitoring equipment
9. Airplanes
10. Helicopters
11. Boats

## News Gathering

In addition to using the regular news staff, some radio stations employ the following techniques in gathering news:

- **Radio Network**: Either full-time for both program and news services or for just news. The type of affiliation is open to contractural agreement between the station and the network. Some radio news networks are set up on a mutual cost basis, with each station sharing in the profit or loss. Some networks offer a news service, which a station can sell, in exchange for periods of time for use by the network either on a commercial or sustaining basis. (The station does not receive any revenue.)

- **Audio Services**: Several news-gathering organizations offer news programming services, on a contractural basis, consisting of telephoned news reports (recorded on tape) edited by the station news department. These services generally offer reports direct from overseas or Washington, D.C., or from other large cities such as New York, Los Angeles, Chicago, etc. They also provide special events reports directly from the scene, such as the launching of space capsules, sporting events, etc.

- **Reciprocal Agreements With Other Stations**: Many news directors work out reciprocating information exchange agreements with a counterpart at other stations, usually by Beeper phone.

- **Reciprocal Agreements With Newspapers**: Similar to the arrangements above many radio stations enter into some sort of exchange agreement with newspaper editors. (If not a news exchange, the newspaper is given a specified number of commercial announcements.) Some stations actually broadcast news directly from newspaper "editorial rooms," with newspaper reporters functioning as newscasters. (This occurs in many cases where the station and newspaper are mutually owned.)

- **News "Stringers"**: Part-time personnel on special assignment are often called "stringers." Or where a station covers a regional area they employ a stringer to gather and furnish local stories from each community. Remuneration is based on a weekly salary or on the stories furnished or used.

- News "tipsters": It is standard practice for some stations to offer rewards in cash or merchandise to any listener (tipster) who phones in a story or a "tip." Remuneration is offered, usually, only when a story is used on the air.

In the preparation of newscasts it must be remembered that the newscaster cannot be seen by his audience. Therefore, the listener will rely solely on what the newscaster says and how he says it. The news writer must remember that a broadcaster cannot use gestures or facial expressions. Broadcast news can't be sustained or supplemented by "props" or other theatrics, only on clearly written concise statements. A good news writer uses simple words and relatively short sentences. On the other hand, the newscaster must remember that he isn't standing on a soap box making a speech. He should strive for an intimate and conversational style delivered in a natural and restrained voice.

## Sports

A "music, news, and sports" format requires more than a morning and an evening "sportscast" gleaned from the newswire. Local high school basketball and football games should be thoroughly covered, with play-by-play broadcasts where possible. They are not only audience builders but also a very good source of revenue from sponsors who ordinarily do not use radio as an advertising medium. We will discuss the sales aspect of this type of program in the chapter on "sales."

Many "special" networks offer play-by-play broadcasts of professional and college baseball, football, and basketball games. Some networks furnish such programs on a cooperative basis at no cost to the station. The network pays for all the broadcast rights, talent, and telephone line charges in exchange for the right to secure advertisers or sponsors for part of the program. The local station may sell the remaining part of the broadcast locally. The network retains the revenue for its share and the local station receives the revenue from its advertisers. Usually, at least half the broadcast is available for local sale. Some networks furnish programs on a direct purchase plan, where the network pays for all broadcast rights, talent, and "line" charges, secures all the advertisers and sponsors, and retains all the revenue. They contract with the local radio station for broadcast time either on a program basis or on a "flat fee" for an entire series of programs. The station is paid by the network for the air time. I must caution you to remember that details of all contracts with networks must be filed with the FCC. Prior approval from the Commission is not necessary but the contract should be filed prior to the beginning of any network broadcasts.

## "All-Talk" Radio

In the 1960s many stations, especially those located in multiple station markets, developed a new format now referred to as "All-Talk." Also known as "conversation" stations in several localities, such formats include little if any music but perhaps more extensive news coverage than all-music stations. The typical all-talk format is devoted almost entirely to talks, discussions, panel type programs, and audience participation shows. As with all specialized formats all-talk stations must depend entirely upon demographic studies and the segment of the audience they wish to reach.

The "telephone interview" is a popular program form and it often comprises a large part of a broadcast day. But in order not to run afoul of FCC rules and regulations this technique requires special equipment so that both sides of the telephone conversation are "delayed" by 5 or 10 seconds, thus allowing sufficient time to "edit" (prevent going on the air) undesirable statements or language. Usually, the telephone conversation is fed into a tape recorder and then on the air, providing an adjustable delay time. Some "talk" stations originate audience participation programs, supervised and hosted by a "master of ceremonies." Invited guests comprise the audience, and the MC "interviews" individuals or small groups, discussing various phases of special topics. The audience participates either by asking questions or commenting upon the subject that is being discussed.

Finding qualified personnel for a talk format is not easy, as is the case with all specialties. Above all else they must be masters of the interview technique and possess a complete command of the language. Excellent memory retention is an asset, obviously, and such an individual must have more than a mere first-hand knowledge of a myriad of subjects. To assist these personalities many stations employ a staff of researchers, as well as a "production" staff to insure an adequate number of participants and a diversification of subject matter. Under current "Fairness Doctrine" rules the "all-talk" entrepreneur must be certain that all opposing views are offered equal time. He must be sure also that he is adequately covered by "libel and slander" insurance and that every possible means is employed to avoid instances that may be embarrassing to the participants, the listeners, or individuals.

## "All-News" Radio

In 1966 Radio Station WINS New York City embarked upon a new format now generally referred to as "all-news." As the title suggests, the entire program schedule is devoted to capsule news, news analysis, and commentary. This format requires a very large staff of newsmen, both at the station and in the field, and a world-wide "stringer" network.

"All-news" stations cover every phase of news, including stock market reports, sporting events, book reviews, movie reviews, theatre, opera, music, etc. A large proportion of the program schedule is devoted to discussion and panel type programs concerned with current events, thus necessitating the employment of a specialized program staff to formulate programs and to serve as a liaison with participants. The heart of an all-news operation, of course, is a large editorial staff capable of rewriting news stories into broadcast language and to prevent reuse of a story in exactly the same language.

The "all-news" station is for all purposes a "newspaper of the air." It cannot expect to have the same constant audience; rather, it strives to build a loyal audience "tune-in" at intervals throughout the day. Its main purpose is to cater to that segment of the total audience who is interested in the events and happenings of the day and who expect immediate and current reports on all phases of the news.

# CHAPTER 4

# Developing a Program Schedule

Clearly, a radio program schedule is not to be developed in a haphazard manner, no more than a manufacturer would literally "throw together" a piece of equipment. In both cases the "product" must reflect serious concern and consideration for the needs and desires of the potential "customers." New and renewal station license applications require attention to community convenience and necessity. To assure compliance with the above the FCC is interested in the applicant's plans in the seven principle areas stated previously and repeated here:

(1) Entertainment; (2) Religion; (3) Agriculture; (4) Education; (5) News; (6) Discussion: and, (7) Talks. Let's examine the Commission's definition of each category:

- Entertainment: Music, drama, variety, comedy, quiz, children's, etc., are viewed as entertainment programs. Disc jockey programs are classified as entertainment, too. If, however, the DJ interrupts a musical portion of the program for interviews, news, extended weather reports, etc., those segments may be classified according to the appropriate category.

- Religion: Includes all sermons, religious news, religious music, and religious drama.

- Agriculture: All programs containing farm or market reports or other information specifically addressed to the interests of farmers or persons interested in "growing things." Weather reports prepared specifically for the farmer, home gardening programs, and hunting and fishing programs where the content is related to the product.

- Education: Programs prepared by or on behalf of educational organizations. The broadcast of a high school athletic event which is programmed in cooperation with educational authorities may be classified in this category. Discussion programs about education do not fall into this category, however, nor does instruction in any subject by any persons other than school authorities. Such programs should be listed under "talk" with a special notation—"educational content."

● <u>News</u>: News reports and commentaries.

● <u>Discussion</u>: Forum, panel, roundtable, and interview programs concerning controversial issues and where opposing points of view are presented; also, interview programs of a non-controversial nature where there is a "give-and-take" discussion.

● <u>Talk</u>: All conversation programs which do not fall into any of the other categories.

For further clarification and to illustrate FCC intent here are several time-proven program ideas in each of the principle categories. While few will seem original to a broadcast veteran, these basic ideas are adaptable to most small markets where it is necessary to reach a large general audience.

## Entertainment

A greater part of most program schedules is devoted to entertainment. In fact, all radio programs should, to a degree, "entertain," accompanying each member of the audience as he pursues his daily routine or relaxes during moments of leisure. Audience participation shows offer excellent entertainment highlights, literally drawing listeners into your programming efforts. And such programs are not limited to very large operations with a staff to match. Here are some typical examples:

<u>The breakfast show</u>: Here is a good 45-minute to 1-hour program designed for live presentation from a hotel ballroom, the cafeteria or dining room of a department store, or a restaurant. The audience is invited to partake of a simple breakfast consisting, for example, of orange juice, coffee, and

toast served at a nominal cost of no more than 25 cents. Corsages are awarded to guests who traveled the furthest distance to attend the program, thus encouraging members of the "studio" audience to bring visiting friends and relatives. Out-of-town visitors are a source of interesting and entertaining interviews. Anniversary and birthday cakes may be presented to those attending the show whose birthdays fall on the exact day of the program. And to add more excitement a "pre-selected" person (selection by drawing prior to air time) is given the opportunity to compete for a prize. If unsuccessful award a "jackpot" prize, created by adding a prize on each consecutive program, or a minor prize as a consolation for those who fail to win the jackpot. In most communities there is a wealth of local entertainment available, anxious for broadcast exposure: theatrical groups, high school choruses, etc. After the program goes off the air you can present door prizes such as theatre passes, 6-packs of soft drinks, etc. The field is wide open for any special games or contests the MC decides to include.

A very logical time for a breakfast show is 9 to 10 AM. Usually, the food and flowers can be obtained for "air" mention. And certainly a local bakery will be glad to provide the birthday or anniversary cake. The recipient is presented with a certificate while the audience sings "Happy Birthday" (or anniversary). Jackpot prizes, theatre passes, 6-packs of soft drinks can be obtained for "air mention," too.

A program of this type is an excellent advertising vehicle for a department store with a cafeteria, for on the day of the broadcast it insures the store manager of a captive audience. Some stations using this type of audience participation show have been successful in selling the program on a participation basis (more than one sponsor). As with all audience participation programs, the breakfast show has a proven record of increasing an audience; generally, it shows up as number one in all audience surveys. People, especially women, are very interested in this type of local program for they are always curious as to who may be attending and called upon to participate, who may be visiting whom, and the answer to the "jackpot" question.

The telephone quiz show: As part of a disc jockey program, or as a separate entity, a telephone quiz is an excellent Monday-through-Friday feature. Soon after the start of the program, the DJ asks the listening audience a question, or to identify a mystery voice or tune, and to telephone him while on the air with their answers. The DJ should ask only the name and the address of the caller and the answer. He can do this while the "mike" is open or during a musical selection. He should not "air" the caller's answer. The answer is never given during the program but at the very end of the show. Prizes are awarded to the first six persons, for example, who call in the correct answer.

Questions should be relatively difficult; never, under any circumstances, make it an easy question. It is amazing how listeners will search to find an answer. And, the more difficult the question, the more people will stay tuned to the program for the answer. Participants should not be permitted to win more than once a week, but at the same time they should be allowed to participate daily. Experience with this type of program shows that people will call in even if they are not eligible to be a winner.

Prizes can be very modest, such as theatre passes, 6-packs of soft drinks, bakery products, etc. All of these can be obtained at no cost to the station merely by mentioning the donor's name. Sponsorship on a participating or "spot" announcement basis is very easy to secure because this type of program is very popular and enjoys high ratings in audience surveys and in surveys indicating listeners' desires and preferences.

Children's program: A children's story hour is a very good Saturday morning program. Try to originate the program at the local library where children can congregate and be entertained by the dramatic reading of a story by either the librarian or a kindergarten, first, or second grade school teacher. If community facilities are inadequate or nonexistent, a department store probably would be glad to loan its space. The size of the live audience should be limited; restrict admission to ticket holders only. You'll find that a program of this type will enlist the support of many. Children who once attend become loyal listeners. Librarians are most anxious to cooperate as they have learned that it increases library participation. And school authorities will encourage children to listen, in many cases by urging parental cooperation. Potential sponsors include establishments who cater to children's needs such as furniture, toys, and clothing.

## Religion

There never seems to be a scarcity of religious program material—both commercial and non-commercial. I have yet to meet a clergyman who is not anxious to appear before the microphone. Although this type of program rates high on the "listener's desire" list, it doesn't often rate high on the audience survey list. Once a station begins broadcasting religious programs it will be swamped with requests for sustaining and commercial time. A good policy is to begin and end the broadcast day with a short sermonette delivered on a rotating basis by area clergymen embracing all religious faiths. If you do decide to broadcast religious programs it is best to schedule them only on Sunday mornings prior to 12 noon. Some stations carry a "live" service from area churches, on a rotating basis, between 11 AM and 12 noon. Be wary of religious programs that solicit funds in every program. But in spite of the drawbacks, there is no doubt—notwithstanding the FCC's statement that it doesn't want to control a radio station's programming—that the Commission expects licensees to devote some part of the broadcast week to such programming. However, the practice is arousing some question. Marcus Cohn, one of the most able, competent and experienced attorneys practicing before the FCC, has raised the question that this requirement may be unconstitutional under the concept of the separation of church and state.

## Agriculture

Stations located in entirely urban areas usually don't find it necessary to program in this category. However, if any of your listeners live in the suburbs it would be well to consider some programming for them. The best all-around agricultural programs are available from, or prepared in cooperation with, the U.S. Agriculture Department Extension Service and state universities. They furnish material of interest not only to the farming community but also to anyone who "grows" anything like flowers, lawns, and trees. Also available from these sources is advice to housewives on food prices and what food products are scarce or plentiful. They also offer information on methods of canning, preserving, freezing foods, etc. In most cases, a representative from such agencies, as well as home economics teachers, the homemaker or home economist from various public utilities, and hospital dieticians will gladly do a regular program series. Scheduled at a regular time each week it becomes a favorite with the listener and always enjoys a loyal audience.

## Education

In this category you must remember the FCC's definition that only such programs prepared by or for educational institutions can be classified as "education." Panels, round-tables, and other discussions concerning educational problems cannot be classified as such. A typical and quite worth-while program is the "You and Your Schools" type. Enlist the aid of a school board member, the board of education or the superintendent of schools.

Another program, very popular on weekends, is the "instructional program" featuring teachers of specialized subjects—an entire series around literature, art, music, history, etc. Do not overlook the possibility of presenting the high school's drama society, glee club, chorus, or orchestra on special occasions, especially when any of these groups are appearing before service clubs or other organizations.

A 15-minute sports program featuring former local sports personalities draws a large listening audience and is very easy to sell to a sponsor. In our case the sports director interviews local people who were at one time or another active in sports on the local level. It should be entirely geared to the "Old Timers"; the former high school football, baseball, basketball or track celebrity.

## Basic Program Schedule

While it is completely beyond the scope of this book to attempt a thorough discussion of all possible program ideas, it is appropriate to consider a basic schedule of proven programs for a typical small market middle-of-the-road station.

## Typical Sunday Schedule

All audience surveys indicate that the least number of people listen to radio on Sunday morning. Therefore, the 6 AM to 12 noon time period may be used to cater to the small special audience segments. For instance, it is an excellent time to schedule "foreign language" programs. Reference here is to a general type foreign program in which the oral content is in English. Only the music is directed to a particular ethnic group. A "Polish Hour" featuring polkas will be enjoyed by Polish speaking people without alienating the rest of your audience. Likewise, an "Italian Hour" featuring operatic arias and neopolitan tunes will appeal to the total audience as well as cater to the ethnic group of Italian descent. All surveys indicate that foreign language program listeners are the most loyal of all audiences, not only to the station but exceptionally so to the sponsors and advertisers. But unless you are a "foreign language" station you should not schedule such programs in which the oral part is in the foreign tongue after 12 noon, since such programs should be scheduled only for that small segment of the total audience. Otherwise, those listeners not in the particular ethnic group will seek other stations for entertainment.

If you are planning to broadcast any foreign language programs be sure that you, as the licensee, are fully aware of the FCC regulations concerning control over the broadcast of foreign language programs. It is necessary for the licensee to make arrangements for responsible persons with a knowledge of the particular language in question to monitor the programs and inform the licensee of the content.

Sunday morning is the best time of the week to schedule religious programs; actually, all religious programming should be restricted to the pre-noon hours. But it must be remembered that this type of programming caters only to a small segment of the total audience and can cause those of other religious denominations to listen to other radio stations during this segment. With the preceding thoughts in mind here is a sample 6 AM to noon Sunday schedule:

6 AM          — Sign On
6:01 - 6:05 — News
6:05 - 8:00 — Foreign or Religious program
8:00 - 8:15 — News
8:15 - 9:00 — Foreign or Religious Program
9:00 - 9:05 — News

9:05 - 10   — Foreign or Religious Program
10  - 10:05 — News
10:05 -  11 — Foreign or Religious Program
11 - 11:05 — News
11:05 - 12  — Live Religious Service

Sunday afternoon programming should be divided into two
segments. One period from 12 noon to 2 PM and the other
from 2 PM to "sign off." The period beginning at 12 noon
should feature an indepth news program, either a 15-minute
or 30-minute newscast. Thereafter until 2 PM, unless programs of a special or seasonal nature are planned, the schedule should be devoted to musical entertainment. This is a
good time for the "familiar" or standard type of music or for
complete albums of musical comedy shows featuring original
cast performances.   The 12 noon to 2 PM schedule may
look like this:

12 noon to 12:15 — News
12:15   - 12:30 — Music or News commentary
12:30   - 1:00 — Music
 1:00  -  1:05 — News
 1:05  -  2:00 — Music

From 2 PM to 6 PM the station can "specialize" and present
those programs established to meet the needs of particular
total audience segments. If you adhere to a "music, news,
and sports" format this is the time to present play-by-play
professional baseball or football games. The average baseball game now takes about 2 1/2 to 3 hours, and the average
football game generally lasts from 2 1/2 to 2 3/4 hours. Adequate program time should be allotted not only for the actual
play-by-play but also for pre-game and post-game commentary. During the spring and summer months if you do not
broadcast professional baseball games you might want to give
consideration to "Little League," "Babe Ruth," "American
Legion," or "semi-pro" baseball games featuring local teams.
If you do not program athletic events try to schedule as many
"talk" or discussion programs as possible during this period.
A typical Sunday afternoon "sports" station program schedule would appear as follows:

```
2  -  2:05  —  News
2:05 - 2:15  —  Pre-Game Show
2:15 - 5:00  —  Play-by-Play and Post-Game show
5:00 - 5:05  —  News
5:05 - 5:15  —  Talk (education, social security, health, etc.)
5:15 - 5:45  —  Discussion Program
5:45 - 6:00  —  Late News Round-Up
```

A typical program schedule for a "non-sports" station would appear as follows:

```
2:00 - 2:05  —  News
2:05 - 2:30  —  Music
2:30 - 3:00  —  Discussion Program
3:00 - 3:05  —  News
3:05 - 3:30  —  Music
3:30 - 4:00  —  Discussion Program
4:00 - 4:05  —  News
4:05 - 4:30  —  Music
4:30 - 5:00  —  Discussion Program
5:00 - 5:05  —  News
5:05 - 5:45  —  Music
5:45 - 6:00  —  Late News Roundup
```

## Typical Weekday Schedule

The Monday-through-Friday broadcast schedule should remain constant for each period of the day. What you schedule for Monday at 6 AM should be the same at 6 AM on Tuesday, Wednesday, Thursday, and Friday. In preparing a weekday schedule you must know who listens to radio at specific times of the day. As indicated previously, studies show that during the period from 6 AM to 9 AM the audience generally consists of teenagers, adult men and women, and older adults. This encompasses practically the entire audience, or at least a sizeable cross section of it. It is necessary, therefore, to understand this audience in relation to its work habits and its desires. It is important to know area school hours and at what time children leave the house to meet the school bus. Are there commuters in the audience? What trains or buses do they "make"? Remember, commuters listen to their automobile radios while on the way to the railroad station or bus terminal. You should also know what newspapers, if any, are delivered, at what time they are delivered, and the time the newspaper "went to bed." All of these things are of utmost importance in planning the 6 AM to 9 AM program schedule. Ask yourself: "What is it that these people want to hear at this particular time?" And then plan accordingly. Most people will answer that what they want is information first and entertainment second. They want to know the time, weather, road conditions, train schedules (if there are delays), and the latest news. But they don't want it "shoved down their throats." They want all this information in an entertaining fashion with the least amount of irritation. Let's look at a typical 6 AM to 9AM Monday-through-Friday schedule:

| | |
|---|---|
| 6 AM | — Sign On |
| 6:01 - 6:03 | — Morning Devotional |
| 6:03 - 6:10 | — News (include weather, short sports report) |
| 6:10 - 6:30 | — Music |
| 6:30 - 6:35 | — News and Weather |
| 6:35 - 7:00 | — Music |
| 7:00 - 7:05 | — News and Weather |
| 7:05 - 7:15 | — Sports |
| 7:15 - 7:30 | — Music |
| 7:30 - 7:35 | — News and Weather |
| 7:35 - 8:00 | — Music |
| 8:00 - 8:15 | — News |
| 8:15 - 9:00 | — Music |

The 9 AM to noon segment of the day, as surveys indicate, finds housewives, adult men, and adult women listening to radio. The tumult of the early hours has subsided by now. The working force is at their place of employment or well on their way to that destination. The school-age child has gone to school. The housewife is ready to relax and begin her daily chores, while older folks in the household begin to experience "loneliness." Retail stores begin opening and managers turn on the radio. This is truly a transitional period.

Many stations refer to this segment as the "Music Hall." It is our suggestion that the "transition" period should not extend beyond 10 AM. From 10 AM to 11 AM the audience needs stimulation. Here is a good spot for features such as a "telephone quiz," intermingled with music with a livelier beat.

From 11 AM until noon a good talk program is appropriate.

The station's women's director is a likely moderator or hostess. It need not be an "all-talk" program necessarily. Intermingled with "music that's easy to listen to" use reports on upcoming movies, theatre presentations, church, club and other social events, household hints, recipes, and short 10-minute interviews with celebrities or representatives of social and civic organizations, but be careful that nothing of a real controversial nature is presented at this time. The program schedule may indicate the following:

| | | |
|---|---|---|
| 9:00 - 9:05 AM | — | News |
| 9:05 - 9:30 | — | Music |
| 9:30 - 9:35 | — | News |
| 9:35 - 10:00 | — | Music |
| 10:00 - 10:05 | — | News |
| 10:05 - 10:30 | — | Music and Quiz Show |
| 10:30 - 10:35 | — | News |
| 10:35 - 11:00 | — | Music and Quiz Show |
| 11:00 - 11:05 | — | News |
| 11:05 - 11:30 | — | "Community Reporter" type program |
| 11:30 - 11:35 | — | News |
| 11:35 - 12:00 noon- | | "Community Reporter" type program |

Between 12 noon and 2 PM preference surveys indicate that the audience is composed of mostly adult women and older adults. If your radio station is located in an area where long lunch hours are in effect, then you will find a great many professional men and merchants in the audience. It is the time of day when people are interested in news, want to relax, and want some information in addition to music. They are ready for a newscast in "depth" and music preferably the "album type" featuring a female or male singer of popular and familiar tunes. This segment should include information about things that affect their own individual life such as Social Security, health reports and medical discussions, school news, etc. The program schedule might appear as follows:

| | | |
|---|---|---|
| 12:00 - 12:15 PM | — | News |
| 12:15 - 12:30 | — | Album Music |
| 12:30 - 12:35 | — | News |
| 12:35 - 1:00 | — | Album Music |
| 1:00 - 1:05 | — | News |

| 1:05 - 1:20 | — | Talk Programs on Social Security, Health, etc. |
| 1:20 - 1:30 | — | Music |
| 1:30 - 1:35 | — | News |
| 1:35 - 2:00 | — | Music |

The period from 2 PM to 6 PM should attract a preponderance of teenagers, young adults, and adult males. The housewife is usually out of the house attending to her shopping chores and when home in the late afternoon busy with preparations for the evening meal. The teenager is home from school and usually dominates the radio. The factory worker also returns during this time and begins listening to the radio. No one is interested in anything of a serious nature at this time of day. They're interested in music, news, and, if available, sports. The tempo of the music should be much livelier and feature the more popular selections of the day. A typical program schedule for this period:

| 2:00 - 2:05 PM | — | News |
| 2:05 - 2:30 | — | Music |
| 2:30 - 2:35 | — | News |
| 2:35 - 3:00 | — | Music |
| 3:00 - 3:05 | — | News |
| 3:05 - 3:30 | — | Music |
| 3:30 - 3:35 | — | News |
| 3:35 - 4:00 | — | Music |
| 4:00 - 4:05 | — | News |
| 4:05 - 4:30 | — | Music |
| 4:30 - 4:35 | — | News |
| 4:35 - 5:00 | — | Music |
| 5:00 - 5:05 | — | News |
| 5:05 - 5:30 | — | Music |
| 5:30 - 5:35 | — | News |
| 5:35 - 5:45 | — | Sports Reports |
| 5:45 - 6:00 | — | Evening News Round-up |

## Typical Saturday Schedule

Saturday is the most difficult day of the week to program. With the advent of the 5-day work schedule practically all professional men and factory workers are at home. In fact, with the exception of retail establishments and certain services everyone, including school children, has a holiday. No two radio stations program their Saturdays alike. Planning a Saturday schedule requires a thorough knowledge of listener likes and desires. Most radio stations continue their Monday through Friday 6 AM to 10 AM schedule on Saturday, but they vary their schedule extensively for the balance of the day. Some cater the 10 AM to 12 noon period to teenagers exclusively. Others schedule a 30-minute children's program, or devote a segment to the female teenager and young adult woman by scheduling a talk program on "Beauty Hints." A Saturday 6 AM to 12 noon program schedule might look like this:

| | |
|---|---|
| 6:00 AM | — Sign On |
| 6:01 - 6:03 | — Morning Devotional |
| 6:03 - 6:10 | — News (include weather, short sports report) |
| 6:10 - 6:30 | — Music |
| 6:30 - 6:35 | — News and Weather |
| 6:35 - 7:00 | — Music |
| 7:00 - 7:05 | — News and Weather |
| 7:05 - 7:15 | — Sports |
| 7:15 - 7:30 | — Music |
| 7:30 - 7:35 | — News and Weather |
| 7:35 - 8:00 | — Music |
| 8:00 - 8:15 | — News |
| 8:15 - 9:00 | — Music |
| 9:00 - 9:05 | — News |
| 9:05 - 9:30 | — Music or "Kiddie Show" |
| 9:30 - 9:35 | — News |
| 9:35 -10:00 | — Music |
| 10:00 -10:05 | — News |
| 10:05- 10:15 | — Talk on Beauty Hints |
| 10:15 -11:00 | — Music for the Teenager |
| 11:00 -11:05 | — News |
| 11:05 -11:30 | — Music for the Teenager |
| 11:30 -11:35 | — News |
| 11:35 -12:00 noon | — Music for the Teenager |

If your radio station caters to a sports-minded audience the Saturday afternoon schedule is fairly easy to program especially during the spring, summer, and fall seasons. Here's a suggested Saturday afternoon schedule:

| 12:00 - 12:15 PM | — | News |
| 12:15 - 12:30 | — | Sports Interviews |
| 12:30 - 1:00 | — | Music (album Type) |
| 1:00 - 1:05 | — | News |
| 1:05 - 1:30 | — | Music (Album Type) |
| 1:30 - 1:35 | — | News |
| 1:35 - 1:50 | — | Music (Album Type) |
| 1:50 - 2:00 | — | Pre-Game show |
| 2:00 - 5:00 | — | Play-by-Play and Post-Game Show |
| 5:00 - 5:05 | — | News |
| 5:05 - 5:30 | — | Music (familiar or standards) |
| 5:05 - 5:35 | — | News |
| 5:35 - 5:45 | — | Sports Round-Up |
| 5:45 - 6:00 | — | Evening News Report |

If your radio station does not program sports the period period from 12:30 PM to 5:00 PM requires a special study as to the musical tastes of your audience. All surveys indicate that radio has a small listening audience during these hours and it is impossible to suggest the type of music for this segment unless one has a complete knowledge of the audience and its listening habits, likes, and desires. Some stations program operas and symphonies during this period; others cater to small segments of the audience and schedule folk music, country and western, or "rock and roll" music.

## Contest Programming

One type of program received favorably by most radio audiences is the "contest." People enjoy playing games; everyone wants to be a winner and get "something for nothing." For the radio station a "contest" can increase the number of listeners. All reputable audience measurement firms specifically mention in their reports that a station was conducting or had just completed a "contest" at the time the survey was made. There is no doubt that radio stations do gain additional and new listeners when they schedule a contest. However, it is also a proven fact that once the "contest" is completed that most, if not all, of the new listeners revert to their previous listening habits. A "contest" should never be considered the "end-all" in creating a permanent audience. It is the total programming that creates the permanent audience. For the sponsor a "contest" should, in most cases, increase his store traffic, stimulate sales, and produce new customers. Researchers indicate that many "new" customers become regular customers. This is a matter completely controlled by the store, its personnel, its policies, and the merchandise and prices offered. Therefore, no radio station can or should ever guarantee that a radio contest, no matter how successful a broadcast vehicle it may be, can ever increase the total business of any establishment over an indefinite period.

There are those who claim that contests can have a reverse effect; that people who do not win become antagonistic to the radio station and the sponsor. Above all else be sure that the contest you program is honest in every respect and that everyone has an equal opportunity to be one of the winners. When contests are legitimate, researchers report, losers do not act adversely toward the radio station or the sponsor. They further report that less than 1/10 of 1% ever complain to the radio station or the sponsor. I very strongly recommend that whenever a complaint is received, either by the station or the sponsor, that the station management immediately answer the complaint. The answer should be in the form of a courteous and honest letter. All complaints and replies should be filed for reference should any question arise concerning them.

There are many types of successful contests, some quite simple, requiring a minimum of listener effort, while others call for thought and initiative. Some of them are:

1. Complete the Sentence. In (25) words or less complete the sentence: "I like to listen to radio station (call letters) because...." or "I like to shop at (name of store) because...." or, "I like to use (name of product) because ....", etc.
2. Complete the last line of a limerick.
3. Identify a "mystery" voice.
4. Identify a particular song.
5. Identify a well-known "talent" or personality.
6. Suggest a name (for a store, product, etc.)
7. The "treasure hunt."
8. The "Lucky number Game." This has proven a most successful audience builder for radio stations, especially in areas where the telephone company does not place any limitation upon the number of local calls made by a sub-

scriber. Periodically throughout the broadcast day a number between 1 and 36 is announced, and the first person calling the station who can match the broadcast number with the last four digits of their phone number receives a prize. Winners are asked to verify their phone number by presenting their telephone bill to collect the prize. The contest is broadcast at the will of the station and at times chosen by the station. No advance notice of contest times is given. It is good practice to "air" the contest at least once an hour and at different segments of the hour.

Before scheduling any contest its cost should be evaluated. The cost of the prizes, advertising and promotion costs, cost of handling mail, additional telephone costs, cost of additional personnel, etc.

It is also very important to devise a set of rules for the contest, and to be sure that every employee adheres strictly to the rules. Once the rules are established never deviate from them or make any exceptions. In devising a set of contest rules some of the essentials to be considered are:

1. The prizes
2. A time limit (the contest must end at a specific time)
3. Opening and closing date for the contest
4. Provisions in case of a "tie"
5. How prizes are to be awarded
6. Rules as to how the contest will be judged
7. Form of "entry"
8. Where "entries" are to be sent
9. Number of entries allowed
10. Eligibility rules
11. How, when, and where winners are to be announced
12. All entries should become the property of the radio station; etc.

In scheduling any contest be sure that it is not a lottery. I would suggest that you re-read the section concerning "lotteries." If the contest is to be a game of "skill" be sure that "skill" is required. Guessing games like the number of beans in a jar have been judged by the courts as "guessing games" and not a game of skill. The courts have included such "guessing games" in the "chance" section in the description of a lottery.

## Station Promotion.

The only "promotable" asset a radio station has is its programming. Unless a radio station has a good solid program schedule which meets the likes and desires of the prospective audience, no amount of exploitation, advertising, or special appeals and promotions will create a listening audience. Available promotion methods are legion, but for the sake of brevity we will consider only some of the most successful methods easily adopted by any radio station.

● Newspaper ads listing the daily program schedule or special programs supplemented by adequate on-air announcements. Billboard advertising calling special attention to the station format and the "spot" on the dial. (A strategic location is important.)

● Movie theatre trailers emphasizing your call letters, frequency, and format.

● Automobile bumper stickers displaying call letters and frequency, or regularly schedule and special shows and/or personalities.

● Dial position (frequency). Too many stations pay more attention to their call letters than to their dial setting. This is perhaps due to FCC requirements concerning station identification. It is good for a station to be known by its call letters, but when a person tunes in a station he does it by the numbers on the dial, not by call letters. TV stations are well aware of the fact as evidenced by newspaper or magazine program schedules listing the channel number instead of call letters. Radio stations should promote their frequency by calling attention to it wherever and whenever possible. Some use the dial setting in program names, such as "Club (frequency)," "(frequency) Radio Row," and they award prize money in amounts equal to their frequency number (800 pennies for a station on 800 kHz) or when the last three or four digits in a contestant's phone number is the same as the station's frequency.

- "Cross Plugs": Announcers, personalities, and DJs "plug" and promote other air personnel and call attention to special programs.

- "Giveaways": Use programs which offer prizes, plus contests and specialized quiz programs.

- Reciprocal Advertising: For example, electric clocks provided at cost in return for advertising contracts with service stations and stores. These clocks display the station's call letters and frequency.

- Surveys: Make full use of all available surveys both in determining the audience and in promoting survey "standings."

- Childrens' Parties: Free theatre parties for children during the Christmas period, and "Easter Egg" rolling contests.

- Automobile Display: License plates for all station personnel displaying call letters and frequency. Also, automobiles with call letters and frequency distinctly painted in strategic locations.

Station promotion must not be a "sometime" thing; such an attitude doesn't speak very well of advertising. If it makes good sense for others to advertise, it certainly should make good sense for a radio station to use every available means and media. It is only through adequate advertising and promotion that a community is made aware of a station and its programs. Good programming will create an audience. Good advertising and promotion will not only aid in keeping the audience but help to increase it, too.

# CHAPTER 5

# Staffing a Station

Like all enterprises, a radio station's success depends to a large degree on the competency of its staff. The finest facilities, ideal location, power, and frequency are greatly diminished in value and importance unless such attributes are combined and implemented by a capable and dedicated staff. However, a licensee cannot absolve himself of all responsibility simply by hiring good people. Certainly the ownership can delegate authority and responsibility, but it must answer to the FCC for the performance of every employee.

## Departmental Organization

Most station organizations comprise eight principal departments:

● Engineering Department
   Chief Engineer
   Transmitter Engineers

● Management
   General Manager
   Station Manager

● Sales Department
   Commercial Manager
   National and Regional Representatives
   Sales Manager
   Time Salesmen
   Copywriters

- Program Department
    Program Director
    Announcers
    Talent
    Continuity Writers
    Music Librarian

- News Department
    News Director
    Newsmen
    Stringers

- Traffic Department
    Traffic Manager

- Clerical Department
    Bookkeeper
    Steno-typists
    Clerks

- Custodial Department
    Custodian

Each department is charged with specific duties under the supervision of a responsible department head, each reporting directly to management. It is not too uncommon in small market operations especially to find more than one "department" under the same supervisor. For example, the manager may function also as the commercial manager, program director, news director, or even as chief engineer. Or, the program director and news director may be the same individual, etc. So in view of the required flexibility in many cases, we will discuss each department separately, considering the factors contributing toward economical operation without risking quality or performance.

### Engineering Department

The engineering department is placed first in our consideration because today the station licensee is often an "absentee owner" or one with little or no broadcast engineering experience. And it is a simple fact that no station can operate without an engineer. He is responsible for equipment operation and maintenance, enabling you to keep the station on the air. The engineer's duties include all necessary repairs and equipment adjustments necessary to satisfy FCC performance standards regarding signal quality and coverage without interference to other stations as specified in the license. You can go so far as to compare the engineer with the ignition key of an automobile. The most expensive car with the best possible engine is useless unless you first have and use the ignition key; likewise, the finest and best broadcasting equipment cannot begin to function without an engineer to supervise and maintain its operation.

To maintain uniform technical standards, the FCC issues six classes of operator licenses:

1. Radiotelephone First Class
2. Radiotelephone Second Class
3. Radiotelephone Third Class
4. Radiotelegraph First Class
5. Radiotelegraph Second Class
6. Radiotelegraph Third Class

There is also another class called a "restricted radiotelephone operator permit," which does not require an oral or written test. The applicant is required to be at least 14 years of age and certify in writing that he has a need for such a permit; that he can receive or transmit spoken messages in English; that he can keep a rough written log in English or a language easily translated into English; that he is familiar with the treaties and laws governing the use of this permit; and that he will keep currently familiar with all such provisions.

Prior to the promulgation of the FCC regulation requiring announcers who handled remote equipment to have a third class license with broadcast endorsement, announcers usually were required to secure a "restricted radiotelephone operator permit." Today, under present regulations all announcers who are required to make meter readings and enter them upon station engineering logs must have a "third class license with broadcast endorsement." Failure to employ operators without such a license can result in heavy fine assessment against the station owner. (Do not misunderstand, an announcer does not need an operator's permit of any kind unless he is to maintain a transmitter log.) Applicants for all other classes of licenses (the six mentioned previously) must take a written examination and receive a grade of at least 75%.

Any applicant who fails an examination element is ineligible to repeat the exam again until two months after the date of the first examination. Holders of radiotelegraph licenses generally are not permitted to operate commercial broadcast or TV stations. Holders of radiotelephone licenses are not permitted to operate stations using telegraphy.

Except at times when station operation is under the immediate supervision of an operator holding a valid radiotelephone first class license, adjustments of the transmitting equipment shall be limited to the following:

1. Those necessary to turn the transmitter on and off.

2. Adjustment of external controls as may be required to compensate for voltage fluctuations in the power supply.

3. Adjustment of external controls to maintain modulation of the transmitter within the prescribed limits.

4. Adjustment of external controls necessary to effect routine changes in operating power which are required by the station license.

5. Adjustment of external controls necessary to effect operation in accordance with a national defense emergency authorization during an emergency action condition.

All stations must employ full-time at least one engineer holding a valid first class radiotelephone license, or alternatively contract in writing for the services on a part-time basis of one or more such engineers (applies to all non-directional AM stations with a power of 10 KW or less). (Stations with directional antenna systems and those over 10 KW directional or non-directional cannot use the contractural alternative.) The engineer with a "first class ticket" shall perform transmitter maintenance and be promptly available at all times to correct conditions of improper operation beyond those allowed to second class or third class operators. If you choose to hire part-time first ticket engineers by contract, it is mandatory that a copy of the contract be available for inspection and that a copy of the contract be placed on file with the FCC and the Engineer in Charge of the radio district in which the station is located.

The FCC also requires that a first class ticket holder shall make a complete inspection of all transmitting equipment in use at least once a day, five days per week, with no less than 12 hours between successive inspections. He must see to it that all necessary repairs and adjustments are made so as to insure operation in conformance with the station's license and good engineering practices. Second and third class ticket holders who are required to make external control adjustments must be properly instructed and able to perform these tasks when the first class is not present. It is suggested that printed step-by-step instructions be posted concerning these operations. It is mandatory that a station "shut down" if the transmitter operation exceeds prescribed tolerances and cannot be returned to proper operation by external control adjustments. A second or third class ticket holder cannot make any internal adjustments except under the direct supervision of a first class licensed engineer.

Many stations today operate remote controlled transmitters when the studio and transmitter are not at the same location. By the use of telephone lines or electronic means the main transmitter can be switched on and off and the meter readings relayed to the studio. The remote control equipment also must be capable of carrying out external transmitter adjustments initiated at the studio. Those stations operating by remote control must employ or contract for the part-time services of a first class radiotelephone license as we discussed above. All licenses and contracts must be prominently displayed at the point of broadcast. I must again caution you that failure to comply with this rule and regulation will result in heavy fines and even cause the FCC to institute revocation proceedings. If you do not plan to operate by "remote control" and if your studio is not at the transmitter site you may find it necessary to employ more than one first class radiotelephone operator. Wherever possible, feasible, and allowed by law, remote control is highly recommended. Though the initial cost of such equipment may be high, the saving in salaries alone will more than offset the cost of the equipment. In addition you eliminate the problem of staff turnover. With the demand for first class radiotelephone license holders by private industry, radio stations are finding it very difficult to find and hire them.

Where it is necessary to have more than one first class engineer, station management usually selects one to be the "chief engineer" and to supervise other engineering employees. He must be given the full authority to carry out his responsibility of maintaining the broadcast equipment so that its performance always complies with the standards of good engineering practice within the limitations as set forth on the station's license. It is the chief engineer's responsibility to see that the transmitter is adequately manned by authorized personnel; that daily tests are made as required by the FCC; that monthly frequency tests are obtained; that the results of yearly "proof of performance" tests are available for FCC inspection; that engineering logs are properly kept; and that second class and third class operators are supervised and instructed. In addition the engineering department head must supervise all studio equipment maintenance including tape recorders, turntables, etc., and purchase needed supplies and equipment. And in many stations it is the chief's job to order telephone lines for "remote" broadcasts and to supervise the engineering aspects of such broadcasts.

The weekly compensation paid to your engineer varies with location and the availability of such personnel. The National Association of Broadcasters reported that in 1966 the average gross weekly compensation on a nationwide basis was $133 for chief engineers and $119 for technicians. For a station located in the southern part of the U.S. serving a market of 50,000 to 100,000 population the compensation was $114 per week for the chief engineer and $79 per week for a technician. A similar station serving the same size market in the northern part of the U.S. paid its chief engineer a weekly salary of $140 and $107 per week to a technician.

In order to cut payroll costs many stations employ a chief engineer capable of doing some air work. Wherever possible the practice is highly recommended as a means of alleviating some of the problems in regard to your announcing staff in addition to lowering your operating cost.

The 1967 financial report published by the National Association of Broadcasters states that engineering department salaries amounted to 10.2% of the typical station payroll. The accompanying table shows a breakdown of engineering depart-

| MARKET SIZE | % OF TOTAL EXPENSE | % OF SALARY TOTAL |
|---|---|---|
| Less than   $ 50,000 | 10.2% | 10.2% |
| $ 56,000 - $ 75,000 | 10.9% | 11.0% |
| $ 75,000 - $100,000 | 10.0% | 10.9% |
| $100,000 - $125,000 | 9.7% | 10.2% |
| $125,000 - $150,000 | 9.0% | 9.1% |
| $150,000 - $200,000 | 9.7% | 9.1% |
| $200,000 - $300,000 | 9.5% | 9.1% |
| $300,000 - $500,000 | 11.2% | 12.8% |
| $500,000 - $750,000 | 11.2% | 14.7% |
| $750,000 - and over | 12.9% | 16.7% |

ment operating costs, including salaries and overhead. Good business practice dictates the necessity of keeping expenses commensurate with revenue. Should problems necessitate higher engineering expenditures, budget adjustments should be made in other non-revenue producing departments. Do not skimp on the engineering budget. You will soon discover that when it comes to equipment the best is cheapest in the long run. Likewise, in hiring personnel; when you employ the best, only then can you be assured of fewer headaches fewer breakdowns, lower maintenance costs, and an acceptable broadcast signal.

## Management

In large stations the management function is divided between a general manager and a station manager. But small stations assign both functions to a general manager. Such an individual must have the broadest possible experience in every aspect of the industry, in addition to being well versed in commercial practices. The best management candidates come from the ranks with experience as an assistant station manager, sales manager, or program director. With a background as a sales manager he should also have some program experience. Likewise, if he is a former program director some times sales experience is needed. But above all else he must be a mature individual capable of commanding respect from all employees, the business community, and the community at large. Since the general manager must supervise and discharge responsibility commensurate with the vested authority, he must be free of malice, prejudice, or bigotry. Before and after his association with the station the manager's personal life must be above reproach, because in the eyes of the general community, the business community, and the staff he is "the station."

A general manager must have a working knowledge of the Communications Act of 1934, as amended, and all FCC rules and regulations including the sections pertaining to engineering. If he happens to have a first class radiotelephone license, it is an added plus. But as a station owner or licensee you must remember that you alone are responsible to the FCC for any infractions or mismanagement. This responsibility cannot be delegated to a general manager. However, his knowledge and constant awareness of the rules and regulations should prevent any problems.

As a perrenial student of audience demographics the astute manager evaluates and re-evaluates listener likes and dislikes, and why (or why not) people listen to your station. He must be completely familiar with the other advertising media in your coverage area, their revenue and from what sources it is derived, and the use made of various media by the business community. As a man whose bread and butter is tied directly to the economics of the area, a manager should be acquainted with statistics such as retail outlets by category and number, service establishments by category and number, the retail sales of each establishment, the amount they are now spending on advertising, and how your sales department can get its fair share of this expenditure. Working with the sales manager and commercial manager he must establish the station "rate card," approve sales, sales activity, sales promotion, in-training programs, special sales events, and the preparation and use of audience surveys.

A thorough knowledge of audience demographics is of invaluable help to the general manager in his supervision of the program department. He must be familiar with the contents of the original or renewal license application to insure that the program department is living up to the promises made to the FCC by the licensee. Cooperating with the program director he approves the hiring and firing of the announcing staff, schedules and rate of pay, station and program promotion, and that program logs are kept in accordance with the rules of the FCC.

The general manager must know when the various FCC reports must be filed and complete or assist in the preparation of reports such as the yearly financial report, the renewal application every three years, ownership changes, etc. A good background in business practices is essential for he must supervise the bookkeeping and clerical staff, see that funds are deposited, approve the payment of bills, and act as the credit manager (otherwise accounts receivable will become a collection of delinquents). He must have a knowledge of the insurance needs of the station and the labor laws relating to each employee. Inasmuch as radio stations generally operate in the "inter-state" category of industry, an understanding of both the Federal and State regulations is necessary. There are certain federal regulations which excuse overtime pay for certain personnel classifications in specific population centers. By knowing all these laws the general manager can effect savings in the number of required personnel and salary expenses. There are many instances on record where the ignorance of labor laws has caused untold harm, both in money and reputation.

Inasmuch as the general manager is regarded as "the station" he must have the ability to make social contacts at every level. By serving on the "boards" of practically every social service, social welfare and civic agency, club or group, the station becomes a further asset to the community. Wherever possible the manager should be a member of the leading country club, service club, and businessmen's club in the area.

By now it must seem that I am suggesting a person who must be all things to all people. If that is your assumption, you are absolutely right. Don't think for one moment that such a person is an impossibility. Interview any general manager of a radio station and ask him about his duties and his work and be prepared for a shock. He will tell you that he performs many, many more tasks than those listed above. As to hours or the work schedule, there just isn't any such thing. A general manager works for the station from the moment he opens his eyes until he goes to sleep at night. Practically every general manager is awakened by a clock radio tuned to his station at "sign on." He listens while washing, getting dressed, and on the way to the office, and whenever possible he keeps listening to it all day, both in and out of the office, until he is ready to retire. Every phase of its operation, no matter how small or large, is his responsibility. His rate of pay varies with the population and revenue potential of the market. Some general managers work on a straight salary basis; some for salary plus a bonus arrangement, and others for salary and a percentage of the profits. Here is a good point to inject a reminder: Any arrangements you make with any personnel promising or guaranteeing a share of the profits or any financial interest in the station must be filed with the FCC. Failure to do so may result in serious consequences.

## Sales Department

A very wise and successful radio station operator once remarked, "Whenever my sales staff pass me I tip my hat." This man knew from actual experience, as you, too, will discover, that this is the principal money-producing department of any radio station. There is no doubt that you would do some business without a sales department, but it would be so small that you would soon find it financially impossible to operate.

The sales staff must seek out and call upon every potential sponsor and advertiser to obtain revenue. However, the responsibility doesn't end there. Every account requires "servicing" in order to achieve the maximum response with timely "copy" or announcement content. A pleased advertiser may be expected to increase his use of radio, while a poorly serviced account will do the opposite. The salesmen are the station's representatives to the business community. They are your "ears" as to how the business community responds to your programming and the image you are creating in the general community. Your sales department is in a good position to keep you advised and posted on the activities of your opposition, on activities in the business community as an aid to credit management, and on plans for future business activity as an aid to your program director.

The sales department is in a position to know what programs have good commercial sales potential and what programs are not being accepted by the business community and cannot be sold. Do not become dismayed or alarmed should you find that the sales department and the program department are constantly at "swords end," bickering and arguing. This is a healthy situation. As a station owner or manager you will soon discover that something is radically wrong if the sales and program departments are in complete accord. Your program director and his staff are creating programs that they feel meet the demands and the needs of the community. They should be creative and imaginative people. Your sales staff, on the other hand, is interested only in those programs they can sell. Its main function is to obtain as much sales revenue and as many sponsors as possible. Your sales staff will be constantly criticizing the announcers, disc jockeys, and other "air" personalities, for they should never be expected to settle for less than something close to perfection. A salesman cannot be expected to sell any commodity unless he is first sold on it. It is management's responsibility to supervise both departments and their inter-relationships so that the conflict does not exceed the "productive" stage where it would disrupt the morale of the entire staff. The manager must be the final arbitor and make the final decision whenever a conflict does arise. He cannot and shouldn't attempt to "pass the buck."

## Commercial Manager

Stations in large or high-medium revenue markets usually employ a commercial manager. It is his responsibility to supervise all commercial aspects of the station as they pertain to the sales department. Following is a list a commercial manager's principal duties:

1. Supervision of the sales manager
2. Developing and securing "national business"
3. Liaison with "national and regional representatives"
4. Producing sales promotion material and advertisements
5. Developing sales promotion programs in cooperation with the program manager
6. Instituting studies concerning area economics and audience potential.

A commercial manager's background must include extensive experience in radio time sales, preferably as sales manager or station manager. In his relationship with the sales department the commercial manager must deal maturely and possess the ability to take and give directions. His personality must be readily acceptable in the business community and all those with whom he comes into contact. Like the general manager he should become involved in a variety of community activities and seek membership in organizations and clubs similar to those of the general manager.

Market-wide economics should be second nature—the amount of potential national advertising; service and commodity distribution for the area and the advertising agencies that serve these clients; how and who to contact in these agencies; plus the ability and tenacity to capture the maximum advertising revenue from "national" and "regional" accounts.

Most commercial managers are compensated on a basis similar to the general manager. Some stations pay a set salary, others a salary plus a bonus depending upon total sales. Occasionally, pay is based on a salary plus a sliding percentage of total sales or a salary plus a percentage of profits and/or a stock incentive. Whatever the agreement it should be in writing. Also, be sure to remember that any and all agreements, verbal or written, that include any references as to "stock" or a share of the profits must, and I repeat, must be filed with the FCC.

## National and Regional Reps

Since most radio stations are geographically distant from New York City, Chicago, Los Angeles, Detroit, Philadelphia, and other cities where the large advertising agencies are located, the cost of maintaining personnel to call upon and service these agencies is prohibitively expensive and unprofitable. Therefore, most stations employ the services of a "national representative" who specializes in this field. The term "national representative" designates a person or firm who represents your station, as part of your sales force, to secure advertising from firms operating on a national basis who maintain distribution and sales in your area. Most "reps" as they are known somewhat affectionately, are located in cities where many advertising agencies are concentrated. "Reps" generally carry a large group of client radio and TV stations as they call on agency "time buyers" and "account executives." Because of their location and contacts, reps know who is buying what and the type markets they're looking for. A rep can be of invaluable help in securing "national" advertising revenue.

While the above arrangement may seem simple enough the best reps, naturally, are interested in bigger market stations or markets where retail sales figures indicate a large volume of name brand products. Small market stations must align themselves with smaller and newer reps. Therefore, such stations tread lightly in acquiring a sales representative. Most reps work on a straight commission basis of 15% to 20% of the net billing they place with a station, and unless they can project a profitable arrangement they are loathe to enter into an agreement to represent a station.

Before signing a contract with a rep, carefully consider what the firm has to offer. Check its track record, and if possible consult several stations already on its client list. It is wise to weigh all aspects before any agreement is made, because it is difficult and usually costly to get out from under an unworkable situation. Following are the basic guidelines to help you choose a rep:

● Experience: A good rep is well experienced in dealing with advertising agency "time buyers" and "account executives." In fact, he should be on a first name basis with such individuals. To function effectively a rep: knows which agencies are handling specific accounts; what accounts are buying radio in what markets and the amount they're spending, and/or accounts planning radio campaigns; is familiar with the stations represented, their competitors, and keeps himself abreast of vital statistics in those markets. Of course, the station must keep the rep advised of new sales ammunition and cooperate with additional market data when requested.

● Size of Staff: Since there are many agencies and offices to visit, a good "rep" has enough personnel to contact each and every firm on an almost daily basis. The more salesmen employed the better the opportunities for his stations, and a large staff enhances the quality of service he can give not only to the stations he represents but also to agency personnel with whom he is involved on a particular account. An adequate staff expedites communications with client stations, too.

● Research and Promotion: Effective and successful reps maintain vigorous research and promotion facilities to aid clients in developing market data, changes in program trends, and specialized programming. In other words, a rep should offer all possible assistance to make each client station's programming—and audience—more attractive to advertisers.

● Type and locations of stations represented: In this age of specialization, many reps handle only stations catering to particular ethnic or racial groups—the "Negro market," foreign language programming, or specific geographic locations such as the "Lobster Network" (Maine) or "The Yankee Network" (New England). Therefore, unless you appeal to a specific audience it would be useless to hire a specialist rep, even if he is interested in your station. Of course, agencies who represent geographic regions may not specialize in ethnic stations. Simply put, you must choose your company—an agency representing stations appealing to a similar or general audience or region.

● The number of stations he serves: Don't be misled into thinking that an extensive client list is any indication of a rep's effectiveness. Representing a large number of stations with an inadequate staff inevitably results in poor performance. Conversely, a rep may have a small list of stations and because of their location, programming, etc., not be able to obtain any national business for them. The criteria is: Does he have an adequate staff to properly serve the number of stations he represents? Where are these stations located? How are they programmed? Are any in similar size markets? Numbers alone never indicate the quality or ability of a national representative. A check with some of his client stations who are in a market similar in population, revenue potential, geographic location, and program format should help you reach a decision.

Some operators in medium or small markets never use a national rep. Because of their proximity to large cities where advertising agencies are located, they believe that they can acquire more national business for themselves than can a rep. They further believe that if and when an agency wants to place advertising on their station the agency will contact the station, so why pay a rep when he isn't instrumental in initiating, developing, or producing the order. In my opinion they are letting the dollar sign blind them to the many advantages a rep has to offer. And for stations located in urban and remote areas it is indeed foolhardy not to employ the services of a national representative.

If the firm you select doesn't have branch offices in other strategic areas or working arrangements with other reps, it becomes necessary to employ a "regional" representative. Though you should not expect the same type or extent of service, do exercise the same care and diligence in choosing a regional representative as you do in employing a national rep. A regional rep is often successful in securing advertising from those accounts whose products and services are being offered to a selected area. Now and then some national business is obtained through a regional rep located in a city where advertising agency branch offices serve "national" accounts on a regional basis.

### Sales Manager

While most stations can depend on some national and regional revenue, you will soon discover that a financially successful operation draws the greatest proportion of its income from the local retailer and local service establishment. This fact is very clearly proven by the 1967 Radio Financial Report issued by the National Association of Broadcasters. The accompanying tables show that the smaller the market—from potential revenue and population standpoints—the greater proportion of local revenue.

It becomes quite evident as you study these figures that it is vitally important to employ and develop an excellent sales force headed by an experienced and qualified sales manager. A sales manager must be mature and personable with a successful record of radio time sales. Not only must he be able to direct a sales staff but also take direction and accept supervision from the commercial manager and general manager. He must become an accepted member of the business community and involve himself in a variety of community activities, especially those associated with the chamber of commerce, board of trade, retail associations, social service and civic groups, and service clubs whose membership is in large number composed of retailers and those in the service field who are prospective customers. A knowledge of area economics, especially pertaining to the retailer and retail

| REVENUE SIZE | % OF NETWORK REVENUE | % OF NATIONAL AND REGIONAL REVENUE | % OF LOCAL ADVERTISING REVENUE |
|---|---|---|---|
| $750,000 and over | 0.4 | 47.5 | 52.1 |
| $500,000 to $750,000 | 2.2 | 40.7 | 57.1 |
| $300,000 to $500,000 | 0.6 | 27.3 | 72.1 |
| $200,000 to $300,000 | 0.3 | 21.3 | 78.4 |
| $150,000 to $200,000 | – | 13.8 | 86.2 |
| $125,000 to $150,000 | – | 11.8 | 88.2 |
| $100,000 to $125,000 | – | 11.5 | 88.5 |
| $ 75,000 to $100,000 | – | 10.0 | 90.0 |
| $ 50,000 to $ 75,000 | – | 9.4 | 90.6 |
| Less than $50,000 | – | 9.5 | 90.5 |

sales, enables the sales manager to help local merchants plan sales peaks and special sales events. In fact, he should try to become a consultant to the retailer. He should know and understand the merchandising problems in each category of retail establishment, including a knowledge of advertising expenditures, how they advertise, and to what extent they are using the various media. To further enhance client confidence he must understand other media and how to use them. And like the general manager and the commercial manager, the

| POPULATION SIZE | % OF NETWORK REVENUE | % OF NATIONAL AND REGIONAL REVENUE | % OF LOCAL ADVERTISING REVENUE |
|---|---|---|---|
| 2.5 million or more ($1 million or more revenue) | – | 59.9 | 40.1 |
| 2.5 million or more (less than $1 million revenue) | – | 17.0 | 83.0 |
| 1 to 2.5 million | – | 25.6 | 74.4 |
| 500,000 to 1 million | – | 34.3 | 65.7 |
| 250,000 to 500,000 | – | 23.3 | 76.7 |
| 100,000 to 250,000 | 0.1 | 19.1 | 80.8 |
| 50,000 to 100,000 | – | 15.6 | 84.4 |
| 25,000 to 50,000 | 0.1 | 14.3 | 85.6 |
| 10,000 to 25,000 | – | 12.1 | 87.9 |
| Less than 10,000 | – | 9.4 | 90.6 |

sales manager should be up-to-date on current audience demographics and know how to interpret and use audience surveys.

A good sales manager also has more than a working knowledge of programming, the station's programming policy, and every program on the station. He must be fully aware of the capabilities and limits of announcers, newsmen, and air **personalities**, as well as the popularity of each of the station's programs and who listens to what programs. It is essential that a sales manager be an expert in all the phases of advertising copy preparation, editing, and production—including the use of "musical jingles," sound effects, "attention grabbers," and the "soft sell" and "hard sell" approach. But above all else he must have the ability to hire, supervise, train, and develop his time salesmen in such a manner that each will produce the greatest amount of advertising revenue for the station. He must assign various accounts to each salesman, set up a schedule that includes account servicing, personal periodic client visits alone and in company with the salesmen, and assist the sales staff wherever necessary and required.

Administrative duties include a constant review of departmental operations: What accounts are advertising; when they advertise. How much money they are spending on the station, their credit rating, and how current they are in the payment of their bills. Periodically the sales manager should sit down with each salesman and review his account list, regarding servicing, the use of station facilities, and ways to increase the advertiser's expenditure. Together with the general manager and the commercial manager, the sales manager should plan the station's sales promotions and create special sales events.

There are many ways of compensating sales managers. In 1966 the National Association of Broadcasters reported an average gross weekly compensation on a nationwide basis of $215. The method used by 40% of the stations is some form of salary plus commission: 19% pay a straight salary; 8% pay a straight commission with no salary; 17% pay a salary plus a bonus; and 12% a guaranteed draw against commission. It is interesting to note the very wide variation among that group paying on the basis of salary plus commission. For instance, in the same market size, to arrive at a figure of $150 per week one group of stations reported $100 per week plus 2% on time sales; another group reported $100 per week plus

1% of the first $13,000 and 5% over $13,000. It is suggested that anyone interested in the many variations obtain this information by writing directly to the National Association of Broadcasters, 1812 K Street N.W., Washington, D.C. 2006. For stations in markets of 50,000 to 100,000 population in the South the average weekly compensation was $186; in the North the salary was $202 per week.

## Salesmen

The number of time salesmen a station employs depends entirely on the size of its market. After all, you can't expect people, especially salesmen, to work for you if it is impossible to earn a living wage. It should be the sales manager's responsibility to know how many salesmen to hire to fully cover the market and at the same time to see that the earnings potential for each salesman is high enough. Salesmen who cannot earn a satisfactory salary usually move on to greener pastures, resulting in a large turnover in the sales force. Inevitably staff turnover results in a poor rapport between the account and the station, deliquent account servicing, and the possible loss of the sponsor. Advertisers do become attached (even emotionally sometimes) to certain salesmen and resent having to do business with a new person. And if it happens with regularity they soon lose all respect for the station. The time spent in wooing a sponsor is lost when that salesman leaves and is replaced by a new man—he simply has to start all over again. Even if the departing salesman's accounts are divided among the remaining sales staff you can run into a plethora of other personnel problems. So, your sales force must not be too large and certainly cannot be too small; it must be adequate to cover the area. Many stations in order to raise status and prestige give salesmen the title of "Account Executive." This sounds and looks good when a salesman presents his calling card. Do not make the mistake of refusing to employ saleswomen. They are excellent sales people and with proper training and supervision can produce better than some men. In fact, several women who started on the sales force are each now managing a station.

What do you look for in a potential salesman? What must he know to be effective: Here is a list to consider:

●Some background in sales, especially intangibles.

- A pleasant personality. Many salesmen, who are obese or have other characteristics which seem unpleasant at first sight, overcome so-called handicaps and become well liked and successful if they possess a personality that is pleasant and appealing. Though appearances are a factor, a charming personality is much more important.

- Salesmen should be extroverts. Introverts have never succeeded in the sales field. A salesman should be totally free from fear when meeting people and in conversations with them. A good command of the language, free from accents, is a necessity.

- Anyone who attempts to sell radio time must be completely "sold" on the medium and the results that can be obtained through its proper use.

- Every salesman on the staff should have a complete and extensive knowledge of every program on the station as to its content, format, and personalities involved.

- Each salesman must know and understand audience surveys and how to interpret them.

- Salesmen should have sufficient knowledge of audience demographics, especially as they pertain to the various programs.

- If in a radio market served by more than one station, he must know the competitors' programming, formats, and personalities.

- He should be an expert on the use of all media and be in a position to intelligently advise them on how to achieve the best possible results from their advertising expenditures.

- He must know the techniques of "hard sell" and "soft sell" and when and to what accounts to apply each technique.

- A salesman should never call upon a prospective account before learning all he can about the account: Some idea of the retail sales revenue; the various products or services the account has to offer; the advertising dollars he is now spending and should be spending; the advertising media now being used by the account and to what extent they are being used.

Always have a well planned presentation on each sales call—either visual material, recorded messages, or a memorized speech.

●It must be impressed upon every member of the sales force that you expect them to "service" each and every account on their list. Too often salesmen are content with just getting the order, while servicing an account can result in increased sales and a contented customer. Accounts who are not serviced on a regular basis are soon lost and very difficult to regain.

●All salesmen should be able to write advertising copy, know what constitutes good radio copy. They must know what approach to use for each retail and service account.

●All salesmen should be licensed drivers and have an automobile, since few accounts are within walking distance, now accessible by public transportation.

Compensation varies with each station. On a nationwide basis in 1966, the National Association of Broadcasters reports an average gross compensation of $152 per week. Some stations pay their salesmen on a flat commission basis ranging from 15% to 20% of net time sales; many use a "drawing account" basis with a set guaranteed figure. Customary in some stations is a straight salary, while others offer a guaranteed weekly salary plus a percentage of sales revenue; still others pay on a sliding scale basis of salary plus percentages that increase in proportion to the increase in sales. According to the NAB here are several pay arrangements totaling $125 per week:

1.  $75 per week, plus 5% of sales up to $2,000 and 10% of sales over $2,000 monthly.

2.  $75 per week plus 1 1/2% on time sales.

| POPULATION SIZE | PERCENTAGE OF SELLING EXPENSE TO TOTAL EXPENSE |
| --- | --- |
| 2 1/2 million or more (large station) | 22 % |
| 2 1/2 million or more (small station) | 19.8% |
| 1 to 2 1/2 million | 21.6% |
| 500,000 to 1 million | 20.8% |
| 250,000 to 500,000 | 19.9% |
| 100,000 to 250,000 | 19.2% |
| 50,000 to 100,000 | 18.8% |
| 25,000 to 50,000 | 17.2% |
| 10,000 to 25,000 | 17.0% |
| Under 10,000 | 15.3% |

3. $110 per week plus 7 1/2% over certain gross income per month, plus a proportionate share of year-end profits.

For a complete report of selected plans for compensating salesmen according to market size, I suggest that you contact the National Association of Broadcasters at 1812 K Street N.W., Washington, D.C. 2006.

To illustrate the cost of operating a sales department, the accompanying tables, based on National Association of Broad-

| REVENUE SIZE | PERCENTAGE OF SELLING EXPENSE TO TOTAL EXPENSE |
| --- | --- |
| $750,000 and over | 21.1% |
| $500,000 to $750,000 | 21.8% |
| $300,000 to $500,000 | 20.7% |
| $200,000 to $300,000 | 20.4% |
| $150,000 to $200,000 | 19.1% |
| $125,000 to $150,000 | 18.8% |
| $100,000 to $125,000 | 16.6% |
| $ 75,000 to $100,000 | 17.0% |
| $ 50,000 to $ 75,000 | 15.5% |
| Under $50,000 | 13.3% |

casters figures, show a comparison of selling cost to over-all operating expense according to population and potential revenue. (The tables exclude agency and rep commissions.) It can readily be seen that as revenue increases the cost of your sales department also increases. This is due mainly to increased staff and supervisory personnel. It should also be noted that as population decreases so does the cost of your sales department. Again, this is due mainly to the smaller staff needed and the allocation of supervising personnel costs to other categories such as general manager, etc. The operations and techniques of sales department operation is covered in a later chapter, but it is appropriate to state here that though salaries will be the largest and major expenditure, the cost of operating the department does include expenditures for travel, telephone, promotion, and other related items. You should always be cognizant of the fact that your sales department is the revenue producer and that you should not expect to get maximum results from your sales staff unless you give them the tools with which to work. Once again I must caution you that any compensation methods, including a share of the profits or a "stock deal," must be reported to the FCC.

## The Copywriter

One of the important people in any sales department is the "copywriter." Many station operators, especially those operating in small to medium markets, require that each salesman prepare the advertising copy or "commercials" for each account. I do not recommend this practice, because it is being penny-wise and dollar-foolish. As I stated, the revenue producer is the salesman. Time consumed in the preparation of advertising copy is time taken away from the necessary activities of soliciting business and servicing accounts. One little sale can more than compensate the cost of a copywriter. It has been established that a sales department needs every possible assistance and the necessary tools with which to perform, and a good copywriter is more than a necessary tool.

Since a copywriter is a specialist, he must possess certain definite attributes. Following are the most basic:

● Some advertising experience: A background in radio is most valuable; otherwise, his experience should be in the field of the printed media or with an advertising agency.

● Formal education: Some college background with an excellent command of the language. The latter is most important as his use of words determines the quality and success of the commercial.

● Knowledge of commercial types: A good copywriter must know how to write "hard sell" and "soft sell" commercials; when to use "sound effects" and "musical backgrounds;" how to employ the technique of "attention grabbers"; and the difference between "institutional" and "merchandising" advertisements.

● Keep commercials up to date: Nothing alienates a sponsor faster, nor causes more harm than to have a "post-dated" or "out-of-date" commercial on the air. This happens much too often. Merchandise offered is no longer on the shelves of the advertiser; Easter copy is broadcast weeks after the holiday; prices are not current; "sales" are being advertised long after the particular event; etc.

● All copywriters should be experienced typists, and also know how to operate duplicating machines.

● A copywriter should also understand the station's programming and talent in order to "fit" the commercial into the mood of the program or style of the air personality.

Many stations in small to medium markets who do not have a full day's work for a copywriter combine the duties with those of the "continuity writer" (discussed later). Copywriter salaries range between $80 to $100 per week on a 40-hour basis.

## The Program Director

To be financially successful a radio station operator knows that the only thing he has to offer his sponsors is "listeners," and the larger the audience the better the opportunities for increased sales of his sponsor's products or services. The person charged with the responsibility of building and maintaining an audience is the program director. Some of the requirements, duties, and responsibilities of the program director are:

●Maturity:  A program director must be a mature individual capable of supervising creative personnel and talent while accepting supervision from management;  he must be thoroughly experienced in broadcasting both as an assistant program director and as a chief announcer;  able to evaluate the effects of various programs and at once recognize those which could alienate groups of listeners; cannot be overly righteous nor overly anxious to present programs that are "way out"; and perform his myriad of duties so as to command the respect of everyone with whom he comes into contact,  both in and out of the station.

●Preparation of Programs:  In order to properly prepare  an overall schedule,  a program director must be fully aware of the licensee's promises to the FCC—know the exact percentages promised in each and every category,  so he can prepare his program schedule to meet exactly these percentages.  Failure to do so requires extensive and detailed reports to the FCC.  And if the Commission isn't satisfied with any deviation between promise and performance,  its license may be delayed or even refused at renewal time.

● FCC Regulations:  It is mandatory that a program director be thoroughly familiar with all FCC rules and regulations, especially those relating to the program department.  He must know the licensing requirements for engineers and operators, particularly if the radio station is operating by remot e control,  and know practically by rote those rules and regulations regarding political broadcasts (Section 315),  the "fairness doctrine," lottery law regulations,  "payola," program logs, operating hours,  and civil defense regulations.  Every program director should have at least an FCC 3rd class radiotelephone license with broadcast endorsement.  I also highly recommend that he familiarize himself with the laws of "libel" and "slander."

● Audience:  Not only must a program director know the numbers of his potential audience, but be able to quote demographics—likes and dislikes, educational background, working hours and if it is an "early or late rising" community, income, how they spend their leisure time, and most of all, listening habits.

● Surveys: A program director should be familiar with surveys and survey techniques: how to institute such surveys; their advantages and disadvantages; how to interpret survey results; and, how to properly program to meet the needs indicated by surveys.

● Work Schedules: It is the program director's responsibility, working with his "chief announcer," if any, to schedule his announcing staff so that the station is fully operable at all times. To do this he must not only know thoroughly each program but the forte of each announcer. Also required is an awareness of labor laws, both federal and state, as they apply to the staff.

● Music: Although some radio stations have adopted an "all talk" format, the majority still program a predominance of music. A program director should carry out the selected music format or image. He should follow appropriate music surveys and use them in formulating musical programs to meet the likes of a particular audience. He should establish communications with record manufacturers and distributors so that the station receives new records as soon as they are released. In fact, most stations have contracts with record distributors; many recording companies and distributors furnish new releases on a complimentary basis.

● Program Logs: FCC regulations specify that a complete record be kept of the program schedule, the time each program begins and ends, commercial contents, advertiser's name, etc. It is the program director's responsibility to oversee the preparation and to check carefully each day's log. At license renewal time the "composite week's" program logs indicate to the Commission whether or not the station has lived up to its promises. It is important that all data (times, program classifications, etc.) entered on a log be reasonably accurate, for occasionally an FCC inspector will log and tape record part or all of a station's program day. It should go without saying that then both should agree.

● Program Book: A good practice to insure a smooth operation is to prepare a daily program book for the announcers containing a written account, minute by minute, of everything that is to be broadcast. Excluding "ad libs," the "book" should include opening and closing formats for each program, program content, and commercial or public service announcements. The pages in the book should conform precisely with the log as prepared by the "traffic" department. It is the program director's responsibility to see that the "book" is ready and in full conformance with the log.

● Promotions: The program director prepares or supervises the preparation of all material used "on the air" to promote the radio station and its various or special programs. Also, he should work with the management in preparing advertisements for other media.

●Announcing Ability: The program director must be able to substitute for or replace all air personnel, requiring of course that he is completely familiar with studio and/or control room operation. In fact, in most small market stations the program director has a regular air shift to cut down on operating costs. Also under the program director's supervision, either directly or indirectly, is the instruction of all air personnel. For this reason he should have enough technical knowhow to explain equipment operation. In most stations today —even in metropolitan markets—the announcer operates his own equipment.

● Remote Broadcasts: The program director should know the rudiments of "remote" broadcasts (programs that originate from points outside the station studios). He should be in a position to estimate the cost of broadcast lines, engineering services, and talent required, as well as order necessary telephone lines in cooperation with the engineering department and see that personnel are assigned to meet the engineering needs of the particular program.

●Special Events: A good program director keeps abreast of all special events scheduled in the community, planning specific programs for special occasions, in addition to those special programs for various local, state, and national holidays. Once such programs are formulated the sales department should be advised of their schedule in sufficient time to secure a commercial sponsor, if the program is to be sponsored.

●Community Service: Rarely will a station receive community support or recognition unless it devotes a good portion of its program schedule to "community affairs." To perform better than adequately a program director should be in constant touch with every community and civic organization in the area served by the radio station. He should be on a "first name" basis

| POPULATION SIZE | WEEKLY COMPENSATION | |
|---|---|---|
| | NORTH | SOUTH |
| 2 1/2 million or more (25 or more employees) | $399 | $399 |
| 2 1/2 million or more (less than 25 employees) | $164 | $164 |
| 1 to 2 1/2 million | $211 | $215 |
| 500,000 to 1 million | $195 | $186 |
| 250,000 to 500,000 | $155 | $158 |
| 100,000 to 250,000 | $153 | $136 |
| 50,000 to 100,000 | $149 | $117 |
| 25,000 to 50,000 | $143 | $124 |
| 10,000 to 25,000 | $130 | $118 |
| Under 10,000 | $123 | $103 |

with the political, community and civic leaders, and be able to inform the continuity writer as to the types of "spot announcements" to write and to instruct the "traffic department" as to where these announcements should be scheduled. The program director is the person who is responsible for the preparation and scheduling of all "public service" and "public affairs" programs. He must seek responsible and knowledgable people in the respective fields and plan and present such programs.

●Training of Personnel: The program director is responsible for hiring his announcing staff. He should be the person who should conduct all auditions and instruct all air personnel, especially newly acquired announcers, as to station policy, how to properly operate the broadcasting equipment, and how to properly maintain the necessary logs. He should originate "in-training" programs especially for those announcers who do not have any previous radio broadcasting experience.

From 1,210 stations answering an inquiry from the National Association of Broadcasters it was determined that the average gross weekly compensation for a program director in 1966 was $142 per week. The accompanying table shows salaries for program directors in various size markets in the Southern and Northern sections of the country during 1966.

## Announcers

Most radio listeners do not care if you are broadcasting from a barn, garage, or a palace. All they are interested in is program content and the "sound." While the engineering department is charged with the responsibility of seeing that your station emits the best possible signal, it is the announcers who create the "sound." The manner in which they speak, their language, and quality of voice all have a great bearing on the creation of a "sound." Of course, your program format is the deciding factor, but the delivery of an announcer can either destroy the best and finest program or create an audience for a poor program. Following are some of the requirements, responsibilities, and duties of the announcing staff:

● Experience: Wherever possible it is always an advantage to employ those with previous broadcast experience, especially if this experience is in the field of announcing. If an applicant is not experienced in air work but meets all other qualifications and requirements do not hesitate to employ him. Practically every major radio or TV "star" and personality received their initial experience at a small radio station. Bob Crane who became California's number one disc jockey and later the "star" of TV's "Hogan's Heroes" made his reputation on a 1000-watt "daytime only" station in Bridgeport, Connecticut, where he started as a $35 per week announcer.

● Education: Though some exposure to a college education is preferable, the main requirement is an excellent command of the English language with the ability to properly pronounce words and to "sight read." Nothing irks a listener more than to have an announcer mispronounce words or stutter and falter in his delivery. In determining the command of the language do not become enamored with the person who uses multi-syllabled words. Bear in mind the educational backgrounds of your listening audience. You don't want announcers who will be talking "over the head" of your listeners, or appear to be "talking down" to them. Persons with some dramatic school or stage experience are very good prospects as announcers, as are those accustomed to addressing audiences or have participated in school debating societies or have had elocution instructions.

●Voice: This aspect of an announcer's qualifications is the most important he has to offer, obviously. The thing to beware of is the presence of any accents or peculiarities such as drawls, "Brooklyneese," inflections, etc. A voice that is too deep (basso profundo) or too high (alto tenor) are not the best qualities for broadcasting purposes. Generally speaking a baritone voice in the upper range is preferred. Other qualities to look for are "the personality" of the voice and the ability to "convince." Remember that an announcer becomes the "air salesman" for the sponsor.

●FCC Requirements: All announcers must familiarize themselves with the FCC rules and regulations as they pertain to their occupation. If the radio station is operating by "remote control" the announcer must obtain at least an FCC 3rd class radiotelephone license with broadcast endorsement before he begins his association with the station. He should also be briefed about the FCC's regulations regarding "lotteries," "payola," "the fairness doctrine," and "Sec. 315" covering political broadcasts. I must again caution that a licensee bears the full responsibility for what is broadcast, regardless of who, willfully or otherwise, violates any of the FCC's rules and regulations. Announcers also should be acquainted with the laws of "libel" and "slander."

●Categories of Announcers: In small markets, announcers are expected to be "jacks of all trades." Usually, in these stations we find announcers who excel in more than one phase or category. A description of several specialty fields follows:

1.  Disc Jockey: Since he is a music specialist a disc jockey must have a thorough up-to-date knowledge of every current recording and surveys or the "charts." He must be capable of quoting biographical data of recording artists, bands, and composers. He must possess the ability to "ad lib," and be able to smoothly integrate his music with his talk. "Timing" is the most essential element possessed by the great disc jockeys.

2.  Newscasts: Small market stations can seldom employ an entire news staff in addition to the announcing staff. Therefore, each announcer is expected to be part of the news department. They must be able to contact various local news sources and edit state and national news as it is received over the teletype machines.

3.  Interviews: Announcers should be able to plan and participate in the "interview" type of program. Each individual must know his limitations though, and not do any interviews if they are not knowledgable in the subject to be discussed, remembering that the listening public is more interested in hearing the "expert" or person being interviewed rather than the announcer. As most interviews are recorded prior to broadcast, each announcer should know how to operate tape recorders.

4.  Sports: There are really two categories in this field—sports reporting and play-by-play reporting. In the former case an announcer must know at least something about the sport and report in such a manner that it is assumed he is an expert. He should have a better than fair acquaintance with the names of individuals and athletes involved in various sporting events. But play-by-play requires expertise. A good baseball play-by-play announcer can be a bad boxing "blow-by-blow" announcer. Or he can do an excellent broadcast of a basketball game, but may turn in a very poor performance when he attempts a football game. When it comes to play-by-play announcing one must be an expert in that particular sport. Remember, people who listen to the broadcasts or sporting events consider themselves experts in that sport and they can tell immediately when an announcer is an amateur and unfamiliar with the sport. Play-by-play

announcers must have a complete command of the language, speak very rapidly, and be able to ad lib when necessary, especially during a pause in play activity or play.

5. Remote Broadcasts: For programs originating outside the studios the announcer must assume the role of a "master of ceremonies" and the duties of an interviewer. One of his best assets is the ability to ad lib and portray in a most descriptive way the activity that is taking place.

6. Miscellaneous: There are many studio programs that require specialization. Among these are "children or kiddie" shows, which require the ability to dramatically portray a story, or the ability to play an instrument or be able to sing; "Ladies Programs" which require a knowledge of household hints, homemaking, recipes, and upcoming events planned by church, social, or civic groups; "Symphony Broadcasts" which require a knowledge of classical music, composers, artists, and instruments.

The salary or wage scale for announcers on a nationwide basis in 1966, as reported by the National Association of Broadcasters, was $109 per week. In the 50,000 to 100,000 population market a station located in the North paid $115 per week, whereas a station in the same size market located in the South paid only $102 per week. As market population increases so does the salary, with stations located in the North paying higher wages than those in the South.

## Continuity Writer

Every program department should have a "continuity writer." In many stations, especially those in the small to medium markets, the duties of the "continuity writer" are performed by either the copywriter or the program director. Here are some of the requirements, responsibilities, and duties of the "continuity writer:"

● Experience: Some experience in writing is essential whether in school or at some facility such as a newspaper, magazine, etc. He should understand radio programming and the FCC requirements concerning the identification of sponsors.

● Education: Some college education is desirable, with a thorough command of the language. Any experience as a writer for school publications, journalism courses, English, drama, or literature is an added factor. The ability to type is essential.

● Duties: The "continuity writer" is expected to produce: (1) the "open" and "close" for each and every program including "newscasts" (2) all "station promos"; (3) all "public service spot announcements"; and, (4) assist in the preparation of all station advertising and promotion properties. Working with the program director and the copywriter, he is also charged with the responsibility to see that the daily "announcer's book" is complete and coincides with the program log in every detail.

In 1966, a continuity writer earned $79 for a 40-hour week on a nationwide basis as reported by the National Association of Broadcasters. In markets with a population of 50,000 to 100,000 the salary varied from $62 to $82 per week.

## News Department

The size of a news staff depends entirely upon the particular programming format. If the format is "all-news" the staff will of necessity be very large. If it is an "all-music," "Music, News, and Sports," or "Rock and Roll" format the news staff can be relatively small. In selecting a news director a station operator should seek a person who has had previous experience as a newsman or newscaster on a radio or TV station, or a person who has worked as a newspaper reporter and has had some exposure to radio. He must possess a "feel" for and know the value of a news story—a "nose for news" as it's called. He should be fully aware of the desires of the people in the community and how much importance these people place on local, state, and national news. A good news director must have a first-hand working knowledge of the "wire services" such as the Associated Press, the United Press International, etc.

Although his voice does not have to be of the same quality as that of an announcer, it must be distinct and clear. He must acquaint himself with all available news sources, communicate with people in all walks of life, and respect confidences. The ability to compile and prepare newscasts is second nature, and also helpful is the ability to operate certain types of equipment such as tape recorders. In most cases the news director reports to the program director; in others the manager. Therefore, he must accept supervision and supervise and schedule the personnel in his department. A college education is helpful, with majors in such courses as journalism, English, and writing. Usually, news directors are paid a "flat" salary, regardless of the hours they work, which varies according to the market and the size of the department. It ranges from $95 to $350 per week. The National Association of Broadcasters reports that in 1966 the average weekly compensation was $132.

Most stations in small markets employ only one person in their news department. If more than one person is employed, one is designated as the news director. All others then are newsmen. Each should possess the same qualifications as the news director and should be expected to perform the same duties as the news director with the exception of supervisory responsibilities. Salaries vary according to the market and the size of the staff, ranging from $80 to $200 per week. The average weekly salary on a nationwide basis in 1966 was $112, as reported by the National Association of Broadcasters. It should be remembered that by an Act of Congress radio stations operating in communities of less than 100,000 are exempt from paying news department personnel overtime rates for work performed over regularly scheduled working hours.

There is a difference between a newsman and a newscaster. The latter simply broadcasts or reads the news as it is prepared by the news department. It is not his function to compile, assemble, or prepare the news. Many stations use regularly-scheduled announcers as newscasters while others have newsmen deliver news. In a majority of the small stations it is not unusual to discover that the "newsman" is a regularly-scheduled announcer with a regular "air" schedule.

## Traffic Manager

An indispensable employee within the program department is the "traffic manager," whose responsibility is to prepare the program log, schedule all announcements, both commercial and noncommercial, and keep the commercial and sales departments advised as to all "times" available for sale. The traffic manager should have a minimum of a high school education and should be an excellent typist. He must be familiar with the various designations listed on the program log, as well as the entire program schedule and the complete list of commercial accounts.

The traffic manager must be acquainted with the nature of each advertiser's business so that conflicting sponsors' messages are kept reasonably spaced throughout the broadcast schedule. It is a strange phenomenon that competitors will not complain when their advertisements appear side by side in a newspaper but will complain bitterly and threaten cancellation should his commercial announcement be broadcast within a short time of his competitors announcement. Many sponsors insist on at least a 15-minute separation between competing products or services, but most will accept a 5-minute separation. It is also the traffic manager's responsibility to alert the sales department when a sponsor's broadcast schedule is about to terminate, thus enabling the salesman to begin his renewal effort. This function also helps the traffic department to keep its time availability list up to date.

The traffic manager works with the program director, continuity writer, copywriter, and sales manager in the preparation of the "announcer's book" and in comparing the "book" to the program log to insure accuracy. In smaller stations a "traffic manager" must be a good stenographer, secretary, file clerk, and "all-round" clerical worker. Depending on the market the salary ranges from $65 to $133 for a 40-hour week. The nationwide average in 1966 was $78 per week.

## Program Department Costs

All of the above categories, beginning with that of the program director, comprise the program department. Of a station's total expenditure about one-third goes into that department. With the exception of those expenditures listed under "general administrative" the operation of a program department is a major factor in determining overall operating cost. The National Association of Broadcasters "1967 Radio Financial Report" compares the program department cost to the total expense for the various market sizes in 1966 as shown in the accompanying tables.

| POPULATION SIZE | % OF PROGRAM DEPARTMENT EXPENSE TO TOTAL EXPENSE |
|---|---|
| 2.5 million or more ($1,000,000 or more revenue) | 37.4 |
| 2.5 million or more (less than $1,000,000 revenue) | 26.8 |
| 1 to 2.5 million | 32.0 |
| 500,000 to 1 million | 32.2 |
| 250,000 to 500,000 | 31.3 |
| 100,000 to 250,000 | 31.6 |
| 50,000 to 100,000 | 33.0 |
| 25,000 to 50,000 | 32.2 |
| 10,000 to 25,000 | 32.3 |
| Less than 10,000 | 32.7 |

| REVENUE SIZE | % OF PROGRAM DEPARTMENT EXPENSE TO TOTAL EXPENSE |
|---|---|
| $750,000 and over | 35.5 |
| $500,000 to $750,000 | 32.0 |
| $300,000 to $500,000 | 30.6 |
| $200,000 to $300,000 | 31.7 |
| $150,000 to $200,000 | 30.6 |
| $125,000 to $150,000 | 32.4 |
| $100,000 to $125,000 | 32.1 |
| $ 75,000 to $100,000 | 31.5 |
| $ 50,000 to $ 75,000 | 32.6 |
| Less than $50,000 | 35.7 |

## Accounting and Clerical

In planning a radio station staff it is necessary that an operator not overlook the need of a bookkeeper and clerical personnel. A bookkeeper must have a complete knowledge of "double entry" ledgers and be an experienced typist. It will be her responsibility to prepare and mail statements to advertisers for broadcast and other services and accurately post the amounts in the accounts receivable ledger. She also must see that payments are properly recorded and that balance due statements are prepared and sent to all accounts. The bookkeeper enters all bills from suppliers in the accounts payable ledger, prepares all checks, and keeps these records accurate and on a day-to-day basis. She must make bank deposits and keep a running account of bank balances.

Other duties include reports required by licensing agents such as ASCAP and BMI, (music licensing agencies), and financial statements and an up-to-date report on all accounts receivable together with a listing of all delinquent accounts by date for the manager. The latter is often referred to as "aging the accounts." In addition, the bookkeeper must prepare the payroll and make the necessary deductions in accordance with regulations of the Internal Revenue Service and other agencies, prepare quarterly tax returns as required by the government, and see that all taxes are paid promptly so as to avoid unnecessary surcharges.

Most small stations insist that a bookkeeper have a knowledge of stenography and act as a secretary, receptionist, and general clerical worker. There are no figures as to the salary scale for bookkeepers.

Many radio station operators, especially those in the small markets, soon discover that they need additional clerical help. This becomes quite apparent as the station's record library begins to enlarge. A good way to overcome this problem is to employ part-time help at a minimum wage level. High school students who are available afternoons and on weekends are an excellent source. Qualifications are, simply, honesty, good moral character, and legible handwriting. The ability to type is a plus factor.

Most stations employ a part-time custodian. Cleanliness is very important in order to maintain the best possible service and to increase personnel morale. It is amazing as to the amount of rubbish which can accumulate in a radio station. Dust and dirt on and around equipment can result in broadcast interruptions, and whenever you are "off the air" your income goes down while your expenses are increased.

# CHAPTER 6

# The Sales Department

No radio station can be financially successful unless it has an adequate and well-trained sales force. And no individual salesman can be successful unless he is imbued with the spirit of selling and is himself convinced of the excellence of the product or service he is offering for sale. If for any reason whatsoever a radio time salesman (or account executive) is not fully convinced that radio can perform the best possible service for the advertiser and that his particular station can do this to a better degree than any other station, that person is foredoomed to failure. Before attempting to sell, a salesman must thoroughly know his product and the product of his competitor. Every radio salesman must thoroughly know the broadcasting business, especially his particlar radio station, its programming, and the programming of the competition. He must have some knowledge of all advertising media, especially those in his particular area, their correct usage, and how they are being utilized by his prospective customers. In markets where there is a daily newspaper, the salesman soon discovers that it is his principal competitor.

### Radio Vs Newspapers

In 1966 a total of over 16 1/2 billion dollars was spent on advertising in the United States. Of this amount a little over 10 billion was placed by national agencies and the remaining 6 1/2 billion was spent locally. The total newspaper revenue was close to 5 billion dollars (about 1 billion came from national advertisers and 4 billion from local advertisers). Radio station income was only 1 billion dollars (about $360,000,000 from national and $640,000,000 from local advertisers). It can readily be seen that the newspaper's revenue was almost 5 times that of radio. National newspaper revenue was a little less than 3 times that of radio and local revenue 6 times better than that of radio. Newspaper competition becomes even more obvious when you consider that the number of newspapers is decreasing while radio receiver sales is constantly increasing. Latest figures show over 230,000,000 radio sets in use in the United States—more than one and one-third sets for every <u>individual</u> in the country.

All newspaper advertising is created for the eye. A person must be able to read in order to understand and get the full purport of the advertisement. A good tool for the radio time salesman is the number of sightless and "illiterates" or people who cannot read that reside in the newspaper's circulation area. On the other hand radio advertisements are created for the ear. A person need not be sighted or literate to get the full benefit and impact of a radio commercial. In fact, they don't even have to have a complete knowledge of the language.

Newspapers are either purchased or borrowed—daily (or weekly). In many instances a person has to leave his house or place of employment to buy a newspaper (and have the ready change where newspapers are sold in vending machines). On the other hand, anyone can listen to a radio set wherever one is present. One radio set playing in an office, store or home can be heard by everyone in the immediate area. Newspapers have to be purchased on a regular basis, whereas the initial investment on a radio set serves for many years. Newspapers are generally purchased on the basis of one to a family and only one person in that family can (conveniently) read a particular part of the newspaper at any given time. Radio, on the other hand, can be enjoyed by all the members of the family at the same time and today each family has at least one radio set for every member of the family. Remember there are over 230,000,000 radio sets in the United States.

Newspaper advertisers pay for special locations on a "space" rate. Radio advertisers have the choice of personality, in most instances, at no extra cost. While a very large newspaper advertisement may gain an advantage over the advertiser with the small ad, a similar advantage in radio is attained by increasing the frequency of his commercials. For the small advertiser, however, one minute is one minute, regardless how large or small the business. In many cases, newspaper advertising material gets more or less supervision from the advertising department. Any mistakes can be corrected only in the next day's edition of the newspaper. Radio commercials receive special and individual attention such as "attention grabbers," musical introductions, musical backgrounds, and sound effects. And any mistakes can be corrected the same day and in many instances within the same hour.

Newspaper circulation figures remain fairly steady on a day-to-day basis, whereas the radio audience improves daily with proper programming, promotion, special events broadcasts, and contests. Newspaper circulation does not show any dramatic rise when something especially newsworthy occurs, whereas radio experiences an instant and dramatic rise in listenership whenever anything of importance happens. However, newspapers have an advantage in that they can quote audited circulation figures for a particular period. But radio stations can quote audience surveys and deliver better demographics of their audience than can newspapers. Another thing to remember when comparing circulation and listening figures is the cost of a newspaper ad per reader to the cost of a one-minute commercial per listener.

To combat the statement that a newspaper ad can be referred to long after its publication, a radio salesman should explain that an ad is placed in a newspaper with a specific purpose and time in mind. If the advertiser wants the same "time" coverage he can achieve it by increasing the frequency of the same commercial over a longer period of time. Also, a newspaper ad may appear side by side with a competing ad, whereas radio stations do guarantee time intervals between competing commercials. A radio time salesman can draw many other comparisons; such as, each newspaper reader must rely on his own individual interpretation, while the radio announcer or personality helps to create the interpretation the advertiser wants; newspapers offer practically no intimacy, whereas by its very nature "radio" offers a great deal of intimacy; it is one person speaking to and with another.


## Sales Tools

To produce his product a master craftsman employs the finest tools available. Likewise, a radio sales craftsman is only as effective as his tools permit. Among the tools used by all productive salesmen are: (a) a complete program schedule and schedule of availabilities; (b) coverage maps of his station and that of his competitors; (c) audience surveys; (d) a portable tape recorder; (e) a supply of rate cards; and (f) a supply of contract forms.

Schedule and availabilities: No radio time salesman should ever call on a prospective customer unless he thoroughly knows his program schedule and what time periods are available for sale. He must also know the program schedule of his competitors and, whenever possible, the time periods they have available for sale. In the first instance he must know what he is selling and realize that he can't sell the same time period to more than one person. Another thing that he has to remember is that he must guarantee a time "spread" between competing commercials. In the latter instance, a knowledge of his competitors' programs and availabilities can be of great help in obtaining an order. For instance, if all your competitors' newscasts are fully sold out and sponsored, your chances of selling the prospect a newscast is much improved. Another similar example is when you have a "spot" availability before a specific newscast and the competition has no such availabilities.

Coverage Maps: Every sponsor desires to know: "How strong is your station?" "How far does your station reach?" and "How many people hear your signal?" The best answer to these questions is the coverage map. The most effective coverage maps indicate as many communities as possible and the extent of the station's signal. The more elaborate coverage maps also include demographic data—retail sales, population, earning power, and purchasing power. The enclosed samples illustrate those circulated by some of the more financially successful radio stations.

Audience Surveys: Wherever available a radio time salesman should make full use of all material dealing with listener "tune-in." If a recognized and reliable research organization has made such a survey the material should be available for use by the sales staff. Radio time salesmen should, however, remember that such surveys generally indicate listening habits and audiences for a specified period of time. Audience surveys usually take from 2 to 4 weeks to plan, at least one or two weeks to perform, and at least 4 to 6 weeks to compile, compute, and publish. Therefore, many things can happen to change an entire survey between the time it begins and the time it reaches the station. When your station is indicated as "number one" the survey can be an excellent selling tool, for it is then incumbent upon your opposition to prove that changes have taken place. Even if your station is not listed as "number one" the survey may still be a valuable selling tool if you can show that your station can deliver more listeners per dollar than the "number one" station. To apply its results more effectively every person who uses an audience survey must know exactly what it is reporting, the technique employed by the researcher, and the methods used in determining the final figures.

Where there is no such survey available, some radio stations use other means to indicate audience size, such as a certification as to the amount of mail received (and from what localities) in answer to a contest or "mail order" commercial; or, a letter from the telephone company indicating the number of phone calls received by the station in reply to a telephone quiz program.

Portable Tape Recorders: Thanks to advances in electronics there are available today a number of battery-operated, portable cartridge tape recorders with excellent reproduction qualities. Every radio time salesman should have one with him at all times, along with a cartridge to demonstrate the ability and technique of each "air" personality and a sample of the station's programming. So equipped a salesman can demonstrate samples of "straight" commercials, dramatic commercials, and musical commercials, plus a cartridge with a sample commercial made especially for the prospective customer. A small transistor radio serves to give the prospective advertiser an idea of what the station sounds like, if he hasn't heard it, but a radio doesn't offer the sales versatility of a portable tape recorder.

Rate Cards: Although the FCC is not empowered to limit the amount of commercial matter a station broadcasts, it is generally agreed throughout the broadcast industry that the Commission has adopted some guide lines for itself when reviewing applications for renewal of licenses. When in the

Commission's opinion it is felt that a station is "over-commercialized" they will expect that station to explain their commercial practices in detail and to state how they are serving the public needs by being so commercial. The FCC has practically accepted the commercial standards set forth by the National Association of Broadcasters, which limit commercial matter to no more than 18 minutes in any one hour with no more than an average of 14 minutes per hour throughout the day. Any radio station applying for a renewal of its license has to list every instance where there has been more than 18 minutes of commercial matter in any one hour

By law the FCC is prohibited from setting rates that a station may charge for advertising or the use of its facilities. Rates depend entirely upon the will and whim of each operator. Cost factors vary in each station, and the amount of profit a station wants to make also varies with the individual operator. The law of "supply and demand" certainly plays a role in setting a rate. The cost per thousand listeners is also a main factor, not only in determining rates but also to the advertiser. There is only one instance in which the FCC does regulate the rate, in a matter of speaking, and that is an insistence that all political candidates be charged the same rate, and the rate may not differ from that charged other commercial users on the basis of coverage.

There is no set formula in establishing a rate card. Moreover, there are as many different rates and rate cards as there are radio stations. By limiting the amount of commercial matter a station may program the FCC has made it easier to plan a rate card. Statistical formulas make it fairly easy to arrive at costs, the percentage of time expected to be sold, and the rate needed in order to insure a profit. For instance, should the projected cost of operation be $65,000 per year, operating 7 days per week from 6 AM to 6 PM, you can arrive at the hourly cost as follows: $65,000 divided by 365 days equals $178.08 per day; divide this by 12 hours (or the actual number) of operating time and you arrive at an hourly cost of $14.83. Or you can take the total number of operating hours, which is 12 hours per day, multiplied by 365 days which equals 4380 hours, and divide that into your operating cost of $65,000, this should equal $14.84 per hour. You now have arrived at your hourly cost of approximately $15 per hour. Figures filed with the FCC indicate that most profit-making stations are commercial 55% to 68% of their total air time. For the purposes of our suggested formula we will use the figure of 50%. We know that the FCC looks with disfavor upon any station with more than an average of 14 minutes of commercial matter per hour in any broadcast day. Consequently, it is easy to see that in order to be financially successful you must sell at least an average of 7 minutes of commercial time per hour per day. This will give you a base rate of about $2.15 per minute commercial. By adding 85 cents to this you come up with a base rate of $3.00 per minute. On a 50% commercial basis this will gross you $21.00 per hour; $252.00 per day; $91,980 per year; for a gross profit of $26,980.00 per year.

As stated previously, there are as many different rate cards and rate structures as there are radio stations. Some operate with two rate cards; one for the "national" advertiser and one for the "local" advertiser. It is our suggestion that radio stations adopt the policy of a single rate card for all advertisers, thus assuring equal service and opportunity for all advertisers. Some stations sell on the basis of special time categories such as AAA, AA, A, B, C, D, etc. Admittedly, there are "prime times" when the station has the largest number of listeners, but we personally frown upon the practice of creating special times. If you have programmed well all your time is valuable and should bring the same rate. Add a talent fee if personalities are involved, but don't advertise the fact that your station doesn't have listeners at a particular time segment. The use of special time rates certainly indicates this fact. Another thing to remember is that your program director has intelligently scheduled his programs according to the demographics and listening habits of your audience. If an advertiser wishes to reach a particular segment of the audience you should have such a program available for him, and regardless of the time period it should bring you your full rate. After all, advertisers should buy commercial time on a cost per thousand "prospective customers."

Briefly, let's look at a hypothetical cost per thousand. Supposing at a specific time you indicate 60,000 listeners. At a $3.00 rate the cost is 20,000 listeners per dollar. If your advertiser is selling a hair preparation, and of the 60,000 listeners 80% are bald, his cost per thousand prospective customers rises sharply to 4,000 listeners per dollar. On the other hand, if you have a period of time which only indicates 30,000 listeners but only 20% are bald then his cost per prospective customer will be 8,000 listeners per dollar. You can readily see why it is necessary to know the make-up of your audience at all times.

Practically every radio station offers a variety of rates depending upon the number or frequency of announcements or programs purchased. Here again there is no set formula for arriving at the "frequency discount" ratio. The main thing to bear in mind in setting up frequency discounts is that you should never sell any of your time at a loss. If your "break-even" point as suggested in our formula is $2.15 per minute no time should ever be sold below that figure. To do so is courting disaster. Some stations create a "weekly" rate card. Others create a "yearly" rate card. This means that they offer special "frequency" discounts for purchases within the week or within the year. A "weekly" rate card shows a basic rate for a one-minute announcement with the offer of "frequency discounts" for 5 announcements per week; 10 announcements per week; 15 announcements per week; 20 announcements per week; and 30 announcements per week. A typical rate card for such a station without classified time categories would look like this:

|  |  |  | Weekly Cost |
|---|---|---|---|
| 1 time | $ 5.00 | = | $ 5.00 |
| 5 times | 4.50 | = | 22.50 |
| 10 times | 4.25 | = | 42.50 |
| 15 times | 4.00 | = | 60.00 |
| 20 times | 3.75 | = | 75.00 |
| 25 times | 3.50 | = | 87.50 |
| 30 times | 3.00 | = | 90.00 |

Above are for one minute announcements.
20/30 seconds are 75% of above rates.
8/10 seconds are 50% of above rates.

The "yearly" rate card provides a basic one-minute announcement rate, with "frequency discounts" for additional time purchased throughout the contract year. There are two methods used in selling this rate structure. The first is to bill the customer at the highest rate, then rebate the amount of the difference between the highest rate and the "earned frequency" rate. The other is to bill at the "earned frequency" rate and rebating on all previously used schedules. Should a sponsor cancel before earning the frequency rate constructed for him, the station re-bills at the actual "earned frequency" rate. This is called "short rate billing" in the trade. A third method, frowned upon by successful radio station operators, is to bill at the lowest rate and then to submit an additional bill for the difference between that rate and the actual "earned frequency" rate. A typical "spot" announcement rate card for a station operating without "classified time categories" looks like this:

### NUMBER OF TIMES

|  | 1 | 13 | 26 |
|---|---|---|---|
| 1 Minute | 5.00 | 4.75 | 4.50 |
| 20/30 Seconds | 3.75 | 3.56 | 3.38 |
| 5/10 Seconds | 2.50 | 2.38 | 2.25 |

| 52 | 104 | 156 | 216 | 260 | 312 |
|---|---|---|---|---|---|
| 4.25 | 4.00 | 3.75 | 3.50 | 3.25 | 3.00 |
| 3.19 | 3.00 | 2.81 | 2.63 | 2.44 | 2.25 |
| 2.13 | 2.00 | 1.88 | 1.75 | 1.63 | 1.50 |

To arrive at program rates we must first consider the hourly cost of operating the station. Previously we arrived at an hourly cost of approximately $15. Still working on the assumption that only 50% of the available time will be sold, this means that you must average $22.50 per hour to break even and to show a profit you must charge at least a basic rate of $25 per hour. Generally speaking the formula used by most stations in establishing program rates is as follows: 1/2-hour programs, 60% of the hourly rate; 1/4 hour programs, 40% of the hourly rate; and 5-minute programs, 50% of the 1/4 - hour rate.

If you are operating on a weekly rate card, you should not allow for any program frequency discounts, since you have established a basic rate allowing only a little over 10% profit. If you do not allow any frequency discounts for programs your "weekly" rate card would look like this:

One Hour — $25.00
1/2 Hour — 15.00
1/4 Hour — 10.00
5 Minutes — 5.00

If you intend to allow for frequency discounts a weekly rate card should look like this:

| | NUMBER OF TIMES IN ONE WEEK | | | | | |
|---|---|---|---|---|---|---|
| | 1 | 5 | 10 | 15 | 20 | 30 |
| One Hour | 41.75 | 37.50 | 35.40 | 33.30 | 31.25 | 25.00 |
| 1/2 Hour | 25.00 | 22.50 | 21.25 | 20.00 | 18.75 | 15.00 |
| 1/4 Hour | 16.65 | 15.00 | 14.15 | 13.30 | 12.50 | 10.00 |
| 5 Minutes | 8.35 | 7.50 | 7.10 | 6.65 | 6.25 | 5.00 |

If you are operating on a yearly "earned frequency" basis without classified time categories your program rate card would look like this:

| | NUMBER OF TIMES | | | |
|---|---|---|---|---|
| | 1 | 13 | 26 | 52 |
| One Hour | 41.65 | 39.50 | 37.50 | 35.40 |
| 1/2 Hour | 25.00 | 23.70 | 22.50 | 21.25 |
| 1/4 Hour | 16.65 | 15.80 | 15.00 | 14.15 |
| 5 Minutes | 8.35 | 7.90 | 7.50 | 7.10 |

| 104 | 156 | 216 | 260 | 312 |
|---|---|---|---|---|
| 33.30 | 31.50 | 29.15 | 27.00 | 25.00 |
| 20.00 | 19.00 | 17.50 | 16.25 | 15.00 |
| 13.30 | 12.50 | 11.65 | 10.80 | 10.00 |
| 6.70 | 6.25 | 5.85 | 5.45 | 5.00 |

Here are some examples of rate cards now in use:

| | CLASS AA | | CLASS A | |
|---|---|---|---|---|
| PER WEEK | 1 MINUTE | 20/30 SECOND | 1 MINUTE | 20/30 SECOND |
| 1-6 × (times) | 12.00 | 10.00 | 10.00 | 8.00 |
| 6 × | 11.00 | 9.00 | 9.00 | 7.50 |
| 12 × | 10.50 | 8.50 | 8.50 | 7.00 |
| 18 × | 10.00 | 8.00 | 8.00 | 6.50 |
| 24 × | 9.50 | 7.50 | 7.50 | 6.00 |
| 30 × | 9.00 | 7.00 | 7.00 | 5.50 |

DISCOUNTS

| 26 weeks | 5% | 52 weeks | 10% |
|---|---|---|---|

Discounts apply to announcement packages only

## TIME RATES

| SPOT ANNOUNCEMENTS | 1 MINUTE | 30 SECONDS | 15 SECONDS |
|---|---|---|---|
| 1 × | 10.00 | 7.50 | 5.00 |
| 13 × | 9.35 | 6.85 | 4.60 |
| 26 × | 8.75 | 6.25 | 4.20 |
| 52 × | 8.10 | 5.75 | 3.95 |
| 104 × | 7.50 | 5.25 | 3.75 |
| 156 × | 6.85 | 4.80 | 3.55 |
| 208 × | 6.25 | 4.40 | 3.35 |
| 260 × | 5.75 | 4.15 | 3.15 |
| 312 × | 5.50 | 3.95 | 2.95 |
| 364 × | 5.25 | 3.75 | 2.75 |
| 520 × | 5.00 | 3.55 | 2.55 |

| PACKAGE PLANS PER WEEK | 1 MINUTE | 30 SECONDS | 15 SECONDS |
|---|---|---|---|
| 10 × | 7.50 | 5.25 | 3.75 |
| 15 × | 6.85 | 4.80 | 3.55 |
| 20 × | 6.25 | 4.40 | 3.35 |
| 25 × | 5.75 | 4.15 | 3.15 |
| 30 × | 5.50 | 3.95 | 2.95 |
| 40 × | 5.25 | 3.75 | 2.75 |
| 50 × | 5.10 | 3.65 | 2.65 |
| 70 × | 5.00 | 3.55 | 2.55 |

| PROGRAM TIME RATES | 1/4 HOUR | 10 MINUTES | 5 MINUTES | 2 MINUTES |
|---|---|---|---|---|
| 1 × | 40.00 | 27.50 | 17.50 | 12.50 |
| 13 × | 37.00 | 25.50 | 16.25 | 11.25 |
| 26 × | 34.00 | 23.75 | 15.00 | 10.45 |
| 52 × | 32.00 | 22.00 | 13.85 | 9.70 |
| 104 × | 30.00 | 20.25 | 12.75 | 9.00 |
| 156 × | 28.00 | 18.50 | 11.65 | 8.35 |
| 208 × | 26.00 | 17.00 | 10.65 | 7.75 |
| 260 × | 24.00 | 16.00 | 10.00 | 7.30 |
| 312 × | 22.00 | 15.00 | 9.45 | 6.90 |
| 364 × | 21.00 | 14.25 | 9.00 | 6.50 |
| 520 × | 20.00 | 13.50 | 8.55 | 6.10 |

## SPOT ANNOUNCEMENTS

### CLASS AA

PER WEEK:

| | | | | |
|---|---|---|---|---|
| Less than 6 × | $ 15.00 | 18 × | $ 11.00 |
| 6 × | 13.00 | 24 × | 10.00 |
| 12 × | 12.00 | | |

### CLASS A

| | | | | |
|---|---|---|---|---|
| Less than 6 × | 13.00 | 18 × | 9.00 |
| 6 × | 11.00 | 24 × | 8.00 |
| 12 × | 10.00 | | |

5 minutes 150% of applicable 1—minute rate
20/30 seconds 75% of applicable 1—minute rate
IDs 50% of applicable 1—minute rate

---

## CONSECUTIVE WEEK DISCOUNTS

| | |
|---|---|
| 13 weeks | 5% |
| 26 weeks | 10% |
| 52 weeks | 15% |

(Discounts apply to announcements or program packages but may not be combined for frequency discount purposes)

---

## PROGRAMS

| | |
|---|---|
| HOUR | 100.00 |
| 1/2 HOUR | 60.00 |
| 1/4 HOUR | 40.00 |

---

## SPECIAL NEWS RATES (3 to 5 Minutes Length)

| | |
|---|---|
| 6 Newscasts weekly | 15.00 each |
| 12 Newscasts weekly | 13.00 each |
| 18 Newscasts weekly | 11.00 each |

Wherever possible, and especially for those stations operating in a small or medium market, we suggest the use of the weekly rate card. It has many advantages:

● Agency and national time buyers like this type of rate card, for they can see at a glance what the total cost of any campaign on a given station will cost without worrying about "earned frequency" discounts or being "short rated" in case of cancellations.

- Local merchants like it for the same reasons.

It enables salesmen to increase the weekly billing for local accounts by offering immediate savings.

- It tends to increase the weekly number of announcements purchased, thereby enhancing the opportunity for a better response to the commercial message.

- It is a tremendous time saver for the bookkeeping department which is not saddled with the problem of keeping track of the number of announcements a sponsor uses during the contract year.

- It does away with the entire practice of rebates at the end of a contract year.

- It negates all necessity for "short rate" billing. Nothing antagonizes a local merchant more than receiving a bill for a "short rate" when he cancels a contract. To him it is an additional expense and one that is most unwelcome and for which he never planned.

- It enables management to project income without worrying about "earned frequency discounts," rebates, or "short rates." At any time a station manager or sales manager chooses, he can easily determine the sales revenue for any given day, week, or month.

- Station management and sales staffs will find that their "one-time" and "15-time" rates are not out of line with the "end rate" which must be maintained to insure profitable operations.

- It is easy to memorize and prices can be quoted without difficulty or much explanation.

- It enables management and the sales staff to maintain the price, offering equal opportunity to all who want to advertise.

- It does away with the "sharpie" and the "chiseler" who always wants the "end rate" for a fewer number of announcements. It is amazing the number of people who will sign contracts for a large number of announcements and insist on the end rate, stating that they understand that if they cancel they will be "short rated," who never intend to fulfill the terms of the contract and who will never pay the "short rate" when they do cancel.

● All salesmen should have a good supply of rate cards in their possession and feel free to exhibit it at all times, leaving one with anyone who may request it. They should also have copies of their competitors and newspaper rate schedules for comparison purposes. All are very important "tools of the trade."

Contracts: I am constantly amazed at the amount of advertising that is broadcast without a written contract. Many advertising orders are accepted by "a shake of the hand," a verbal OK in person or over the phone, or, by the exchange of a letter. The reason I am amazed is that the percentage of people who refuse to pay for advertising on radio stations, on the grounds that they did not order it, is so infinitesimal as to be virtually nonexistent. Yet, contracts are an essential part of any business, especially a "service" such as broadcasting. The contract becomes a permanent record of any agreement and a wonderful source for referral purposes. The sponsor has a written record of what and when he ordered, and the station has a written record of what was ordered for what specific period of time. Also, remember that a record of all purchases of and requests for political purposes must, by law, be available for public inspection.

There is no specific type or contract form required by the FCC. Each individual station is free to originate its own. The type of contract generally used by the broadcast industry was developed by the A.A.A.A. (Advertising Association). Many advertising agencies have their own individual contracts, though most of them use the type approved by the A.A.A.A. I know of many radio stations who never insist on a formal "contract" except for political advertising purposes. A manager of one such station operating in a small market explained his reason to me as follows. "If a sponsor wants to cancel a contract on a moment's notice I accede to his request, for if he isn't satisfied with the results he is getting from his commercials on my station I don't want to black-mail him to remain on the station. If I did insist on his living up to the contract the chances of ever getting him back as a sponsor is nil. When I agree to the cancellation without any penalities I'm the "good guy" and always can try to get him back as a sponsor."

It is my suggestion that a contract should always be executed in any transaction, especially in the sale of radio time. It decreases the possibility of any misunderstandings and does away with the requirement of remembering what was said and what was promised. Too often radio time salesmen offer the moon in order to get an order, and when the station doesn't deliver the result is a much dissatisfied customer. Hence, a written contract insures against any claims for implied ser-vices made by the sales staff. For political programs or an-nouncements we suggest that radio stations use the contract forms illustrated here. This particular contract serves the dual purpose of alerting the sales staff to FCC rules and regu-lations and advises the sponsor of his responsibilities and the laws by which the station must operate. The other contract form is suggested for commercial broadcasts other than political programs or announcements. It does not go into any great detail or explanation, yet covers everything needed to serve as an agreement between the sponsor and the station. The contract recommended by the National Association of Broadcasters and the A.A.A.A. goes into great lengths in detailing and explaining everything from a definition of a "time period" to rights of cancellation and "short rates."

## Planning Sales Calls

Every salesman has his own particular technique of selling a specific product or service and every industry and trade has its individual peculiarities. To attempt to fully describe the technique required to be a successful radio time salesman is an impossibility, but there are some methods and techniques that have been proven to be universally accepted within the radio industry. When properly applied they almost always meet with success.

No radio time salesman should ever call upon a sponsor or prospect without a pre-arranged visit. If there is anything that a sponsor or prospective advertiser detests, it is the radio time salesman who comes into his establishment and says, "Do you want to advertise, or buy time, on Radio Station (call letters)?" It is so easy for the prospect to say "No." But should the prospect be interested he usually says "What have you got."

All people, especially merchants, like to be flattered. They want to feel that a salesman has a particular interest in them and their establishment. The salesman who can win the confidence of the merchant is the person who indicates that he has made some special effort in behalf of the prospect. No radio time salesman should ever call upon a prospective customer unless he has a planned sales message and advertising program tailor-made for that specific prospect. To do this the radio time salesman must have a knowledge of the individual, his business, the type of merchandise he carries, his customers, the amount he is spending on advertising, where he is spending it, the amount he should be spending on advertising, and how much he can afford to and should be spending for radio advertising.

In addition, the salesman should know his station's programming and what particular programs are geared to the particular prospect's customers. He must know what time segments within or adjacent to these programs are available for sale. In the jargon of the broadcasting trade this is referred to as the pre-selection of the audience.

One technique employed by successful radio stations is to periodically review the program schedule and concentrate on unsponsored programs by setting up a sales plan program by program. Program "A" is selected. A study is made as to its popularity, the number of listeners, and the demographics of these listeners. Once the audience is defined, attempts are made to match it to those sponsors whose customers meet the specifications. Then the "copy" department prepares commercial samples for the prospects. The program department produces the full program (on tape) with the commercials just as if the sponsor had already purchased the program. The sales department then sets up an audition schedule with the sponsor. If it fails to interest him the same process is employed for the next prospect, and the next, until the program is sold. And so it goes with each program until it is sold. Another approach is to first have the sales department survey the business community for prospects who are not presently using the station as an advertising medium. In consultation with the program department the sales staff endeavors to match available programs to the requirements of each prospect. Copy and continuity is prepared, the program is tape recorded, the audition is scheduled, and so on until the prospect is sold.

Should the merchant choose not to buy the particular program the station is in a most favorable position. It has indicated to the prospect its desire to be of service to him. It has flattered him by showing an interest in him and his establishment. The prospect in rejecting the offer generally states the reasons behind his refusal to buy, thereby giving the salesman new material with which to work. The door has now become permanently opened, and if enough effort is expended and enough good advertising ideas presented, the prospect must sooner or later become a sponsor.


## Merchandising

Many, and in my opinion far too many, sponsors always seek to obtain more for themselves than they are paying for. Too many want to know, and actually demand from radio time salesmen, what the radio station will do for them over and above what they are paying for advertising. Because some stations, in order to "out-do" their competition or for other reasons, offer advertiser assistance in various ways other than "on the air" promotions, many sponsors demand that all stations perform in the same manner. This practice, called "merchandising" by some, has become far too prevalent in the radio broadcasting industry to be overlooked. Actually, I don't feel that any station should "merchandise" in behalf of a sponsor. What the sponsor is buying from a radio station is an audience, its programming, and its personalities. Radio stations would be much wiser and operate at a better rate of efficiency if they would only remember that they are an advertising medium and that all other problems, especially those related to "merchandising" are the problems of the sponsor or his agency. It costs money and calls for the expenditure of station personnel time for which it is very seldom if ever compensated. But, inasmuch as this practice has become a necessary evil within the industry we feel that it should be considered here.

At the outset it should be made perfectly clear that there is a distinction between "station or program promotion" and "merchandising." Station or program promotion is used mainly for the sole purpose of increasing the station's audience and to build the station's image or prestige. "Merchandising," on the other hand, merely purposes to help the sponsor to sell or increase the sales of his product or services, and is performed over and above the regular advertising schedule for which the sponsor is paying. Window displays, posters, billboards, bumper stickers, etc., which emphasize the advertised product are forms of "merchandising," whereas announcements or other forms of advertising that call attention to a particular program is "station promotion." The main purpose of the latter is to increase the number of listeners to a certain program; the radio station is simply serving its own interests—the larger the audience the better the chance for the sponsor to sell his product or service, and if the sponsor gets good results the chances are he will increase his expenditure with the station. We also know that as we increase the audience the better are our opportunities to sell other sponsors. "Advertising" is the radio station's forte and responsibility. "Merchandising" is the responsibility of the sponsor or his advertising agency.

Some radio stations list the "merchandising" services they offer. Though demands for "merchandising" are made by at least 60% of all advertisers, only about 25% of broadcasters comply. Such demands cover the entire spectrum of an individual's imagination, ranging from "letters to the trade," displays, answering the telephone, surveys of distribution and sales, etc. Following is a listing of some of the "merchandising" demands that are being made upon radio stations from sponsors:

1. Letters to the trade, on station letterhead, carrying the signature of the manager (or a "jumbo" postcard) are mailed to the wholesalers and/or retailers in the area that stock or who are prospective customers for the sale of the product. The purpose behind such letters, of course, is to announce that the producer or manufacturer has contracted to purchase a program or a schedule of announcements.

2. Courtesy announcements broadcast without remuneration, call attention to the fact that a particular product or service

will soon be advertised on the station, or that a certain manufacturer or product will soon sponsor a particular program. Calling attention to a particular broadcast or program without mentioning the sponsor's name or product is "station promotion," not merchandising.)

3. Newspaper advertising: The station pays for newspaper advertising in which the sponsor's name or product is mentioned. (Advertising which does not contain the sponsor's name or product is "station promotion.")

4. Publicity releases: Some sponsor's expect radio stations to arrange for newspapers to publicize in an editorial fashion or as a news story the fact that the sponsor will present a certain program or personality. They may also expect the station to arrange for the appearance of similar releases in magazines, periodicals, or "house organs."

5. Displays. Some sponsors even go so far as to expect a radio station to obtain preferential display of their merchandise on retailer shelves. And it may or may not seem surprising that some stations actually contract for such services with supermarkets and other stores by an exchange of "time" for "space." Sponsors will also request that the station print and place signs "as advertised over (radio station's call letters)" on counters in retail establishments where the merchandise is displayed, or print, distribute, and cause to be displayed such things as counter cards, window posters, streamers, etc. Some also insist on bus cards and automobile bumper stickers, all carrying the name or product.

6. Trade calls. It is not too unusual for some advertisers to ask a station to conduct a survey of all area retail stores to determine if they are merchandising the particular product, and if so how much of the product they are selling. During the radio advertising campaign these same sponsors will expect a progress report on the sales increase of the product.

7. Sales seminars. There are some sponsors who insist that radio station personnel attend their sales meetings and give their sales staff a "pep talk" concerning the radio advertising campaign.

8.   Free samples.  Occasionally an advertiser will expect the station to offer free samples of their product to its listeners. The station is expected to "plug" the item and to arrange for its delivery, all at station expense.

9.   Telephone service.  Some sponsors will advertise and suggest that the listeners call the radio station and place an order for a product or service.  The sponsor expects station personnel to answer all these telephone calls and advise him of the orders.

These are but a few of the "merchandising" requests that radio station operators receive.  The question as to whether or not a station should offer "merchandising" is of course up to the individual operator.  My suggestion is that if you intend to offer "merchandising," set forth a clear policy and program.  Arrive at a set figure or percentage of the revenue you can economically afford to spend and offer this plan to all sponsors.  There are some radio stations that maintain their positions in competitive markets only by offering aggressive "merchandising" services.

## Sales Promotion

Apart from merchandising and station promotion, sales promotion is an activity solely to be used in developing and building the sale of programs and announcements.  It must never be confused with any activity in behalf of promoting listenership or the sale of a sponsor's product.  Every detail of this operation must have but one goal in mind—to "sell" the station as an advertising medium.  All activity must be geared to interest the prospective user of the station's facilities and to stimulate a desire in him to advertise on the station.  Sales promotion material should prominently display the station's call letters, its telephone number and its address.  In addition, it should call attention to its power and coverage.  The "spot" on the radio dial is not always essential, though it can be used as follows: "Your clear channel station on 800," etc.

Every sales promotion campaign should employ every available advertising means, including "giveaways" such as pens, pencils, calendars, diaries, etc., and advertisements in trade journals and magazines or other reading matter subscribed to by the users and purchasers of radio time. Here are some other ways to enhance your "sales promotion" efforts:

1.  Create a colorful and descriptive brochure containing the station's rate card, coverage map, pertinent statistics concerning population, retail sales, audience surveys, demographics, family and per capita income, etc.

2.  Duplicates of all "copy" should be sent to the sponsor on stationery that is attractive and descriptive.

3.  Present all time buyers and other customers with "memo pads" that feature your call letters, phone number, frequency, address, and name of the station salesman. This is a low-cost way to build goodwill and have your "call letters" where your client will be reminded of the station every day.

4.  Call letter lapel buttons should be worn by every salesman. Some stations furnish their salesmen with cuff links and tie bars featuring the station call letters.

5.  Automobile bumper stickers which read: "Your ad is heard by more people when you advertise on radio (call letters)," or some other suitable slogan.

6.  All salesmen should be furnished with an ample supply of distinctive engraved business cards that are "attention grabbers."

7.  Present time buyers and other customers with a distinctive ash tray featuring the station call letters and location.

8.  Conduct a "golf tournament" to which you invite time buyers and other customers. Local golf pros are invited to play in foursomes along with your clients. Suitable prizes carrying the station "call letters" and location are awarded.

9.  Conduct a picnic for the time buyers and customers and urge them to include their families.

10. Invite time buyers and other customers to a day or night ball game.

11. Provide adequate expense accounts for salesmen to entertain clients.

The efforts expended in sales promotion campaigns should aim to create a preference for your station as an advertising medium and to establish and maintain goodwill. It should always be in good taste, appealing, and of such character as to permanently establish your station call letters and facilities in the mind of the client.

## The Sales Manager

One of the sales manager's primary responsibilities is to train and supervise the sales staff. To accomplish this goal a sales manager must:

—Know his area, the listening habits and the demographics of station audience.

—Know his business community and have a complete list of every person and establishment in the area who might be a prospective sponsor or advertiser. No business, or person, should be excluded from this list regardless of the size of the establishment.

—Know each individual and "air personality" the station will use to broadcast its programs.

—Know the abilities and idiosyncrasies, the "strong" and weak points, of each person on the sales staff.

—Know every technique required to sell radio time and service accounts and how to impart this knowledge to every member of the sales staff.

The manner of assigning accounts to individual salesmen differs from station to station. Some sales managers assign a diversified "list" to each salesman; others, certain territories; and still others assign on the basis of "categories." Some stations let it up to the first salesman to "close" and "bring in" the account. Of all these the latter is the poorest, for many times it results in more than one salesman calling on the same account with different "sales pitches," thereby confusing the prospect. The prospect many times also feels that too much pressure is being placed upon him by the station. It can also cause a great deal of conflict between members of the sales staff.

The assignment of a "diversified list" has proven to be the best means of operation, especially for those stations operating in small to medium markets. It allows the sales manager, on the basis of his knowledge of the account and the salesman, to fit the salesman to the prospect or client. It also allows the sales manager to shift accounts from one salesman to another and one account to another. Every sales manager employs this technique whenever he feels that a particular salesman is not "closing" the account or when an account is not using the station as much as should be expected. Salesmen must be impressed with the fact that they are not allowed to call any account unless the sales manager has assigned it to them, thus eliminating the possibility of more than one salesman calling on a single prospect.

The assignment of "territories" can be detrimental to a successful operation. Though the assignment of accounts is a very simple matter it does not allow the sales manager to "tailor" the account to the salesman nor the salesman to the account. It can also prove to be a financial advantage to one salesman over another salesman. In small to medium retail markets most of the large advertisers are concentrated in one particular area and you can readily see the problems that can be caused by the use of "territorial" assignments.

In areas where there may be a great amount of duplication of retail outlets, some sales managers assign salesman to "categories." For example, one salesman would be assigned all financial institutions such as banks, lending companies, and stock brokerage houses; another would be assigned to all department stores; another all furniture stores; another all the jewelry stores; etc.; or a combination of such categories. In some instances this has worked very successfully, for it allows a salesman to concentrate on a particular "category" and learn everything about it and those businessmen operating in that particular field. He soon learns what type of advertising they are using and the amounts they are spending, and which account should be spending more. There are several disadvantages to the "category" method of allocating accounts. It does not allow matching the salesman to the account or the account to the salesman. Many sponsors object to the same salesman servicing them and their competitor at the same time, fearing that the salesman is telling trade secrets to their competitors. They sometimes place the salesmen in the awkward position of having him discuss the competitor's business. Some sponsors expect "first refusal" rights, and when they don't get it the salesman is accused of "playing favoritism" because a competitor was offered a particular program, announcement, contest, etc.

Regardless of what system a sales manager uses, he must make it a practice to hold sales meetings at specific times, preferably at least once a week. And if he is supervising a large staff, he should meet with individual salesmen, in addition to the full sales staff meeting, and discuss every single account assigned to him and receive a full report on the salesman's activity relative to each account. This report should cover also the customer's reactions, whether or not he is on the air at the moment. Decisions concerning the assignment or reassignment of accounts should be made at these meetings, for if an account is to be reassigned it would help the "new" salesman to get as much information concerning the account and the reassignment at an open meeting.

Sales meetings should be used also to devise new approaches to prospects who are not on the air and discuss programs which are not sponsored, hopefully resulting in recommendations to the program department and station management. Station programming and the programming of any competitive stations should be included on the agenda, at least occasionally, with recommendations to the program department and management concerning any new programs or changes in the station program format or announcing staff. It should be the sales manager's responsibility and concern to discuss with each salesman any accounts which are delinquent. It may be true that "salesmen should sell and not collect bills, but I know of no one who can be more effective in collecting from a past due account, without antagonizing the account, than the salesman. This discussion also alerts the salesman as to the account's credit and how far he can go in "selling" the account.

Sales meetings can be a most effective vehicle for "mass training"; however, individual attention and training can never be surpassed. The sales manager should make it a practice to spend as much time as possible in the field with each salesman, so he can observe how the salesman operates, how he is received, and discuss with the sponsor his relationship with the station. Sponsors are always flattered when they receive visits from station "brass." By means of these visits the sales manager can observe the extent to which the salesmen are using the "tools" made available to them.

## The Rep

Unless a radio station has personnel assigned to cover the advertising agencies in the large cities, such as New York, Philadelphia, Chicago, etc., it will not be the recipient of much "national" advertising. The "national rep" is the individual or firm who represents the station in its quest for this "national" business. A radio station, however, should not expect the impossible from its national reps. There must be very close cooperation and excellent rapport between the rep and the station sales or commercial manager, and the rep must be supplied with all the "tools" that it makes available to its own sales staff, plus a complete description of the station's programming; all audience surveys, not only as to the number of listeners but also the complete demographic breakdown program by program; coverage maps; rate cards; sample tapes of the station's programs and personalities; reports on "special events" programs; and a report on any and all available merchandising programs.

Even with all this the national rep must have the complete cooperation of the sales or commercial manager in developing national advertising. In many instances the station sales staff has to perform the necessary "groundwork" in the local community before the national rep can get the advertising agency's contract. Therefore, the sales manager must know the local distributor of all nationally advertised products. Following are some examples of how this type of knowledge and cooperation produced excellent results in the quest for "national business."

A radio station operating in a small market did not have a single beer account using its facilities. The station sales manager surveyed the area and determined the distribution and sales of the brand-name beers and the distributor for each brewery. He then reported his findings to the station's national rep who visited the various advertising agencies serving individual beer concerns. The national rep reported to the station sales manager the results of these visits, advising him as to why the agency was not placing advertising on the station. With this information, in addition to the results of his distribution study, the sales manager called upon the distributor and interested him in advertising his beer on the radio station. The distributor contacted the brewery's sales manager, who contacted the brewery's advertising manager, who in turn approved the use of the local station as an advertising medium. With this "spade work," which was done at the local level, the national rep now went to work on the agency and secured the account for the station. The same process was duplicated for the other beers distributed in the area, and with the added "ammunition" of a competitor using the station the national rep was able to convince other advertising agencies to use the station for their client. Where this station had never had a beer account on the air they soon had six different breweries using its facilities.

A national representative informed a station sales manager that it was not on the "agency's list" for an advertising campaign to be shortly scheduled for an automobile account. The sales manager contacted the automobile dealer and advised him of this fact. So, the dealer contacted the manufacturer's representative and complained of the omission and requested that he see that the station was placed on the "agency's list." He in turn requested a report from the automobile manufacturer's advertising manager. With enough pressure placed by the local dealer the car manufacturer's advertising manager requested the agency to include the local radio station in its advertising schedule. The agency contacted the station's national rep and the order was secured. Thereafter this station has been included on any "agency's list" for this automobile account.

A national rep informed the station's sales manager that the time buyer of an agency reported that it would be willing to place a schedule on the station for a "bread" account, if they could get approval for the expenditure from the bakery. The station sales manager paid a personal visit to the bakery and discussed the matter with the plant manager. He in turn, anxious for as much advertising help as possible, contacted his supervisor and received the approval and the national rep secured the order.

The above three cases indicate how close cooperation between a sales manager and national rep can work to the benefit of the station. They also point up something that all sales managers should know: The distributor of any product knows the value of advertising, but too often they are not familiar with the advertising plans of the firms whose products they distribute. When made aware of these plans, and how he is being omitted from this activity, the local distributor will actively cooperate with the radio station to secure the advertising. Too often he is too busy with his own internal problems to originate requests for advertising allowances or programs. They must be prodded into activity and the station sales manager is the person who can do it. Securing national business is always a "two-way street" between the national representative and the station. No station should ever expect its national rep to go it alone. Since the rep is part of the station's sales force he must receive the fullest cooperation at all times. It is also suggested that at least twice a year the station manager and sales manager visit the rep and have him pre-arrange appointments with the advertising agency time buyers and account executives. Agency personnel are not only accustomed to visits by radio station operators and staff but actually welcome such visits. It gives them the opportunity to meet the people with whom they are doing business and get to know a little about them. These visits also give the station personnel the opportunity to get to know the agency people and to personally tell them all about their facility and its operations.

Many radio station operators are not aware of the fact that the majority of advertising agencies have a complete file and portfolio on key staff people. Each file and portfolio contains information for use by agency personnel on the experience and character of each individual, his idiosyncrasies, the cooperation that can be expected, and his mode of operation. A face-to-face meeting is of great help to agency personnel in determining the veracity of these reports. Likewise, these visits can be of invaluable aid to the station personnel in getting to know the agency staff, often resulting in many "first-name relationships.

Advertiser Budgets:

A very successful small-market broadcast facility created

a "budget" plan for it's sponsors, an arrangement which has proven so successful for both the station and sponsors that it deserves careful consideration here.

The operator of the facility realized there were many small merchants in his area who wanted to advertise but felt that it was too expensive. Because of their particular type of operation these merchants did not need advertising every day of the week; or, at least did not have the money or the business volume to afford radio advertising on a continuing basis. They did, however, need and want to advertise during sales and special events. When these periods arrived their advertising budgets were so small that they could not afford both newspaper and radio advertising. Since most businesses in the area were completely newspaper-oriented all of their advertising budgets were spent entirely with the newspaper.

Since the weekly "end rate" or 100-time rate on this particular radio station was $3.60, the station sales manager set up a special "package" calling for 100 "spots" not to exceed 100 words per announcement for a total of $360. The merchant could use these spots at anytime he desired throughout the year. Each month the merchant is billed at the rate of $30, regardless of the number of "spots" used during that month. Even if the merchant did not use any "spots" during a particular month he still was billed the $30 for that month. Thereby, the small merchant could budget his radio advertising on a yearly basis at a low monthly figure. It also means that he won't be faced with a large advertising bill at the end of a month in which he ran a special event or sale. It worked out well for the radio station, too. It had a large group of merchants who were billed on a regular basis each month, assuring a certain minimum income.

This method also resulted in additional business from these accounts. As the end of the year approached many discovered that they had already used their allocated 100 spots and, because they were now "sold" on radio advertising, purchased additional time on the station. In billing these accounts the bookkeeping department must be instructed to indicate on each bill the number of spots used in the current month, the "number of spots used to date, and the "number of spots remaining against the contract. The station in preparing its contract with the merchant should be sure to include a statement that if the 100 spots are not used during the contract period each announcement will be refigured at the "one-time" rate. The contract should also include a statement that any additional "spots" over the 100 will be billed at the rate of $3.60 per spot.

A good suggestion for those stations who may adopt this plan is for the sales manager to review every account each month. When an account has used its 100 spots prior to the end of the contract the salesman is instructed to contact the merchant and secure a new contract from him with a new beginning and ending date. For the few months remaining on the old contract the station bills the merchant at a monthly rate of $60. For those stations using a weekly rate card this may sound like rate cutting. In these instances it is suggested that this plan be made available only to a select group of small merchants or those merchants who may be located on the fringe area of the business section of the community. Excellent prospects for this type of sales promotion are small ladies' specialty shops, small mens' furnishing stores, "independent" shoe stores; "independent" neighborhood grocer or market, etc.

## Why Advertise?

Many years ago a very wise and experienced advertising agency executive coined the phrase, "If your business isn't worth advertising—advertise it for sale." Advertising is one of the most important elements of "business." Anyone who may doubt this should be challenged to name a single business that is truly successful without using advertising in every one of its phases in all existing media. Concerns who are the most consistent users of advertising are usually the most successful in their particular field. Frank E. Pillegrin, a former (1941) National Association of Broadcasters Director of Broadcast Advertising, listed what he believed to be the reasons why business must advertise in order to exist. They are:

1. Most consumers prefer to buy advertised brands, and to patronize those stores which make the best impression with their advertising.

2. The result of advertising is greater production, more employment, higher wages, and a higher standard of living for all.

3. Advertising provides a quicker and more economical method of distributing goods, thereby saving time and money. It is a low-cost form of selling, an important point for consumers as well as for business men.

4. Advertising is the most effective and almost the only economical way to introduce a new product, improvements in old products, and new uses for existing articles.

5. Advertising is especially helpful in establishing trademarks, which enables customers to know whose brand of merchandise they are buying and consequently what quality to expect.

6. Advertising promotes competition, the kind of competition that builds business, makes business strive harder to anticipate customer's wants, and to give them more for their money.

7. Business must advertise to maintain volume, payroll, dividends, and profits; to protect its market for the future; to safeguard its routes of distribution; to build and hold goodwill.

It follows that if advertising is essential to business it is equally profitable to the consumer, for by selling the masses it creates the volume needed for low prices. The point is well illustrated by the public utility companies that furnish us with electricity. As more and more electrical products were advertised, bought, and used, electricity consumption increased accordingly. Notwithstanding the facts that all costs—labor, raw materials, construction, taxes—have increased markedly during the past several decades, the cost of electricity per kilowatt hour has steadily decreased. It was advertising that brought these products to the attention of the mass buying public; it was advertising that "moved the minds" of this mass buying group to desire and purchase the products; it was advertising that brought about the use of these products; and it was advertising that brought about the increased use of electricity and resulting lower electric rates. Just as advertising is an important element of business, radio advertising has become as important an element and an integral part of the American economy. Because of its quality and diversification, radio advertising creates a degree of prestige for a product that will make its brand name a household byword. Radio advertising keeps the product or service before the prospective buyer in a dignified and entertaining manner by delivering the commercial message surrounded by music, information, and entertainment that attracts buyers and customers.

Any one person who aspires to become a successful radio time salesman must know everything there is to know about the medium, in addition to having a full and comprehensive knowledge of all other advertising media. He must always adhere to the policy of selecting the right time for each product and sponsor—to fit the audience to the product and the product to the audience. He should be aware of the fact that to achieve the best results there must be a spirit of full cooperation between the sponsor and virtually every department at the station.

Successful radio time salesmen soon discover the importance and time-saving factor of making their "pitch" to the right person—the individual who has the authority to buy or place advertising. Too often a time salesman will make a presentation to a store operator who, though impressed, will say "let me talk it over with my (partner, boss, manager, etc.)." This was a poor choice of a prospect, for the presentation should have been made to the partner, boss, manager, etc., to begin with. In addition, too often the impact of the sales effort is lost when described by a third party. Radio time salesmen should remember also that in addition to making their presentation to the "right" person they must know the establishment, what it has to offer, who its customers are and above all else they must know something about that particular "right" person. What kind of a person is he? Should he use the serious, friendly, or comedy approach? What is his particular attitude towards advertising, especially radio advertising? How does he use the advertising media available? How much is he spending and how much should he be spending on advertising? etc.

Some other questions to be considered are: Is he interested in "cost per thousand," or only in results per dollar spent? Does he measure his advertising expense on "what will it cost" instead of "how much should I spend to get results?" Does he compare newspaper rates with the station's rate? If he does he should be quickly advised that in a one-minute radio commercial there are between 125 to 150 words, all directed at the listener and all pertaining to his products and services. The average number of words in a full page newspaper ad is less than 500. Radio time salesmen must be convinced, and be able to convince others, that radio advertising is the most effective and economical of all the advertising media. It delivers more selling impacts for every penny spent. There is no other advertising media that has a greater impact upon the mind and lives of the people in our country. It is certainly more human, more personal, more flexible, more informative, more entertaining, more effective, more penetrating, more believable, more timely, more selective, and more popular than any advertising media now in operation.

With a firm belief in all this, with the "tools" available, with the vast amount of research available, and with the use of the proper techniques, properly oriented personnel will produce results beyond those reasonably expected. Radio time sales is one of the most challenging, and at the same time, most rewarding of professions. It is an experience that must be encountered and enjoyed by all who aspire to succeed in any phase of the radio broadcasting industry. Upon the shoulders of the sales department rests the entire financial structure and life of any radio station. A smart and successful operator always tips his hat whenever a member of the sales department passes by.

# CHAPTER 7

# Special Sales Considerations

During certain periods emphasis should be concentrated on specific sales efforts. Almost every month there are several special events or holidays with a potential commercial tie-in. Every such occasion is an opportunity to increase revenue and build station prestige.

## Special Sales Campaigns

The sales department (with the help of the program department) should never wait until the last moment to firm up advertising campaigns for special events, such as: anniversary sales; January clearances, warehouse sales, pre- and post-Easter and Christmas sales. There are holidays in practically every month of the year, and of course the merchant always makes plans far in advance of the event. The salesman should always contact the sponsor or prospect at least a month in advance of the event.

Let us examine month by month some of the special events and holidays in which radiobroadcasting can participate, both in programming and in sales.

JANUARY:

1. "The New Year's Day Review of the News," a special program prepared by the news department presenting the highlights of the news events of the past year. It can be either a half-hour or a one-hour program. Excellent prospects for this program are banks, insurance companies, and public utility concerns. Contacts should be made prior to December 20th.

2. The "First Baby of the Year" contest. Immediately after

Christmas Day the radio station begins to announce that it will award a group of gifts to the first baby born at a selected hospital on January first or during the New Year. Arrangements are made with the hospital to furnish the radio station with this information. Beginning around December 15th, the sales department signs up a group of merchants, banks, photographers, etc., to co-sponsor the promotion. The amount charged each participant depends on the amount of commercial time devoted to the event. Each sponsor is also required to furnish a gift for the first baby.

3. January Clearance Sales. Practically every retailer in the country holds such a sales event. Contacts to reserve time for the sponsor should be made around December 15th.

4. January "White Sales." This has been an annual event for all merchants who sell pillow cases and sheets, in most areas beginning immediately after New Year's Day. Contacts should be made no later than December 15th.

5. Robert E. Lee's Birthday. Falling on January 19th, this day is a legal holiday in 12 states. If your facility is located in any of these states contacts should be made immediately after the first of the year. Excellent prospects for a "special" radio program are manufacturers in the area who generally do not advertise on radio but will sponsor this type of program on a goodwill basis.

FEBRUARY:

1. Lincoln's Birthday. February 12th. It can be a good source of income, similar to that mentioned for "Robert E. Lee" above. Contacts should be completed by February 1st.

2. St. Valentine's Day. February 14th. Excellent sales prospects are jewelry stores, candy shops, and ladies' apparel stores. Sales efforts should begin on February 1st.

3. Washington's Birthday. February 22nd. Prospects similar to the "Robert E. Lee" and "Abraham Lincoln" programs. Contacts should be made by February 10th. In addition, many communities run a one-day retail sale of very large propor-

tions. Merchants generally offer several products at practically no cost to the consumer if they shop early. In cities like Washington, D.C., this sale receives nationwide publicity. It is an excellent sales event and should be in operation in every area. Contacts should begin on February 1st and be firmed up no later than February 15th.

4. February Fur Sales. Practically every retail furrier runs a special sale during this month. Contacts should begin about January 15th.

5. February Furniture Sales. Should be treated as suggested for the February "Fur Sales."

MARCH AND APRIL:

1. Easter. The sales effort should begin at least three weeks in advance of the exact date of the holiday. All clothing stores are excellent prospects. In addition, large mercantile establishments, bands, and industrial concerns will sponsor on an institutional basis special "Good Friday" and "Easter Sunday" programs. Contacts for the latter should be made no later than one week before the event.

2. Fur Storage. This is the time to begin scheduling fur storage spots. The period extends through July 4th. Contacts should be made no later than April 10th.

MAY:

1. Mother's Day: Observed on the second Sunday in May, Mother's Day sales are tendered by ladies shops, jewelry stores, and restaurants. It is wise to allow three weeks to obtain sponsors. Some stations run a "Mother of the Year" contest in connection with retail establishments, restaurants, and travel agencies on a basis similar to the "First Baby of the Year" contest. The winner may be chosen from letters of nomination or on a "popularity" basis.

2. Memorial Day. Most communities hold special parades on this day; therefore many stations broadcast a description of the parade, sponsored by industrial concerns, insurance

companies, and banks. Contacts should be made early in the month and all plans fully formulated no later than May 20th.

JUNE:

1. Jefferson Davis' Birthday. Celebrated in 9 states on June 3rd. Special programs should be planned and sponsors contacted by May 20th. Good prospects in those states where June 3rd is a legal holiday are banks, insurance companies, automobile dealers, and industrial concerns.

2. Flag Day. June 14th. Some stations run contests in which American Flags are awarded as prizes. Banks and insurance agencies are very good prospects for this type of promotion, usually scheduled to begin on June 1st.

3. Father's Day. Celebrated on the third Sunday of the month; therefore sales contacts should be completed no later than the first Sunday of the month. Excellent prospects are sporting goods stores and mens' furnishing shops.

4. Father of the Year. This is the same type of program suggested for "Mother of the Year."

JULY:

1. Independence Day. Celebrated on July 4th, it can be treated in the same manner suggested for Memorial Day.

2. Shoe Store Sales. Practically every shoe store runs a July clearance sale especially for their summer shoe stock. Contacts must be made no later than June 15th.

AUGUST:

1. Furniture Clearance Sales. All furniture stores schedule sales, especially on summer furniture. Sales contacts should be completed by July 21st, though.

2. August Fur Sales. This is the big month for retail furriers' sales. Contacts should be completed by July 21st.

3. World War II Victory Day, usually observed either August 12th, 13th or 14th. It may be handled in the same manner as "Washington's Birthday", etc.

## SEPTEMBER:

1. Labor Day. Celebrated on the first Monday of September. Special programs may appeal to industry and labor unions. Contacts should be completed by August 15th.

## OCTOBER:

1. Columbus Day. October 12th. Excellent sponsorship prospects for special programs are the local and regional Knights of Columbus.

## NOVEMBER:

1. Election Day. With adequate advance planning, radio is able to give speedy and complete coverage to election returns, an effort usually very easy to sell. Among sponsor prospects are banks, insurance companies, public utilities, and moving and storage firms. Many stations have this program sold a year in advance of the broadcast.

2. Veterans's Day. November 11th. It can be treated in the same manner as "Washington's Birthday," etc. It is appropriate to program at least one special event, such as the playing of "taps" at exactly 11 AM.

3. Thanksgiving Day. The last Thursday of the month, a holiday traditionally associated with eating. Excellent sales prospects are food stores and restaurants. Most restaurants start advertising at least 10 days to 2 weeks prior to the holiday. Contacts must be made at least 3 weeks before the event. Other good advertising prospects during the 2-week period prior to the holiday are stores featuring table linen, crystalware, and china.

## DECEMBER:

1. This is the busiest month of the year for every retailer

and radio station. Contacts for pre-holiday advertising dur-
this month should be completed in November. Also not to be
overlooked is the period between Christmas Day and New
year's Day. Many retailers report that this period is one of
their busiest and most profitable weeks.

2. Christmas Greetings. Many radio stations create a special
"package plan" of 20-second announcements in which retail
establishments, manufacturing concerns, and service firms
can extend "Christmas and New Year's greetings on the air.
Many stations schedule such announcements on December
23rd, 24th and 25th. Every person and concern in the business community is a prospect. Contacts, which should be
started immediately after Thanksgiving Day, should be, and
are usually made by telephone. Some stations employ part-
time help to contact every business firm listed in the Yellow
Pages of the telephone directory or other directories that
may be available.
   Most program directors delight in creating special programs
for Christmas Day. Such programs can be sold at premium
rates to the larger concerns and establishments. There is
absolutely no excuse for any radio station not to be completely
sold out on Christmas Day or the shopping days preceding the
25th.

## Local Sports Programming

   In the small to medium markets local high school football and
basketball athletic events produce some of the largest listening audiences, especially those games played away from home.
In spite of this, many times we hear of station managers who
are reluctant to schedule these broadcasts because of the cost
and personnel involved, plus the fact that some sales managers report difficulty in selling these programs. Let's consider the techniques to produce and sell these events.

Staff requirements are:

1. Play-by-play announcer.
2. Announcer for "color," commercials, and to spell the
   play-by-play announcer during time-out periods.
3. Two spotters to assist the play-by-play announcer.
4. An engineer to operate the remote control equipment.

Since the qualifications for a play-by-play announcer are considered in the chapter on staffing a station, we won't repeat them here. If there isn't such an announcer on the staff one can be obtained on a per game contractural basis from neighboring stations and colleges. Former athletes who have excelled in the sport sometimes are good play-by-play announcers. The color announcer can be any member of the announcing staff who is a good "ad libber" and knows something about the game. "Spotters" can be obtained by asking the coaches of the schools involved to assign willing students. The engineer's primary job is to simply "ride gain" during the broadcast.

The cost of production and time for these broadcasts on a one-game basis can be figured, approximately, as follows:

- Telephone line charges—$20

- Play-by-play announcer—$25 to $40

- Color announcer—$10 to $15

- Two spotters @ $3.00 each—$6

- Engineer—$10

The total cost, less program time, amounts to $71 to $91 per game. The average basketball game including pre-game and post-game programs runs between 1 1/2 to 1 3/4 hours. The average football game including pre-game and post-game programs run about 2 1/2 hours. If we figure the station's hourly rate of $60 per game, the average basketball game will have a cost of $155 to $175 and the average football game from $220 to $250.

The usual high school football schedule averages 9 games per season. To be on the safe side a station should figure that the entire schedule will carry a price tag of $2500 to produce, promote, and broadcast. Notice this figure includes the full hourly time rate.

The average high school basketball schedule is 18 games per season. To produce, promote, and broadcast the entire schedule will cost about $3500 including the station's full hourly rate.

If the radio station is located in a small market a sales manager can readily see the almost impossible task he faces in getting a single client to sponsor either of the entire schedules. If he tries to sell each game on a per game basis he has to get $275 per football game and $195 per basketball game. This means 9 separate sponsors for football and 18 for basketball games. In such markets it is almost an impossibility to get a sponsor to spend $200 to $300 on a one-time basis. Small-market retailers seldom spend this much in a month on radio advertising. Obviously an alternative method must be devised to sell such programming. Here's how one packaged his high school football schedule:

- 5-minute newscast prior to the game—$100 per season

- One-minute "spot" prior to the game—$50 per season

- Pre-game show }
- Game } 11 sponsors @—$200 per season each
- Post-game show }

- One-minute "spot" after the game—$50 per season

- 5-minute newscast after the game—$100 per season

The total revenue for the entire season amounted to $2500. Sponsors were billed at three intervals—October 1st, November 1st, and December 1st. In this way the maximum monthly cost to each advertiser was $17, $34, or $67, depending on whether he bought a spot, newscast, or a participation in the schedule. Commercials were rotated throughout the pre-game show, the game itself, half-time, and the post-game show.

This same station operator did not broadcast the full high school basketball schedule. He chose the ten most popular games and used the same package plan, charging participating sponsors $150 each. Billing was spread over a 4-month period beginning in January so that the maximum monthly cost to each sponsor was $12.50, $25, or $37.50.

This sales method has proven itself most successful and the station has a waiting list of sponsors who wish to participate. In fact some of the participating sponsors are anxious to purchase a double participation. There of course are some draw-backs. Instead of dealing with one sponsor or a maximum of ten sponsors you are dealing with and billing 15 separate accounts and the copywriter has to prepare commercials for 15 different sponsors. However, if given careful attention you can create 15 happy and satisfied customers who will use your station for other advertising campaigns. The package method also makes it possible to obtain sponsors from business concerns that ordinarily would not use the station. Many factories participate in this type of a schedule, and waive their commercials for public service announcements for the benefit of "blood bank," "safety," "United Fund," "Community Chest," or "hospital."

## The Importance of Good Copy

No radio time salesman can hope to be successful unless he has the full cooperation of a capable commercial "copywriter." The salesman can ascertain what the sponsor wishes to include in his commercial. But it is the "copywriter's" responsibility to formulate and construct the commercial; to create the vehicle that reaches out to that very segment of the broad mass audience, the potential customer who has a particular need for a product or service not necessarily desired by others.

The copywriter must know the station's program schedule and exactly in what segment the sponsor's message will be broadcast. He must know the aims of that particular segment and the audience it reaches. In other words he must strive for ultimate results by appealing to the special interests of those potential customers, realizing that the value of the station to the sponsor is measured in terms of how many people who hear the commercial are in the market for the sponsor's product or service.

Some time ago The Harvard Business Review, in an article discussing advertising practices, mentioned the case of the "Rubber Girdle," where the deciding factor in whether or not a consumer would purchase these girdles hinged on the need for a product with very strong figure control. This means, simply, that a sponsor wishing to advertise rubber girdles should not only look for a radio program predominantly aimed at women but for a women's radio program whose listeners are made up of a majority of women with weight problems.

Researchers have proven time and time again that when a radio commercial is used skillfully it can be the most powerful sales weapon. It can sell goods or services at the lowest advertising cost. It has the power to move people to buy specific products and services. These same researchers also report that good radio commercials influence more purchases of a specific article or service than any other advertising medium.

Radio copywriters, in the quest for effectiveness and dynamism, must adhere rigorously to honesty and truthfulness. It is not only bad public relations but also unlawful: The Federal Trade Commission's rules and regulations very clearly state that it is "unlawful for any person, partnership or Corporation to disseminate, or cause to be disseminated, any false advertisement." There are many excellent and worthwhile books, written by the most competent authorities, on how to write a successful radio commercial. Therefore, it would be pure folly to attempt a full treatment here. We will, however, endeavor to list what is considered the most pertinent points as a means of initiating the unfamiliar:

1. Before beginning to write commercial copy you should know your sponsor, his products, and customers;
2. The radio commercial must have meaningfulness;
3. It must make sense;
4. It must be believable;
5. It must be honest;
6. It must be interesting;
7. It must be thought-provoking and stimulate the mind to conjure up sensory pleasures associated with the product or service as well as the benefits of the product;
8. The commercial should be written in a manner that makes it very easy for the listener to identify the product;
9. Use phrases and wording that coincide with the ideas, feelings, and images already created in the minds of listeners in regard to well-known products;
10. Spend more time on items that are easy to describe and less time on those that may be difficult to describe;
11. The commercial should at all times be written with a specific audience in mind;
12. It must be appealing;

13. It must be forceful;

14. Strive for effectiveness;

15. It should be as brief as possible;

16. It should always be in good taste;

17. It should be informative, informal, and friendly;

18. Try to create an "institutional" theme for the sponsor;

19. Try to create a "slogan" for the sponsor;

20. Make use of "attention grabbers," jingles, echo chambers, multiple-voice commercials, etc.;

21. Remember that radio is an entertainment medium so try to be a showman;

22. Fit the commercial into the style or spirit of the program in which it is to be broadcast;

23. Always have the commercial speak to the audience in terms of "you" and "your";

24. Be specific;

25. The commercial should impel action, and to do this it must contain the "what," "when," "whose," and "when-to-buy" elements;

26. The commercial should be written so that it is "tailor made" for the announcer who will read it on the air;

27. When writing commercials for sales events try to avoid using phrases such as 40% savings, 15% off, etc.; instead use the actual dollar figure such as "formerly $50 now only $40, a $10 savings," etc.;

28. Commercials should be intensely liked—never disliked;

29. Use the law of association and repetition;

30. Keep the number of different items in any one commercial at a minimum. Where more than one item is being offered divide the commercial into distinct parts by using two voices;

31. Use a style of rhythmic language;

32. Be sure to repeat points not easily understood;

33. Put the best idea at the end of the commercial.

There same authors also agree that there are certain things to be avoided in the writing of a good radio commercial:

1. Don't play games with the listener. Be sure that the product or service advertised is easily identified in the commercial;

2. Avoid flippancy;

3. Do not over-emphasize minor details;

4. Don't confuse the listener;

5. Don't use exaggerated or hard-to-believe claims;

6. Don't make statements that may be construed by the listener as unreal, absurd, or "phony";

7. Don't bore the listener with excessive repetitions;

8. Don't put the listener in a position where he has to assume the role of a critic;

Here is the basic information that a copywriter needs before planning a commercial. The salesman should give the copywriter:

1. A description of the item;

2. The "name brand" of the item;

3. Price of the item;

4. Is there a special sale on the item, or is it being made available because of a special purchase, or is it a regular priced item?

5. What are the sizes, if this is a factor?

6. What colors?

7. What is the single most important selling point for this particular item?

8. What are the other selling points in order of their importance?

9. Who are the prospective buyers for this particular item?

A copywriter must always remember that he is writing for the ear and not the eye. Because he is writing to be heard, and not to be seen and studied, he should remember that if the syntax is difficult or if the sentence is rambling, the listener may not get the message. If the listener does not get the message the product just won't sell. That is why, at times, it becomes necessary to repeat certain points in a radio commercial; for example the price of the article. If a pair of shoes sells for $14.95 the copywriter must repeat the price within the radio commercial to be sure the listener hears it. Where two items with different prices are to be offered in the same commercial be sure to adequately separate the items and the prices.

Flowery or extravagant language should be avoided. However, strive for originality of phrasing and description. The commercial should be a straightforward statement of why the listener should buy the item or service and why he should do it now! Don't waste words in leading up to the hard facts and be sure to avoid timidity about making urgent statements when the facts justify the urgency. Every commercial should be written with every one of the station's announcers in mind, especially if the commercial is to be broadcast on several different programs. The copywriter should be aware of the fact that each announcer reads differently and at different speeds.

Radio commercials, just like radio programs, can have a format of their own. It should consist of 1. a headline, or lead, that states the item or items that are being offered, or which directs attention to the major selling feature; 2. specific selling features of the item or items being offered; and 3. a repeat and summary of the item or items. The "lead" may be just a few words or a complete sentence. It should arrest the attention of the listener. Never use a general or a long-winded introduction to try to gain the listener's attention.

The Radio Advertising Bureau, Inc., a nonprofit association supported by radio stations, networks, and station representatives has prepared a chart for the use of copywriters and radio time buyers indicating the composition of the radio audience, hour by hour, in the nation's largest metropolitan markets. Your particular area may differ slightly but will not show substantially different listening habits. True, the "peak" audience periods may vary, depending on the size of the community and the work habits of the population; however, the "peak" listening time will usually be that time when people are getting up and going to work. The chart indicates the following:

| | | Radio Audience Composition in % | | |
|---|---|---|---|---|
| | Women | Men | Teenagers | Children |
| 6 – 7 AM | 46 | 47 | 4 | 3 |
| 7 – 8 AM | 44 | 44 | 9 | 3 |
| 8 – 9 AM | 50 | 39 | 8 | 3 |
| 9 – 10 AM | 64 | 26 | 5 | 5 |
| 10 – 11 AM | 67 | 23 | 5 | 5 |
| 11 – 12 N | 67 | 24 | 4 | 5 |
| 12N– 1 PM | 65 | 25 | 5 | 5 |
| 1 – 2 PM | 67 | 23 | 5 | 5 |
| 2 – 3 PM | 63 | 26 | 7 | 4 |
| 3 – 4 PM | 60 | 24 | 12 | 4 |
| 4 – 5 PM | 45 | 42 | 10 | 3 |
| 5 – 6 PM | 48 | 38 | 11 | 3 |
| 6 – 7 PM | 42 | 45 | 11 | 2 |
| 7 – 8 PM | 43 | 45 | 10 | 2 |
| 8 – 9 PM | 44 | 45 | 9 | 2 |
| 9 – 10 PM | 44 | 45 | 9 | 2 |
| 10 – 11 PM | 45 | 47 | 7 | 1 |
| 11 – 12 M | 46 | 49 | 5 | – |

The statistics in the above chart should be compared with local surveys of listening habits. This information can be of tremendous help to the copywriter, especially when a sponsor orders a series of commercials to be broadcast throughout the day. Knowing the audience composition for a particular hour enables the copywriter to produce a commercial aimed at a specific group within the total audience; remember, men react differently to commercials than do women, and the same holds true for teenagers.

The experts and the researchers list four major elements in a radio commercial contributing to effectiveness and results:

1. The commercial must have significant content: The listener must feel that he has received some meaningful information. It doesn't have to be earth shattering or something that is brand new. It can simply corroborate a thought or idea he already possesses. It must however be honest, accurate, and believable.

2. The commercial must be thought provoking: It must arouse

the listener's thoughts and feelings concerning the product or service offered. For example, it must change his "thinking about playing golf" to "buying that sport shirt," etc.

3. The listener must be able to identify himself with the product or service. The commercial is actually a group of words that surreptitiously imposes upon the listener's mind a picture that his imagination completes. The woman must be able to imagine how slim she will look in the new girdle; the man must be able to imagine how well-groomed he will appear in that special shirt, etc.

4. The commercial must meet the preconceived standards, feelings, and ideas of the listener concerning the product or service offered; such as: Banks charge the lowest rate of interest on loans; a certain soap product gets clothes whiter; snow tread tires are best for winter driving; etc. The listener must be able to feel that the commercial actually represents his own personal feeling about the product or service.

Conversely, there are four basic elements to be avoided in radio commercials:

1. Never offend the listener. Avoid creating frustration by the use of non-understandable dialects, impossible messages, and ridiculous statements. A radio commercial should never irritate or annoy the listener. Those that do create animosity toward both the station and the sponsor's product or service;

2. Don't exaggerate. If the listener feels that the commercial is phony, unreal, or absurd and unbelievable it will cause him to have doubts about everything he hears on the station, in addition to doubts about the items or service being advertised.

3. Don't confuse the listener. Commercials that are not clear or understandable to the listener always result in distraction and confusion. Never talk about one product in a commercial while trying to sell another product;

4. Avoid excessive repetitions. Radio commercials that

seem to repeat the same words over and over are sure to be dull and quite annoying to the listener. Never make the listener feel that he is wasting his time by listening to your station. Such a feeling also results in animosity toward the sponsor's product or service.

Several approaches are used in commercial preparation and delivery:

1.  The straight announcement is a straightforward sales talk or advertising message delivered by an announcer without the use of "gimmicks," sound effects, or musical backgrounds;

2.  The dramatized announcement is a commercial employing two or more voices generally presented in the form of a play or skit;

3.  The dialogue announcement is a discussion between two or more persons concerning the product or service. It differs from the dramatized announcement in that it is not delivered in the form of a play or skit;

4.  The comedy announcement is a commercial in which the copywriter coats the sales message in a humorous atmosphere;

5.  The "punch" announcement, also referred to as the "hard-sell" announcement, is emphatic and urgent and requires a well-controlled delivery on the part of the announcer.

6.  The "soft-sell" announcement is "easy-going" and requires that the announcer create the relaxed atmosphere of a face-to-face conversation;

7.  The singing jingle announcement is set entirely in music with the commercial message as a part of a song;

8.  The musical announcement is a combination of talk and music; music is used to either introduce or finish the announcement or held softly in the background while the announcer reads the message.

Special effects may be used to accentuate the message or to gain the listener's attention; for example, an echo chamber, or extraneous sounds either during or to open and close the message.

The following is intended as a guide in determining the number of words required to fill the most frequently used announcement lengths. Obviously, the actual number depends on reading speed.

- 8 to 10 seconds—15 words
- 15 seconds—38-40 words
- 20 seconds—50 words
- 30 seconds—75 words
- 60 seconds—125 words

## Why Advertise

The advertising director of a large agency who was in charge of the Borden Company account once defined the purpose and meaning of advertising in four little words: "TO MOVE A MIND." That is the real purpose of all advertising—to stimulate the prospect to purchase a specific product or service. No one is ever free from the influences of advertising. From the very moment we awake until we go to sleep we are constantly bombarded with advertising messages and slogans and names. When we awake and look at the clock, there on the face of the clock is the name of the manufacturer or the brand name of the clock. The cake of soap we wash with is likewise imprinted. We turn on the radio and are greeted with commercials. The can of coffee has advertising all over the outside; the oven has a name emblazoned on it, even the coffee pot is similiarly stamped. The bread wrapper, the jar of jam, etc., all have advertising messages or identifications.

Our car manufacturer has his name stamped upon the dashboard. The automobile radio blares our commercials. Even the tires carry advertising. As we drive to the railroad station or our place of employment we pass billboards and see an ocean of advertising on and in every shop window. If we take a train, the front, back, and top of the car is plastered with ads. You cannot get into a taxicab today without some advertising message staring you in the face. At the office the pens and pencils we use all bear advertising of one kind or another. At lunch, the menu, the bottles, and practically everything subtly competes for your attention. And so it goes, until exhausted you finally fall asleep.

All this advertising has but one purpose—"to move a mind." Go into any supermarket today and you will be overcome by the amount of advertising awaiting your gaze. In that same supermarket, if you take the time to look, there are from 65 to 85 different brands of soaps and detergents. Stop and think about what makes a woman reach for one brand in preference to another. After all, every one of these products is intended for essentially the same purpose. "Packaging" and "position" on the shelf may have some bearing on the customers' choice. Experience in the use of the particular brand and recommendations from other users of a particular product may also have some bearing on the purchase. But, mainly, and surely, it is the advertising that is the real motivation that rings a bell in the subconscious mind.

The study of "motivation" is a science unto itself, far exceeding the limitations existing here. There is one thing, however, that all researchers in the field of motivation and "marketing" agree upon; that is the necessity of an adequate and sound advertising program. To have an adequate and sound advertising program, a potential radio sponsor must know the station's coverage, its popularity, its programming, the audience demographics, and what program promotions and merchandising services are available. Even with all this knowledge, any sponsor who uses radio, just for the sake of being on the air, without the use of creative advertising copy, is just wasting his money. And even the best advertising copy can be ruined by poor or flippant announcers. Announcers must never shout or appear to be bullying the listener. A hard-sell commercial can be direct and forceful, without shouting or bullying. All commercials should be read in a distinct manner. A garbled message only tends to confuse the listener and may drive him to frustration and a dislike for the radio station, the sponsor, and the product or service offered. Unclear messages escape the listener's comprehension. All commercials can be delivered in an intimate, relaxed, lively, and sociable style. A good announcer can add personal warmth and intimacy without interfering with or distracting from the commercial message. Good advertising copy delivered in the proper manner is remembered to a high degree and can "move a mind."

Another thing that some sponsors will ask of radio time salesmen is whether to spend their advertising dollars in sponsoring a program or shall they spend this money on a series of "spot" announcements.

## Program vs Spot Announcements

Should an advertiser sponsor a program or buy an announcement schedule? It all depends on his goal. Programs offer the following advantages:

1. Radio programs are scheduled and broadcast at a specific time period and people know when to expect the program, whereas spot announcements generally are not pre-advertised to call the listener's attention to the broadcast;

2. Radio programs attract a more consistent audience. If the program is geared to a special segment of the total audience, because the program director knows that the particular segment of the audience wants and likes this type of show, it should have a loyal group of listeners. On the other hand, "spot" announcements should be placed in or adjacent to programs appealing to the advertiser's potential customers.

3. Radio programs tend to build greater product identification. Such identification is difficult to achieve with spot announcements.

4. Programs tend to build goodwill for the sponsor, his product, and for the station. People always like to get something for nothing, and when a radio station presents enjoyable and entertaining programs, listeners show their gratitude by referring to the station in glowing terms and in buying the sponsor's advertised product or service. Radio audiences seldom associate a "spot" announcement with any particular program, no matter how popular the program or how often a particular spot announcement is heard within that program;

5. Programs produce a much higher level of dignity and prestige for a sponsor.

Spot announcements offer these:

1. There is more flexibility in scheduling spot announcements; they may be scheduled throughout the day according
to audience demographics and listening habits. Programs
are usually scheduled at a specific time within the broadcast
day;

2. Spot announcements, due to the greater frequency alone,
reach a wider audience. In a 5-minute program the sponsor
usually gets an opening and closing mention, plus a one-
minute commercial; in a 15-minute program a sponsor usually gets an opening and closing mention plus two commercials. In a 30-minute program there is an opening and closing mention, plus three to four commercials; in an hour program the sponsor gets an opening, closing, and middle-of-
the-program mention, plus four commercials. An investment in spot announcements provides more commercials for
the dollar spent.

Both methods, spot announcements or programs, can produce good results for a sponsor if they are intelligently scheduled. My suggestion is that a radio time salesman should
endeavor to sell a sponsor a combination of both programs
and spot announcements whenever possible.

# CHAPTER 8

# Internal Operations

All effort expended in selling, programming, planning, and promoting is in vain if a radio station itself doesn't operate like a well-oiled machine. If orders and schedules aren't executed exactly as intended, if program material isn't prepared in accordance with instructions, if any facet of station operation is left to chance, it is only a matter of time until the station is in deep financial trouble. Therefore, it is vitally important that we adopt rules to govern internal operations, just as we have policies to guide salesmen and rules regulating the technical aspects of broadcasting. So, let's take up each area one by one.

### Routing Sales Orders

The only source of revenue a radio station has is the sale of its time. However, the mere fact that a salesman, or an account executive as I like to refer to him, has sold a client or secured a sponsor does not necessarily mean that the station will receive the full benefit or revenue from the sale. Adequate measures must be adopted to insure the actual broadcast of the commercial announcement or program. It is not a rare occurrence for a client to purchase time and then discover that for one reason or another his program or commercial message was not broadcast. When this happens all the confidence the sponsor has in his dealings with the station representative may be undermined and all effort in securing the account may be irretrievably lost.

When a sponsor purchases time he rightfully expects that his program or commercial announcement will be broadcast on the day and at the time agreed upon. If the purchase was made to coincide with a sales effort or plan, the failure of the station to deliver on its part of the contract may mean the failure of such a sales event or project. It will not do the sponsor any good to have an announcement broadcast on a Wednesday concerning a sale that was scheduled for the previous Monday. Likewise, it would be foolish for a merchant to run a sale unless he was sure that the public knew he was running such a sale.

Each radio station has its own method of routing sales orders. It is amazing, however, to discover how slip-shod some of these methods are. The method we are suggesting, though to some may appear to be cumbersome and to others have certain faults, has proven to be most successful, at least for many stations. Here's how it works:

1. All orders, regardless of who obtains it or the manner in which it was obtained, should be routed to the sales manager.

2. The sales manager makes sure the time is available and then routes the sales order to the station manager who either approves or disapproves the order.

3. If the station manager disapproves the order he should immediately notify the sales manager and state the reason for disapproval. The sales manager likewise informs the salesman, account executive, or other person who obtained the order.

4. If the station manager approves the order he dispatches it to the program manager to alert him of the sale of a program on a specific time of the broadcast day.

5. At the same time the station manager routes the order to the traffic department for inclusion on the program schedule and log.

6. Simultaneously the station manager routes a copy of the order to the bookkeeping department to alert it for billing purposes.

7. At the same time he informs the sales manager of his approval of the sales order.

8. The sales manager advises the copywriter of the sale and instructs that department to create the commercial continuity and to forward it to the program director.

9. The program director then proceeds to include the commercial in the program schedule and the "daily broadcast book."

10. At the specific time on the designated date the announcer broadcasts the commercial matter.

Station operators, especially those in small to medium markets, know that radio time sales do not always originate with the salesman or account executive. Many requests for radio time are made through the mail and are received by telephone. If the radio station has a national rep his orders will invariably be received through the mail, though sometimes by telephone or telegram. But, regardless of how the order is received the suggested routing of the order should be followed. We offer the following as examples of the forms that might be utilized in carrying out the suggested method of routing.

When an order is received, regardless by whom or by what means, the person receiving or obtaining the order should immediately complete, in triplicate, a form similar to that shown here. (The radio station's "call letters" can be printed above the legend "Order to Broadcast.") This is for those accounts whose orders originate through an advertising agency. In these cases it is suggested that the agency's name and address be listed on the first line and the company's name or product written on the second line. The reason for this suggestion is that the "billing" will be going to the agency but the "traffic" department and program department will be listing the company or product on the traffic control board and program logs. Should the space provided for "schedule and instructions be insufficient, a separate sheet should be stapled to the form.

When completed, all copies of this form should be routed to the sales manager. If he approves the order, the third copy is retained and the remaining two are forwarded to the station manager for his approval.

If the station manager disapproves the order he should immediately return both copies to the sales manager with the reason for disapproval. The sales manager in turn notifies the salesman who then notifies the client. If the station manager approves the order he returns the second copy to the sales manager stamped "approved" and signed by the station manager. The sales manager retains the second copy and now stamps "approved" on the third copy, signs it and returns it to the salesman for his files. At the time of approval the sales manager notifies the copywriter of the order and instructs him to create the commercial continuity for the account and to forward the commercial to the program department. A copy of the continuity should also be forwarded to the salesman for delivery to the client. The station manager,

# Order to Broadcast

DATE _____

CLIENT _____

ADDRESS _____

CONTRACT BEGINNING _____ ENDING _____

SALESMAN _____

SCHEDULE AND INSTRUCTIONS

RATE _____

TOTAL CHARGE _____

CLIENT: _____

_____

ADDRESS: _____

SALESMAN: _____ TYPE OF PROGRAM _____

BEGIN BROADCAST _____     SCHEDULE: _____
          time    date

_____

_____

_____

_____

_____

_____

AUTHORIZED BY: _____     DATE: _____

INSTRUCTIONS: _____

using the "Order to Broadcast" form, now prepares in quad-
ruplicate a form similar to that included here. He retains
the original, forwards the second copy to the bookkeeping department, the third copy to the program director and the
fourth copy to the "traffic" department.

In completing this form the agency's name and address, if
any, should be used. The company or product name should
be entered on the second line. Next to "type of program"
should be inserted the phrase one-minute announcement, 30-
second announcement, or the name of the program, depending on what the order calls for. The exact times and beginning and ending dates should be clearly stated. In the space
marked "schedule" insert the exact information as ordered.
If a program has been ordered, the day of the week and the
time of the program should be inserted such as Mon., Wed.,
and Fri., 10:05 to 10:15 AM or Tuesday 12:30 to 1 PM, etc.
If there is insufficient space for the entire schedule a notation
should be made—"see attached"—and a copy of the complete

schedule should be stapled to each of the four copies of the forms. Under "instructions" the station manager should list all pertinent information required by the program department and the bookkeeping department, such as: 1. rates and discounts; 2. "bills in duplicate or triplicate"; 3. affidavit and copy of commercials required; etc.

The manager sets up a file or book in alphabetical sequence according to the client's name, and retains this file after an order has been completed or cancelled. By using this file he can check the program logs daily to insure that every commercial was broadcast. He can also use it to determine, in advance, the revenue expected from committed orders for any particular period of time. The bookkeeping department sets up a similar file or book and each month prepares the bills from this file, thus it is no longer necessary for the bookkeeping department to "bill" from the program logs.

The program manager, upon receipt of the "traffic order" is immediately alerted as to what to schedule, announcers to assign, continuity to be prepared, tapes to be produced, etc. He is expected to receive the commercial continuity from the copywriter. The program manager should maintain an alphabetical file in which his copy of the form is held until the order has been fulfilled. Once the broadcast schedule is completed his copy of the order is destroyed.

Upon receipt of the form the "traffic" department makes the necessary entries on the "traffic board." An alphabetical file is also set up as a daily check against the program log. This should be done before the daily program log is given to the program manager. Upon completion of the broadcast schedule the form is destroyed.

In those cases where a cancellation occurs the salesman servicing the account is immediately notified. He completes 6 copies of the "stop order" form, retaining one copy for himself and forwarding the other 5 copies to the sales manager. This reminds the sales manager to discuss the reason for cancellation with the salesman. After assuring himself that the cancellation is in order the sales manager retains one copy for himself and forwards the other copies as follows: one to the program department, one to the "traffic" department, one to the bookkeeping department, and one to the station manager. He also notifies the copywriter of the cancellation.

When the program manager receives his copy the appropri-

CLIENT:_____

_____

ADDRESS:_____

SALESMAN:_____TYPE OF PROGRAM_____

LAST BROADCAST_____ _____
                time   date

REMARKS:_____

_____

_____

_____

_____

AUTHORIZED BY:_____DATE:_____

ate "start order" is destroyed after deleting all the necessary material from the active file. Likewise, the traffic department also destroys both the corresponding "start" and "stop" orders after deleting all the necessary material from the traffic board, program logs, and program books. The bookkeeping department immediately attaches the corresponding "start" order to the "stop" order and bills the account for the programs or announcements that were broadcast, making the appropriate notation on the reverse side of the "start" order, indicating that the account was "billed", and files both copies in the account's folder.

The station manager, after assuring himself that the account was properly billed destroys both the "start" and the "stop" orders. It is also suggested that each form be printed on a different color paper; the color itself signifies that an order has been cancelled.

## Bookkeeping

One of the most important departments in any radio station is the bookkeeping department. In addition to keeping a full set of double-entry books the bookkeeper must be able to maintain proper payroll accounts; prepare the payroll and prepare the payroll checks for the required signatures; make all deposits; bill all the accounts; prepare checks for all bills payable; issue monthly statements to all accounts from whom money is due; and, prepare a monthly profit-and-loss statement for the station manager.

We are convinced that a bookkeeper must be very prompt and accurate in sending bills to all accounts. This insures faster payment and holds the list of accounts receivable at a realistic level. To do this in a systematic, thorough, and correct manner we suggest the following procedure:

1. Maintain an accurate and complete "start order" file.
2. Check this file against each program log on a day-by-day basis to insure that every account for which there is a "start order" has received his due, and to insure that there is a "start order" for every commercial entry on the program log.
3. Immediately upon the completion of any broadcast schedule prepare the necessary bills from the "start order" and forward them to the manager for his examination and mailing.
4. On the first business day of the month immediately prepare all the bills from the "start orders" and forward them to the manager for his examination and mailing.
5. On the reverse side of the "start order" indicate the date, invoice number, and amount of each bill that was prepared.
6. No later than the 10th of each month prepare a statement of amounts due by month and invoice number for all accounts who may owe the station for services rendered during any prior months. These statements should be on the station manager's desk no later than on the 11th day of the month so that he may examine them, make any necessary notations and see that they are immediately mailed.
7. Take appropriate steps to file alphabetically all "start and stop orders" in a permanent bookkeeping file.

There are several advantages to the above described procedure:

It provides for an accurate check to insure that all accounts are billed for all announcements or programs that were broadcast.

It provides for an accurate check to insure that all programs or announcements that were ordered were actually broadcast.

All billing is done directly from the start order, thus expediting the billing procedure.

A record of all "billings" is permanently retained.

Bills are rendered immediately upon the completion or cancellation of a start order. This not only facilitates the "billing" operation at the beginning of the month but in many cases results in prompt payment of bills.

All accounts more than 30 days past due are notified as to any money they may owe the station.

It allows for the station manager to check all bills and statements that are sent to the sponsors.

## Financial Statements

A station manager needs several types of monthly financial statements so as to properly ascertain the financial condition of the station. The following have been found to be most helpful. The figures which are to be supplied should be for the last day of each month.

CURRENT ASSETS:

1. Cash, by amounts in each bank and banking account;
2. Accounts receivable;
3. Expense account;
4. Employee's advances (this may be drawing accounts paid out to salesmen against commissions, loans to employees, etc.);
5. Merchandise inventory (do not list any fixed assets in this category).

The above is the actual "current assets" total. This is an important figure to watch, along with the station's "current liabilities." Station operators should strive for a ratio of at least 2 1/2 to 1 of "current assets" over "current liabilities." Anything less than this ratio will generally indicate a lack of sufficient cash to maintain an orderly operation.

## FIXED ASSETS:

1. Land;
2. Buildings;
3. Transmitting equipment;
4. Radiating system;
5. Technical studio equipment;
6. Studio furniture and fixtures;
7. Office furniture and fixtures;
8. Automobiles;
9. Leasehold improvements;
10. Emergency generators;

All of the above figures should be net figures after depreciation.

## DEFERRED CHARGES:

1. Prepaid taxes (by category i.e., city, state or federal);
2. Prepaid insurance;
3. Prepaid salaries (all advances against future earnings such as vacation pay, etc.);
4. Prepaid interest charges.

## LIABILITIES:

1. Accounts payable, including:
   a. all bills payable;
   b. accrued interest;
   c. accrued payroll;
2. Taxes payable:
   a. Federal OAB;
   b. Federal unemployment;
   c. State unemployment;
   d. State sales tax;
   e. Employees' withholding;
   f. State prior taxes;
   g. State current taxes;
   h. Federal prior taxes;
   i. Federal current taxes;
3. Reserves:
   a. Doubtful accounts;

b. Auditing;

c. Legal;

d. Advertising (this is for all advertising contracted for, especially in cases where the station is to furnish advertising on its facility for which it has already received money or articles).

4. Commissions payable: This should consist of a figure for each person to whom a commission is due, including all national and regional representatives.

5. Capital stock: This should consist of a figure for every class of stock issued and outstanding.

6. Surplus or (Deficit): This should be a current figure for the amount of profit or loss since the facility began operating. Of course all dividends paid out should be deducted from the "profit" figure before it is listed.

OPERATING STATEMENT:

1. Direct Expenses: Under this category the bookkeeper should list all expenses for:

a. Agency Commissions—all money paid to agencies or deducted from gross amounts when preparing bills. Do not list commissions due salesmen or national and regional representatives.

b. Cost of talent sold: Some station operators charge clients a talent over and above what they actually pay the talent. This may be due to the extra cost in billing, social security payments, etc. The gross amount actually billed to the sponsor is reported under income.

c. Cost of special wire facilities: Some radio stations charge clients for "radio wire service" over and above what they actually pay the telephone company. This may be justified for many different reasons.

d. Cost of news service: Some stations arrive at a set figure for this expense. The balance of the actual cost is allocated to program expense. Some insist on a percentage breakdown of the cost of news services according to the number of newscasts that are commercial and those that are sustaining.

2. Technical Department:

a. Salaries.
b. Power and light: Radio stations should insist on separate utility bills for the operation of the transmitters, tower lights, etc., apart from the power required for studio and office operation. Some operators even insist on separate bills for the operation of the studio and include this as a program department expense, where it rightfully belongs.
c. Fuel.
d. Maintenance and repair of transmitter buildings and grounds.
e. Maintenance and repair of technical equipment.
f. Tubes.
g. Transmitter lines.
h. Outside engineering expense. Some stations employ consulting engineers or others for proof-of-performance tests and for operating remote broadcasts.
i. Transmitter telephone.
j. Other technical expense.

3. Program Department:

a. Salaries, including all salaries paid out to all employees of the program department, supervisory or other.
b. Maintenance and repair of studio.
c. Purchase of music, records, tapes, or recordings.
d. News service (discussed under "Direct Expenses.")
e. Royalties and license fees: All money paid out to such organizations as ASCAP, BMI, etc.
f. Purchase of programs: Some stations purchase syndicated or other prepared programs. The purchase price is generally added to the broadcast time when the sponsor is billed and is included in the gross amount of reported income.
g. Prizes: The cost of all prizes offered and awarded by the station are reported here. If the sponsor has been charged for this it is included in gross income. The cost of prizes not as yet awarded is reported in the "accounts payable" and carried as a "current asset" under "merchandise inventory."

h. Program advertising: List only those expenses incurred to advertise programs. Do not list "sales promotion or advertising" under this category.

i. Other program expenses.

4. <u>Sales</u> <u>Department</u>:

a. Sales commissions and salaries.

b. Commissions to national and regional representatives (should be listed separately by name).

c. Advertising: List only those expenses incurred for sales promotion and advertising.

d. Other sales expense: Some stations list travel and entertainment expenses incurred by their sales department. Many in small markets list such an expense under "general and administrative." For an actual cost of a sales department we suggest a separate listing under the "sales department" expenses.

5. <u>General</u> and <u>Administrative</u>: These are the items that should be listed under this category.

a. Officers salaries.

b. Director fees.

c. Office salaries.

d. Rent.

e. Light and heat.

f. Maintenance and repair of office equipment.

g. Travel and entertainment (do not list any items relating to the operation of an automobile such as gas, tires, etc.).

h. Telephone and telegraph.

i. Dues and subscriptions.

j. Stationery and supplies.

k. Postage.

l. Contributions.

m. Freight and express.

n. Auto expense.

o. Bad debts.

p. Insurance.

q. Legal and auditing.

r. Collection expense.

s. City taxes.

t.   State unemployment.
u.   Federal OAB.
v.   Federal unemployment.
w.   Sales taxes.
x.   Interest expenses.
y.   Miscellaneous (this can become quite large and it is suggested that this entry be reviewed periodically to determine if a separate category should be established for a particular item.)

Accountants employed by radio stations usually set up a planned depreciation schedule and advise the bookkeeping department as to the monthly figure to be used in figuring this expense.

Another good practice is to have the bookkeeper maintain a running list of all accounts payable and to prepare a daily record on bank balances by bank and account after all checks are received and deposited. The manager can then inform the bookkeeping department as to what bills are to be paid. This practice spreads accounts payable throughout the month and allows the manager to plan for all forseeable expenses. With savings banks now paying interest from the date of deposit to date of withdrawal, it also creates the opportunity for additional income. Those stations using this additional income feature deposit all funds in a savings account and withdraw for deposit in the checking account only those funds needed to pay salaries and bills.

## The Traffic Department

Seldom does one hear much about the all-important traffic department, but no commercial radio station can function without it. Very appropriately named, its principal objective is to see that everything goes on the air as planned. Some of the functions are:

1.   To maintain an up-to-the-minute record of the program schedule with all commercial commitments;
2.   To maintain an up-to-the-minute record of all time available for commercial purposes;
3.   To advise the sales department of all commercial time availabilities for any particular account;
4.   To work with the sales department in scheduling commercial time for all accounts.

5. To prepare the daily program log.
6. To work with the program director and check the announcer's book with the daily program log.

Unless the sales department knows exactly what time is sold and what times are available for commercial broadcasts it is impossible for it to adequately perform. Obvious problems arise when the same period of time is sold to two different sponsors, and similar problems result when sponsors featuring the same or similar products or services are sold time adjacent to each other. Though advertisers do not object when their ads appear next to each other in a newspaper they complain bitterly or refuse to advertise on radio if they are not guaranteed a spread between their commercial message and their competitor's. Some advertisers insist on at least a 15-minute spread. Now, the generally accepted practice is to guarantee at least a 5-minute spread.

Generally, some method is employed to keep a master log for each day of the week. Such a log shows each program (or each hour), its sponsor (if commercial), and long-term announcement schedules calling for specific times. (Short-term and run-of-schedule orders are not entered on most master logs for obvious reasons.) In some stations the master log is mounted on a convenient wall (called a traffic board) and lists the schedule for each day of the week, or a separate, smaller board is used for each day. Others use a file containing 3x5-inch cards (a Cardex file, for example) with a card for each hour of the day. Different colors are used to designate various programs and sponsors. Trade journals and office suppliers list a variety of equipment suitable for the purpose. No matter which method you decide to use, be sure there is enough space to clearly indicate the names of the sponsors and the exact date on which their particular contract ends. At the completion or cancellation of a broadcast order the sponsor's name is simply deleted.

It is always best that the sales department request specific time availabilities such as "traffic times," "news adjacencies," "afternoon or morning time," etc. In advising the sales department of time availabilities the traffic manager should always be aware of the FCC implied ruling concerning the amount of commercial matter that should be scheduled in any one hour and the average per hour for the total day. Some traffic managers keep a running account, hour by hour, of the

# AM and FM Program Log

To be retained for two years from date.—F.C.C.

DATE

LEGEND

L—Local
NET—Network
REC—Recorded
CM—Commercial Matter
CC—Commercial Continuity
CA—Commercial Announcement
PSA—Public Service Announcement
ET—Electrical Transcription
REM—Remote
ID—Station Identification
AS—Announced as sponsored

LEGEND

A—Agricultural
E—Entertainment
N—News
PA—Public Affairs
R—Religion
I—Instructional
S—Sports
O—Other
EDIT—Editorials
POL—Political
ED—Educational Institution

ANNOUNCERS:

| Stn. ID Given at | Program Actually | | PROGRAM Sched: | SPONSOR | Anncr | Comm Ancmt Given | Sponsor Ancmt Given | Source/Type |
|---|---|---|---|---|---|---|---|---|
| | ON | OFF | | | | | | |
| | | | | | | | | |
| | | | | | | | | |
| | | | | | | | | |
| | | | | | | | | |

exact amount of commercial matter that is scheduled, a tremendous time saving factor when availability requests are made.

Actual log preparation, though time consuming, is a fairly easy process. Everything on the "log" should be typed in black, except commercial programs, announcements, and legends pertaining to the same, which should be typed in red. Adequate spaces should be left between programs to allow for the insertion of at least 20 lines of entries per hour, unless a 1/4-hour, 1/2-hour, or one-hour program is commercial. The exact date of broadcast, not the date of preparation, should be inserted in the proper place. The FCC frowns upon the practice of preparation far in advance of the broadcast date. They also insist on legibility and that all insertions or deletions be dated and signed by the person who actually makes the entry or deletion. In the space marked "announcers" the "traffic" manager should insert the names of all announcers who will be broadcasting on that date. It is mandatory by the FCC regulations that no announcer be omitted.

The traffic manager prepares only those sections of the log under "program schedule, sponsor, and source/type." All other entries are made in writing by the announcers. Under "program" the exact time for the start of each program is listed, the name of the program, the name of the sponsor and the exact amount of "commercial matter" in the program. Under "source/type" the exact "legend" is typed. A typical "log" entry looks like this:

6:30  News      City National Bank      cc 1 1/2 min  LN

The above would all be in red and would indicate that a commercial program was scheduled for 6:30, that its name was "News," the sponsor of the program, the exact time in minutes of commercial matter, and, that it was a live local news program. Here is another example of an entry:

12:15  Jerry Vale Show  Bethel Food    cc 3 min   REC E

The above would all be in red also, indicating a fully-sponsored program, time, name, sponsor, amount of commercial matter, and that it was a recorded program of an entertainment nature.

Should a program not be fully sponsored by one client but co-sponsored by a group of clients it is referred to as a "participation" program. The log entries appear as follows:

| 1:30 | Club 800 | music | | REC E |
| | Atlantic Refining | cc 1 | min | CA TAPE |
| | Ford | cc 1/2 | min | CA TAPE |
| | First National Stores | cc 1 | min | CA |
| | Social Security | | | PSA |

The first line indicating the time, name, and content of the program and the source/type is all typed in black, since the program is not sponsored entirely by a single account. The sponsor names, the commercial time, and source/type are in red. "Social Security" and "PSA" are in black. The above entries indicate that at 1:30 a musical participating program called "Club 800" is scheduled and that it is a "recorded-entertainment" program with 3 commercial announcements for the named sponsors amounting to 2 1/2 minutes of commercial matter and one public service announcement. It also indicates in red the commercial announcement by the legend "CA" and that the commercial announcement is to be read "live" by the announcer. If a "tape" was used, instead of the announcer reading the commercial, it would be indicated by "CA-TAPE." The use of the latter symbol alerts the announcer that he must play a "tape" or "recorded" message.

All other entries on the "program log" are made by the announcer on duty at the time of broadcast. Under "Sta. ID given at" he inserts the exact time he broadcasts a station identification. Under "program actually on/off" he inserts the exact time he began the program and the exact time the program finished. Due to many factors these times may differ from the time entered by the traffic department. The thing to insist upon is that the exact actual time be entered by the announcer in the appropriate spaces. Under the column "anncr" the announcer's initials signify that he made the entry or read the commercial. Under "comm ancmt given" he enters the exact time the commercial announcement was broadcast. Under "sponsor ancmt given" he inserts his initials to indicate that he has broadcast an announcement identifying the sponsor of a commercial program. At the time they begin on-air duty all announcers must sign the log and enter the time. When their tour of duty is finished they should also sign and again enter the exact time they finished.

Each day's log must be kept for a period of at least two years. Most stations retain them for at least three years. Program logs are all important at the time a licensee applies for a renewal of his license, since the log for each day of the FCC's composite week must accompany the application.

## FCC Logging Rules

The FCC requires all commercial radio stations to maintain three logs: 1) program; 2) operating; and 3) maintenance. The general requirements are:

1. Each log shall be kept by employees competent to do so, having actual knowledge of the facts required, who shall sign the appropriate log when starting duty and again when going off duty.

2. The logs shall be kept in an orderly and legible manner, in suitable form, and in such detail that the data required is readily available. Key letters or abbreviations are permitted if their proper meaning is contained on the log. Each sheet shall be numbered and dated. Time entries shall be in either local standard or daylight saving time and shall be accordingly indicated.

3. No log, or portion of a log, shall be erased, obliterated, or destroyed within the period of retention. Any corrections which are necessary shall be made by striking out the erroneous portion or by making a corrective explanation on the log. Such deletions or entries shall be initialed and dated by the person making the entry or deletion.

The Program Log requires the following entries:

For Each Program: 1. An entry identifying the program by name and title; 2. An entry of the time each program be-

# Transmitter Operating Log

DATE _____

CARRIER ON _____ OFF _____

PROGRAM ON _____ OFF _____

CRYSTAL IN USE (L) _____ (R) _____

| OPERATOR | | ON | OFF |
|---|---|---|---|
| | | | |

| TIME | PLATE VOLTS | PLATE CURRENT | R. F. CURRENT | XTAL TEMP. | FREQ. DEV. | REMARKS |
|---|---|---|---|---|---|---|
| | | | | | | TOWER LIGHTS OBSERVED AT |
| | | | | | | |
| | | | | | | |
| | | | | | | |
| | | | | | | |
| | | | | | | |
| | | | | | | |
| | | | | | | |

gins and ends; 3. An entry classifying each program as to "type;" 4. An entry classifying each program as to source (if a network program the name of the network must also be given—i.e., "Network - CBS"); and 5. An entry showing the name and party affiliation of all candidates who appear on political programs.

For Commercial Matter: 1. An entry identifying the sponsor of the program and/or the person paying for the program; 2. An entry showing the total amount of commercial continuity within each sponsored program; 3. An entry showing the duration of each commercial announcement and an entry which shows the beginning time of such announcements; 4. An entry indicating that sponsorship of a program has been broadcast.

For Public Service Announcements: An entry must be made showing that such an announcement was broadcast, together with the name of the organization on whose behalf it was made.

For Other Announcements: 1. An entry of the time that each required station identification announcement was made; 2. An entry for each announcement presenting a political candidate on a non-commercial program showing his name and party affiliation; 3. An entry for each announcement made pursuant to the "local notice" requirements—i.e., filing for a renewal; change of ownership; pending applications before the FCC, etc.; 4. An entry showing the use of a mechanical reproduction announcement.

The Operating Log: The following entries shall be made only by the properly licensed operator in actual charge of the transmitting apparatus: a. The time the station begins to supply power to the antenna and the time it stops; b. An entry of each interruption of the carrier wave, its cause and duration. (This entry should be signed by the person who restored the operation of the apparatus.); c. An entry, at the beginning of operation, and at intervals not exceeding 1/2 hour, of the following actual meter readings observed prior to making any adjustments to the equipment and, when appropriate, an indication of corrections made to restore parameters to normal operating values: a. Operating constants of the last radio amplifier stage (total plate voltage and plate current); b. Antenna current without modulation; and c. Frequency monitor reading; d. An entry each day of the antenna base currents without modulation; e. Any other entries required by the license issued to the station by the FCC; f. Any necessary corrections on the log shall be made only by the person making the original entry. Such corrections must be signed and dated by that person.

The Maintenance Log: The following entries must be made each week: a. A notation indicating the readings of the tower base current ammeters and the associated remote antenna ammeters (these must be the actual readings observed prior to remote antenna ammeter recalibration) and an indication that the remote ammeters were calibrated against the tower base ammeters; b. Time and result of auxiliary transmitter tests; c. A notation of all frequency checks and measurements made independent of the frequency monitor and of the correlation of these measurements with frequency monitor indications; d. A notation of the calibration check of automatic recording devices. Other entries required on the logs are: 1) An entry of the date and time of removal from and restoration to service of equipment that becomes defective; 2. A record of the inspection of the tower lights; 3. A full description of any experimental operation; 4. All other entries that may be required by the specific license granted to the station by the FCC.

As in the case of the program logs, the Commission requires that the operating logs and maintenance logs be retained for a period of two years. Here again we suggest that they be retained for at least three years, for they will be needed as part of the engineering section of the license renewal application.

At some time during a license period each station is visited by a representative of the Commission. The field engineer will request the following: a. The program log; b. The operating log; c. The maintenance log; d. "Proof-of-performance" tests and reports which are required to be made at least once a year; e. A copy of the most recent antenna resistance or common-point impedance measurements submitted to the Commission; and f. If you are a "directional" station, a copy of the most recent field intensity measurements to establish the performance of directional antennas. All must be available upon request.

## Required FCC Reports

Every commercially licensed AM, FM, TV, or International Broadcasting station must file an annual <u>financial report</u> with the FCC on or before April 1st of each year, using FCC Form 324. The station is required to report its total revenue from the sale of broadcast time, with separate listings for network income, non-network income, commissions paid by the station, incidental broadcast revenue such as talent fees, sale of the use of facilities, material or services, etc. In addition the station has to report all revenue received from political broadcasts. The report must include also a breakdown of expenses into the four categories we previously discussed—technical expenses, program expenses, selling expenses, and general and administrative expenses, plus salaries, wages, and bonuses paid to officers and employees.

The station must also report its annual depreciation and amortization; expenses related to film and tape rentals; records and transcriptions; outside news service; talent expenses; music license fees; and, other performance or program rights. In a separate section of this form there is a provision for listing the total number of people who are receiving salary, whether or not they are officers or employees, and if this number is greater than 15 a departmental breakdown must be included. The last section of the form calls for the dollar value of all tangible property owned and devoted exclusively to broadcast service such as: land and buildings, tower and antenna systems, transmitter equipment, etc. A station should not make the mistake of filing its own audited financial statement in lieu of the required form. The FCC insists that Form 324 be used.

The FCC also requires and insists that radio stations file <u>copies</u> of the <u>following</u> contracts, <u>instruments</u>, and <u>documents</u> within 30 days of the execution of such agreements. If oral contracts are consummated the station must file a written report of such agreements: 1. Contracts relating to network services; all network contracts whether or not it is a national network like CBS, NBC, ABC, or Mutual. There are special networks supplying specialized programs such as the "Sports Network," "Ivy Broadcasting System," etc., plus regional networks to which stations may belong on a mutual basis. Contracts with organizations such as ASCAP, BMI, SESAC, etc.

(which grant music performance rights) need not be filed. 2. All contracts that relate to ownership, whether or not these relate to the present or future ownership of the station or if they refer to the "stock" rights or interests of the station. Included in this category are "articles" of partnership, association, or incorporation, by-laws and changes in the by-laws; station sales agreements; voting rights; pledges; trusts; "stock" options; proxies; mortgage and loan agreements; changes in officers, directors, or stockholders. 3. Any contract relating to the sale of station time to other persons for re-sale (these "other persons" are usually referred to as "time brokers"). 4. All contracts which call for the same sponsor to be provided four or more hours of daily broadcast time. Excluded from this requirement are contracts for athletic events, musical concert presentations, operas, etc. 5. Management consultant agreements, except those with officers, directors, or regular employees who may be hired to act in a managerial capacity. 6. Any contract which calls for a share in the profit or loss of station operation.

Contracts which need not be filed with the Commission are: 1. Agreements between the station and regularly employed personnel such as general managers, station managers, sales managers, and salesmen, providing there is no provision in the contract calling for "profit-loss" agreements or stock acquisition or purchase plans; regularly employed chief engineers or other engineers, attorneys, accountants, consulting engineers, performers, and national or regional representatives. 2. Any contract or agreement between the station and labor unions.

All commercial stations must file an ownership report with the FCC, using FCC Form 323, at the time of license renewal application. The Commission requires that it be informed as to who owns the station. If only one person is the owner and the facility is not incorporated or is not a partnership there is but one requirement and that is the individual's name. If it is a partnership the Commission must be informed as to the names of the partners and the interest each partner has in the concern. Any change in the partnership requires prior consent from the FCC. If it is a corporation, association, trust, estate, or a receivership, the following information must be filed with the Commission: 1. The name, residence, citizenship status, and amount of stock owned by all the officers, directors, stockholders, etc. 2. Information concerning the family or business relationship between any 2 officers, directors, stockholders, etc. 3. A complete report as to the capitalization of the concern as to the amount and class of stock authorized and issued, as well as a full report relative to the voting power of all stock authorized and issued. 4. Where other corporations or entities own stock in the station a full report must be made concerning that corporation's officers, directors, and the person voting the station's stock for the corporation or entity. 5. A list of all the contracts still in effect of the nature that must be filed with the FCC. 6. All interests the station may have in other licensed broadcast stations.

In addition to the above, a licensee must file a revised ownership report every time there is a change in the following: 1. Any change in capitalization or organization; 2. Any change in the officers or directors; 3. Any transfer of stock; 4. Any issuance of new stock; 5. Any disposition, sale, or retirement, etc., of treasury stock; 6. Any change in the officers or directors of a corporation owning stock in the radio station; or, the person who is to vote that stock for the corporation.

Any change in stock ownership which results in any one person, partnership, corporation, or association having 50% or more of the stock is a change of control and must have the prior approval of the FCC. This may occur voluntarily or involuntarily. For example, when a death or legal disability results in a change of holdings by a person, corporation, partnership, trustee, executor, or administrator, the change is involuntary. In such cases an application on FCC Form 316 should be filed with the Commission within 30 days of the occurrence. Although licensees are allowed 30 days to file Form 316 they must immediately notify the FCC, by letter, of the death or legal disability of a person, partner, or stockholder whose holdings may effect the control of the station.

## Cost Factors

Inasmuch as we are discussing the successful financial operation of a radio station we have reserved this last section for a discussion concerning "cost factors."

## Salaries and Payroll

The largest continuing expenditure is devoted to salaries, including officers, management, and all other employees. It is impossible to state typical salaries for each and every employee, as these will differ depending on "supply and demand," the area in which the station is located, market population and revenue, and the quality a station is seeking. It might be appropriate here to refer to the chapter on staffing a station again or to the National Association of Broadcasters' Manual on "wages, hours and employment" which is issued each year.

We are living in a financial era where the cost of living is constantly on the rise and employees are expecting more and more wage increases. Therefore, it is usually profitable to set a starting salary that allows for periodic increases. All employees expect to receive increases as their value to the employer increases, but there are those who feel that they should receive increases based upon the calendar. The longer they work for a concern the more they expect to receive, whether or not the capacity in which they are serving warrants such an increase. At the time they are hired employees should be informed as to the maximum they should expect to earn regardless of their tenure. It is a far better and more economical practice to grant "bonuses" rather than salary increases. "Bonuses" can vary from time to time, whereas once a salary increase is granted it cannot be rescinded without causing discontent.

Overtime pay is another factor to be carefully studied and watched. Once an employee becomes accustomed to a certain income they resent any decrease, even though they may not be working the extra hours. It is better to hire additional staff for the time you may need them than to pay the time-and-a-half and double-time for overtime. It often pays to hire the beginner at a lower salary and train him than to pay for the experienced worker. However, in the radio broadcast business, management should strive never to sacrifice quality for the sake of a few dollars. This is especially true when it applies to air personalities.

## Land and Facilities

The rent expenditure for transmitter and studio sites should be very carefully considered, too. We firmly believe that every station should own the property on which its transmitter, towers, and buildings are located. No matter how cheap the rental for such land may seem, remember there comes a time when leases do expire and you will then fine yourself at the mercy of a landowner. You just cannot get up and move your tower because the engineering upon which your license was granted is based on the present tower location. A change in location may not be possible even if you decided to move. Or at best, a change will require new engineering studies and the expenditure of large sums for the consulting engineer and attorney fees. Prior approval must be obtained from the FCC for any change in the location of towers or transmitting equipment. Though the land you have selected for the transmitter and tower site may be far over-priced, not readily resellable, and does not carry a bookkeeping depreciation benefit, it is still more advantageous to own the land than to rent it. We say this knowing full well that this is non-income producing property which ties up cash that could be invested in income producing properties.

Studios, on the other hand, can be rented, but while renting such space an operator should seek as long a term lease as possible with renewal privileges. Just an average move from one studio location to another can run into a figure ranging from two to four thousand dollars. This should be taken into consideration when entering into a lease agreement. It is not wise—or necessary—to emulate the networks in planning studio facilities. Remember, the average listener will never visit your studios and doesn't care whether you are broadcasting from a barn or a castle; all he wants is good reception and entertaining programs. It is better to sacrifice appearance for better equipment.

## Equipment

Since the quality of the signal your station emits is probably the most important factor in retaining your audience, equipment should not be acquired on a "bargain-barn" plan. Good programming certainly entices and builds an audience for any station, but unless that program can be heard with clarity and fidelity the listener will soon become annoyed and switch to another station whose signal is stronger and clearer. Station operators, on the other hand, should beware of the extravagance of purchasing too much equipment. An adequate amount, plus a proper supply of "spares," is of course mandatory for good operations. But an over-abundance is just a plain waste of money and tends to make personnel wasteful and careless in the handling of the equipment.

In purchasing broadcast equipment, one can't be "penny-wise and dollar-foolish." Buy the best that you need to meet the requirements established by your facility. Although we recommend that you check with your engineer for his advice concerning equipment, be careful not to purchase those things which on the surface look necessary but are in reality a bit of "tinsel." There are stations that have "remote microphones," portable 2-way radios, parabolic microphones, and an assortment of other equipment which at first hand appeared necessary, but they were used only once or twice and are now gathering dust—and probably will never again be used. Expensive broadcast equipment is not easily resold, and then it brings only a fraction of the original cost. To save money some stations construct some equipment by purchasing the parts. We caution those who might make this a general practice. Remember that the transmitting equipment must be approved and licensed by the FCC. Furthermore, a careful study will generally indicate that when the cost of the parts and the engineer's time is added up the piece of equipment could have been bought from a recognized and licensed manufacturer at about the same price. We are speaking about turntables, speakers, cartridge tape machines, monitors, and even transmitters. There should be enough work around a radio station to keep an engineer busy at all times. Don't saddle him with extraneous work.

## Accounting and Auditing

Filing tax returns and FCC financial reports should be handled by an outside firm familiar with these practices. Accounting services are quite costly today, and the amount a station should pay for these services depends entirely upon the work required of the accountant and the number of visits and reports the station wants from him. It should not be too difficult for a qualified bookkeeper to perform those duties which we previously outlined. If this monthly report is furnished by the bookkeeper, most small-market stations will find that an accountant need only visit the station twice a year, at mid-year and at the close of the books for the year-end and filing necessary tax forms. Assistance with other reports needed in the interim can be obtained by telephone and mail from the accountant. In cases of absentee ownership it may be necessary for an accountant to visit the station and issue a monthly or a quarterly report. But it is our opinion that all stations in small to medium markets only need these services on a twice-a-year basis at most.

## Attorneys

Stations in small to medium markets generally do not need to retain a local attorney, once they have received all necessary clearances and licenses and are operating. Any local legal matters can be dealt with on a case-to-case basis. Most often a local attorney is needed only to collect overdue accounts. In these instances most attorneys have a regular fee schedule ranging from 25% to 40% of the amount collected.

The situation is quite different though when it comes to dealing with the FCC. In this instance we strongly recommend that every station have an adequate arrangement with an attorney who is qualified to practice before the Commission. The business of operating a broadcast facility is quite complicated. By their nature and intent the Communications Act and some rules and regulations are quite difficult to understand. They require constant interpretation. Any action taken by the FCC can have a distinct bearing on the operations of your facility, and you, as a licensee, should have someone who is constantly on the alert to protect your interests by advice and action. The amount charged by such an attorney depends directly on the work they have to do. We know of small to medium market stations who retain an FCC attorney at a $900 to $1200 annual fee, plus an extra charge at the time they apply for a license renewal. To me this is a sensible agreement, for it guarantees, at a very small cost, that the station operator has a trained, qualified representative to call upon for any legal or other advice concerning his relationship with the federal government and also that at the time of requesting a renewal of his license he has a qualified attorney to advise him and check his application, file it, and see it through to a grant.

## Telephone

Unwarranted and wasteful telephone calls can be costly to a station. Though some small-market stations may have arrangements for unlimited local calls many do not. The cost of long distance calls can also be a drain on station resources. A saving of $50 to $75 per month can pay for that extra piece of equipment you may need, or be applied to that extra employee needed in the clerical department, or for that $10 weekly raise you want to give to a deserving employee. It is a good business practice to consult with the local telephone company concerning the type of service you need. We would caution you, however, to review their recommendation very thoroughly, taking into consideration your total revenue and anticipated operating costs. Naturally, telephone company representatives always recommend the ultimum in service. You should determine exactly what you need at the present and in the foreseeable future and only order that kind of service.

If your facility is a small- or medium-sized operation, beware of the installation of a switch board. There are other types of installations that do not require the constant attention of a staff member. In planning your telephone service be sure to consider a separate telephone service for the control room. Also be sure that adequate phones are included for the use of your sales and news departments.

We strongly suggest that you initiate a method for the control and checking of all long distance calls. All personnel should be discouraged from using the station's phones for personal purposes, whether it is for in-coming or out-going calls. A very good method used by many stations is for each person to report all telephone calls on a specially prepared form which is turned into the station manager for his examination and routing to the bookkeeping department where it is checked against the monthly telephone bills. The report should include the following: 1. date; 2. person making the call; 3. number called; 4. person called; 5. reason for the call.

## Insurance

In simple terms "insurance" is a contract whereby, in return for a fixed payment, a person is guaranteed that he will be paid a specific sum for a specific loss. Insurance is not an investment. No one should ever expect that they will make a profit from insurance. They should only expect compensation to a certain degree for a specific loss, and in many cases the compensation seldom covers the full financial loss. It is actually protection against the outlay of large sums of money at a time of catastrophe. By the payment of small sums at specific times the insured is building up an equity or reserve to cover the major costs of replacement. There are some other benefits from insurance such as "peace of mind" and the ability to assume risks that would otherwise be avoided.

Some forms of insurance are mandatory. Practically every business today is required to carry "employee compensation insurance." This type of coverage protects both the employee and the employer. There is also "unemployment insurance," sustained by employer contributions, which solely benefits the employee. It is good business practice to consult with other station owners before determining the amount and kind of insurance you should buy. Some stations are way over-insured, while some are very vulnerable because of a meager insurance plan. Inasmuch as everything under the sun is insurable today, and since insurance companies are able to underwrite virtually every kind of a business or enterprise, it is our suggestion that broadcasters seeking insurance contact at least three companies experienced in the field for their advice and suggestions, then discuss these plans with other station owners and his attorneys before entering into a final agreement. We must stress the importance of consulting an attorney regarding all such agreements, for if a catastrophe occurs and the remuneration becomes a matter of contest it will be your attorney who will have to represent you. It is prudent to get his advice even though you may never have to use his services in relation to any claims for reimbursement.

In addition to "employees compensation" and "unemployment" insurance, all stations should insure towers, buildings, equipment, furniture, automobiles, etc. Also imperative is liability insurance against personal injury, as the public will visit the studios and other facilities. Some stations carry "business interruption," "copying and rewriting," "vandalism," "mysterious disappearance," "theft," and a myriad of other types of insurance. You can be over-insured as well as under-insured. Only you can make the decision as to the types and amount of insurance you wish to carry. But, remember, all you are buying is protection—not an income producing expenditure.

In the quest for competent personnel today, industry is offering many fringe benefits such as hospitalization, medical, life, retirement, and other types of insurance to their employees. Many radio stations find that they must do likewise in order to compete for personnel. Here, again, the entire matter is one of individual perrogative If your staff consists of all young unmarried people they will not be too interested in life insurance or even health insurance plans. Retirement plans that do not carry any benefits upon separation will not appeal to them either. On the other hand, if your staff consists of married people, older in age, all of these insurance plans are welcomed. In considering cost factors you should bear in mind that once these plans are established it becomes an impossibility to drop them, for the employee will consider this as a cut in pay. Also, once you have established these plans you must make them available to all employees, otherwise you will create a feeling of bias and discrimination.

There is one type of insurance program that I urge all radio station operators to consider, especially if the facility is owned by a closely knit group of stockholders: it is an agreement to insure the principals so that upon the death of any one his stock becomes the property of the corporation upon payment of the "insurance policy." In the case of a partnership I strongly urge the consummation of a "partnership insurance" agreement. It is needless to go into details, but too few give this matter adequate consideration, until it is too late, and find themselves associated with "trustees," widows, and others who may be stumbling blocks in the development of their business. Many a principal has had to sell a profitable establishment against his will because no such arrangements were considered.

## Promotion Costs

Sales promotion, program promotion, and marketing, if not managed properly, can become a financial drain on the profits of your organization. Similar to any other business enterprise, you should determine very early in the planning stage how much you spend on these phases of operation. Earlier we discussed some of the percentages generally used by various business enterprises for advertising purposes. Radio

222

stations should also govern themselves accordingly and adopt an advertising policy. In adopting such a policy, though, the dollar amount or percentages need not include the cost for broadcast time. The cost of production, however, should be included, as this is a direct outlay of money. Though the amount spent on promotions varies from station to station, and although most operators decide on the amount to spend on a program-to-program or sponsor-to-sponsor basis, good sound business practice calls for a definite plan. We suggest the following yardstick as a guide in establishing such a plan. Let us first discuss sales promotion.

Sales promotion cost should never exceed 4% of the total sales volume—i.e., when it comes to promotion for a particular sponsor, such as we discussed under the topic of "marketing," or in other media than the station's own facilities, the cost should never exceed 4%. In other words, should a sponsor buy a particular program or group of announcements for $100, the station should not spend more than $4.00 total. These costs should include production, employee time, etc. If a sponsor wants a more expensive type of promotion he should be asked to pay for the additional amount needed for the promotion he desires. Spending more than this amount on one promotion for any one sponsor is a mistake. Too often we find operators who feel that, inasmuch as they haven't spent any funds for other sponsors, they can devote such unused funds to offset the excess cost to meet the demands of a particular sponsor. This, in our opinion, is a very poor practice. The unexpended funds should be used for other types of sales promotions, station, and program promotions.

First consideration should always be given to sales promotion and marketing, with the latter being discouraged wherever possible. Program promotions, though necessary, should be evaluated very carefully. Remember that you have one of the best of all the advertising media at your disposal. If your station is a good producer for its sponsors it should also be a good producer for you. This does not mean that you should put all your eggs in one basket and use your broadcast facilities exclusively. You should use all available advertising media in your area, but they should be used judiciously. The amount of money you should spend on this phase of your operation should depend on the amount of money left after you have budgeted for sales promotions.

In order to increase the amount of station and program promotion it is a frequent practice to enter into trade deals with newspapers and movie houses. Some newspapers will accept a dollar-for-dollar exchange for time. Some stations sell time to the newspaper for one-half cash and the balance in space. But too often when the cost of the space is totaled many stations find they have far exceeded the amount they should have budgeted. Many movie houses trade the use of movie "trailers" for time on the air. A movie screen is an excellent promotion medium, providing that the agreement is for at least one full year. It is estimated that practically every person in a given area will visit the movie house at least twice in any one year. If you plan to use this medium be sure that the copy is changed at least every 3 months. The cost of producing a trailer is quite small and is generally assumed by the movie house. Here again the cost of the time you give in exchange for the screen advertising should be figured when computing your promotion costs.

Just as retail establishments, in planning their advertising budgets, set aside funds for special events, you should also set aside funds for special broadcasts such as contests, baseball, football, Christmas shows, etc. Audience surveys, though helpful to and used by the program department, are generally used by the sales department and should be charged to sales promotion expense.

### Dues and Subscriptions

Another necessary expense item may be classified as "dues and subscriptions." Two trade magazines that are a must are Broadcasting, published weekly, and Broadcast Management/ Engineering (BM/E), published on a monthly basis. The number of copies you need depends entirely on the size of your staff. Other publications that you might want to consider are Standard Rate and Data, Sales Management Surveys, and Sponsor. Your program department will also want subscriptions to such periodicals as Cash Box, Variety, Billboard, etc., and your news department will want copies of several dailies. In deciding upon periodicals, particular attention must be paid to whether or not they will be used. It is just a waste of dollars to have periodicals floating around that no one reads. It is also a waste of money to have your staff read these periodicals and not take advantage of some of the many worthwhile articles and suggestions they publish. There is no use to subscribe to Cash Box or Billboard for use in your program department if no attention is paid to the record charts when scheduling musical programs, etc.

The matter of "dues" is much more complicated and depends entirely upon the financial position of each station. We know it is a good business practice to have at least one member of your staff, preferably from the sales staff, become a member of each service club (Rotary, Lions, Kiwanis, etc.). It is also a good business expenditure, if a station can afford it, to have management personnel join the local country club. Whether or not the station pays for these memberships is strictly a personal option; some pay the full dues, others pay half the dues, and others insist upon their staff becoming members in these organizations at the individual's own expense.

There are some "trade" organizations to which all stations should belong. One of these is the Chamber of Commerce. An active Chamber of Commerce means more business and business growth in an area, both industrial and mercantile. It needs and deserves your support. If your station is located in an area that has both a Chamber of Commerce and a trade retail board it is suggested that you join both. We know of a new radio station which refused to join the Chamber of Commerce because of the cost. By this action the operator immediately sounded his death knell. In fact the poor publicity he received by refusing to join the Chamber was so difficult to overcome that in a very short period of time he was forced to sell his facility at a great loss. Everyone loves a winner, so do not advertise your poverty where it is apt to get widespread publicity.

For new licensees we urgently suggest that they consider joining the state association of broadcasters. This is the surest and fastest way to become acquainted with all broadcasting facilities in your state and area. Broadcast licensees are a rather strange breed of people. They love to meet and discuss all their problems and offer suggestions. It never ceases to amaze me how often and with what pride a broadcaster will divulge a successful operation or promotion to his fellow broadcasters. These organizations are of great help in the field of legislation, personnel relationship and acquisition, sales promotion, etc.

Another trade organization that all broadcasters should give consideration to joining is the National Association of Broadcasters. This organization has performed yeoman work in behalf of the broadcaster and the industry. It would require a separate volume to discuss and describe the work of this organization and its contributions and assistance to the individual licensee. If you are first entering the field as a licensee it will be money well spent to become a member. Various departments issue manuals of operation covering everything from legal intricacies to the actual operation of a radio station. The broadcasting industry would never have survived or reached its present stature if it weren't for the National Association of Broadcasters. There are other trade organizations that have also contributed to the success of our industry that should be given consideration. There is the "Code Authority" that governs good taste in advertising; the "Radio Advertising Bureau" (RAB) which constantly promotes the use of radio as an advertising medium, and many others. There also are specialized trade organizations such as the "Clear Channel" group; the "Daytimer's Association," etc. There are so many good and worthwhile organizations that if a station joined all of them it would soon be in financial trouble. The matter of which organization to join is strictly a personal choice. Each organization should be considered according to its value to you as an individual operator and your financial ability to pay for the privilege of becoming a member.

## Travel and Entertainment

Travel and entertainment alone will cost you from 5% to 7 1/2% of your total income. It is one of the most necessary expenditures, and if used in a properly planned and judicious manner should create much goodwill for your station, in addition to increasing your revenue. It is one of the first items that an Internal Revenue Service auditor examines when he processes your income tax return. You must make every effort to enforce a policy that meets the standards of the tax people. Failure to do so may result in additional taxes and penalties. No payment should be made to any employee or officer who does not present a voucher approved by both his superior and the station manager.

An expense voucher should contain specific information. A travel voucher should bear the actual date the trip was made, location by location report, purpose of the trip, and the exact amount spent. It can even be in a narrative form, providing it lists all of the above. Here is a typical acceptable travel voucher:

| Feb. 1, 1968 | Trip to N.Y.C. | |
| Visit to agencies | Total $66.00 | |
| Cab to railroad station | | $ 1.50 |
| Railroad fare, New Haven to N.Y.C. | | 9.75 |
| Taxi to hotel | | 1.25 |
| Lunch | | 2.50 |
| Taxi to B.B.D. & O. | | 1.00 |
| Taxi to Y & R | | 1.00 |
| Dinner | | 6.50 |
| Hotel (see bill attached) | | 16.00 |
| Breakfast | | 2.00 |
| Taxi to Bates | | 1.00 |
| Luncheon with Mr. X of Bates | | 10.00 |
| Taxi to Hotel | | 1.00 |
| Taxi to R.R. Station | | 1.25 |
| Railroad N.Y.C. to New Haven | | 9.75 |
| Taxi to home | | 1.50 |

An example of an acceptable voucher for entertainment follows:

Feb. 1, 1968   Luncheon with Mr. X of XYZ Co.   6.50
Discussed possible sponsorship of the 10 AM news.

Feb. 2, 1968   Entertainment Mr. X of XYZ Co.   15.00
Two tickets for ballgame      5.00
Dinner                        10.00
Discussed sponsorship of 10 AM news, etc.

All vouchers should bear the printed name and signature of the person who is to be reimbursed, the approval signature of his supervisor and the approval signature of the station manager before the bookkeeping department issues a check for reimbursement.

Entertainment and travel is a necessary expenditure and there are stations who are liberal in their attitude toward this cost of operation—they're usually the financially successful operations. Salesmen should be encouraged to entertain sponsors and prospective clients. They should never be hampered in their desire to travel and visit a potential customer. The sales manager and/or the commercial manager, along with the station manager, should make periodic visits to their national representative and the agencies. A very financially successful radio station operating in a small population market insists that its sales staff have lunch or dinner with at least one sponsor or potential customer every day of the week. Though operating in a market of less than 50,000 people this station's revenue is $200,000 per year with 30% of this amount representing national and regional accounts.

## Contributions

Because of the nature of the business every radio station is deluged with requests from practically every organization seeking charitable funds. Not only are these requests for dollars but for "free time" to solicit public support and financial contributions. Unless a firm policy is established and strictly adhered to, the demands for monetary contributions will be overwhelming and very costly. Overlook one sponsor's pet charity after contributing to another will bring the wrath of disfavor upon the station and a probable loss of revenue. Also, a token contribution to one charity will only bring criticism if you have made a larger contribution to another charity. To avoid trouble and possible resentment some radio stations adopt a policy of not making any cash contributions, only free announcement time for all charities. It is not a bad idea at the completion of a charity air promotion to prepare a statement listing the total number of announcements and the amount they would have cost at regular commercial rates. The bill is stamped "paid—contribution of Radio Station (call letters)." Such statements are not included of course in the station's revenue but held in a separate file for future reference. None of these contributions are tax deductable, inasmuch as all production costs and salaries, etc., are absorbed as part of the station's regular operating costs. This policy achieves several things. It eliminates the necessity of cash contributions to any charity; it is a permanent record of its charitable contributions "in kind;" and it substantially increases the actual number of public service announcements broadcast.

In adopting this policy some stations add an additional provision. If the charity has an advertising budget or is spending money in any other media they insist that it spend some of that money for paid commercials. In order not to sound too greedy they guarantee the charity from one to two free announcements for every paid announcement. In these cases the paid announcements are listed on the program log in red and classified as "CA." Free announcements are listed on the program log in black and classified as "PSA." Upon the completion of the schedule the "charity" is billed separately for the commercial announcements and for the "PSAs." The first amount is treated as regular revenue; the second statement lists the number and dollar value as before. No matter what policy you adopt we strongly stress the importance of strictly adhering to the stated policy. Should you adopt the second method and give a charity free time, then discover that it is paying for advertising on another medium, it is suggested that you immediately contact the "fund raiser" or president of the charity and advise them that you are taking them off the air because they misled you. Be sure that you do take them off the air. Don't make idle threats or statements; the failure to take corrective action will open a pandora's box and is unfair to those charities which accept and abide by your stated policy. To make your free-time policy perfectly clear, give mimeographed copies of the following to every charity requesting funds and/or free time on the air:

## Statement of Policy Regarding Contributions

It is not the policy of Radio Station (call letters) to make cash contributions to any charities. We do, however, offer the services of our staff and management and the use of our facilities to all worthwhile and deserving charities and causes on the following basis:

1. If your organization is not paying for advertising, directly or indirectly, in any newspaper or with any broadcasting facility, we will broadcast an adequate amount of announcements consistent with your needs and appeal. These broadcasts will be our contribution to your organization.

2. If your organization is paying for advertising, directly or indirectly, in any newspaper or with any broadcasting facility, we expect that you will also engage our services on a commercial basis. However, for every dollar spent on this

station by your organization, Radio Station (call letters) will broadcast an additional (state number) announcement (s) free of charge. These free announcements will be our contribution to your organization.

3. Any deviation by your organization from the above stated policy will result in the immediate cancellation of all scheduled announcements.

Do not be misled into thinking that the adoption of the above policy will be the end-all answer to the problem of contributions. There is no doubt that you will be faced with requests for funds, as a member of a select group, for a specific project such as "Junior Achievement" whose operating capital comes from contributions by the industrial and commercial community, not from public solicitation, or requests for funds to meet the payment for "Christmas lights and decorations" in the retail areas, etc. The only yardstick you should use is to determine whether or not the request is from an organization that is contacting the general public for funds. If it is, routine policy applies. If the request is of a special nature you will have to make your individual decision.

# CHAPTER 9

# Establishing a Radio Station

Establishing a radio station can be one of the most frustrating experiences you'll ever encounter. In addition to the procedures required by the Federal Communications Commission, and the myriad unforeseen problems arising from the simple act of filing an application for permission to construct a broadcast facility, the applicant also becomes involved with governmental agencies on the state, local, and national level.

## THE INITIAL STEPS

On the state level one must deal with the secretary of state and/or other officials and agencies charged with the responsibility of regulating the establishment and conduct of business or commercial enterprises. Corporations, partnerships, and, in some cases, noncorporate or nonpartnership firms must make application through specified state agencies before the start of operations. Trade or corporate names must be cleared and approved. In the case of corporations or limited partnerships it is absolutely essential that you obtain state approval and legal recognition.

On the local level the prospective applicant necessarily becomes involved with planning and development commissions and with zoning boards or authorities. Practically every community limits the areas where business and commercial enterprises may locate. Many communities have specific regulations concerning the height and location of towers. Restrictions on tower installations may forestall, and even make it prohibitory, for the applicant to select any number of desirable transmitter sites, thereby negating all efforts already expended in trying to establish a radio broadcast facility in a particular community. Prospective radio station applicants must <u>know</u>—and I cannot stress this too strongly—all rules, regulations, and requirements of local agencies, especially the planning and development commission and the local zoning board or authority. For it is within these agencies where you may encounter all sorts of unusual and unexpected problems.

On the federal level an applicant will very likely become involved with several agencies other than the Federal Communications Commission. He will have to negotiate with the director of the National Radio Astronomy Observatory located in Green Bank, West Virginia, should the proposed facility be located within the area bounded on the north by $39^o$ 15' N, on the east by $78^o$ 30' W, on the south by $37^o$ 30' N, and on the west by $80^o$ 30'. For the benefit of the Observatory this area is protected by federal regulations, but in rare instances where interference will be minimal permission can be obtained by application to the director of the National Radio Observatory. Should the applicant desire to erect his station on land controlled or owned by the federal government he must obtain permission from one or more of the following federal agencies:

- The U.S. Forest Service
- The U.S. Department of Agriculture
- The U.S. Bureau of Land Management
- The U.S. Department of the Interior

Several radio stations do have their facilities on government controlled or owned land, and generally such permission is not too difficult to obtain, but it may prove time consuming and costly.

In some areas the location and height of towers may become an insurmountable obstacle. All tower installations must be approved by the Federal Aviation Agency, the office charged with the responsibility of knowing the exact location of every structure that may be a hazard to air navigation. Every effort should be made to locate the tower so that it is not in the "approach path" or "departure lane" of aircraft operating in or above the community. Before the FCC will give any consideration to any application for a construction permit the applicant must have received prior approval of his tower site from the Federal Aviation Agency. In the main, however, of all federal agencies most of your dealings will be with the Federal Communications Commission, located in the new Post Office Building, 13th Street and Pennsylvania Avenue N.W., Washington, D.C. Requests for information or applications can be obtained by writing to this address. The FCC also maintains field offices in various cities throughout the country. These are generally staffed by an "Engineer in Charge" who is responsible for specialized investigations for the Commission and engineering supervision for the area they serve.

The Commission's staff is composed of the following department - ments:

- Executive Director
- Chief Engineer
- General Counsel
- Secretary
- Reports and Information
- Broadcast Bureau
- Common Carrier Bureau
- Field Engineering Bureau
- Safety and Special Radio Services Bureau
- Office of Hearing Examiners
- Review Board
- Office of Opinion and Review
- Defense Commissioner

Relating to the broadcast industry, the FCC is responsible for the following functions:

1. The consideration of all applications relating to construction and operation of broadcast facilities.

2. The assignment of specific operating frequencies.

3. The assignment of the radiated power of broadcast facilities.

4. The assignment of station "call letters" or means of identification.

5. The establishment of operating policies, including hours.

6. Inspection of equipment.

7. Supervising the engineering aspects of operation.

8. Ruling upon requests for transfer or assignment of licenses.

9. Renewing licenses (commercial broadcast station licenses must be renewed every three years).

10. Licensing of transmitting equipment.

11. Licensing of transmitter operating personnel.

12. Reviewing the program operations of licensed stations.

In order to avoid monopolization of broadcast facilities, the Federal Communications Commission will not allow a person, firm, corporation, or any group of persons to operate more than one AM, FM, and TV station in any one locality; nor will the Commission allow a person, firm, corporation, or any group of persons to operate more than seven AM, seven FM and seven TV stations throughout the country. And of the seven TV stations only five can be VHF (Channels 2-13); the other two must be UHF (Channels 14-83) and of the five VHF stations only three can be in the top fifty markets.

The next chapter discusses the steps to be taken in applying for a license, but inasmuch as we have used, and will be using certain terms, definition of these terms is appropriate:

AM is the abbreviation for "amplitude modulation," in which audio signals are impressed on the carrier wave in a manner to cause its power to vary with the audio-wave variations. The frequency of the carrier remains constant. In AM broadcasting use is made of what are called "medium-length waves" i.e., 540,000 to 1,600,000 waves a second (the more waves per second the shorter their "length"). For example a station operating on 540 kHz (kHz = kiloHertz) is emitting 540,000 waves a second; on 800 kHz a station is emitting 800,000 waves a second; etc. The FCC refers to AM stations as "Standard Broadcast Stations," licensed for radiotelephone transmissions primarily intended for the general public. Within the standard broadcast band there are 107 carrier frequencies running in successive 10-kHz steps from 540 to 1600 kHz.

FM stands for "frequency modulation," in which the power remains constant but the carrier frequency is varied in a manner corresponding to the voice or music being transmitted. Commercial FM broadcast stations operate in the region from 92.1 MHz to 107.1 MHz on channels 200 kHz apart.

TV or television is the process of transmitting visual scenes by radio (sometimes by direct wire). An electronic tube, either orthicon or ionoscope, converts light rays into electronic impulses which amplitude-modulate a carrier wave. The receiver reconverts these impulses into electronic beams that are projected against a luminous screen reproducing the original image. Commercial VHF TV stations operate on Channels 2 through 13 (54 to 216 MHz), and UHF stations occupy Channels 13 to 83 (470 to 890 MHz).

The Primary Service Area of a broadcasting station means that area in which the groundwave is not subject to objectionable interference or objectionable fading.

The Secondary Area of a broadcasting station is that area served by the "skywave" (waves reflected back to earth by atmospheric layers) and is not subject to objectionable interference. The signal is, however, subject to intermittent variations in intensity (fading).

The Intermittent Service Area of a broadcast station means that area receiving service from the groundwave but beyond the primary service area and subject to some interference and fading.

Power is the term used to describe the force or the energy used in the transmission of radio waves. Commercial AM broadcasting stations operate with power outputs, as assigned by the Federal Communications Commission, varying from 250 watts to 50,000 watts, the present maximum allowed by the Commission.

From the embryonic thought to commercial sign-on, the following steps have become more or less standard procedure in establishing a broadcast facility.

1. Assure adequate financing.

2. Select attorneys.

3. Select a consulting engineer.

4. Select an area for location of the facility.

5. Begin a search for an available frequency.

6. Select a site for the transmitter and tower location.

7. Select a site for the studio location.

8. Apply to the FCC for a construction permit.

9. Give adequate public notice.

10. The FCC decides on the application.

11. Be on the alert for competing applications.

12. Attend hearings before the FCC Examiners in cases where there are conflicts.

13. Be on the alert for petitions requesting reconsideration.

14. Begin construction of the facility when the construction permit is granted.

15. Apply for call letters.

16. Conduct equipment tests.

17. File for the actual license.

18. Request permission to conduct program tests.

19. The license grant.

20. Begin commercial operations.

## Financing

The need for adequate financing cannot be stressed too strongly. Although the FCC requires that all applicants be financially qualified (at the time of filing the application for a construction permit he must indicate financial ability to operate the facility for a minimum of one year), a large amount of money will have to be spent prior to the filing of the application, after the construction permit has been granted, during the period that the facility is being built, and in the time elapsing between the completion of construction and the beginning of commercial operations. However, the total amount of cash needed does not have to be on hand. Letters from banks or other institutions or financially responsible people as to the availability of the necessary funds satisfies the Commission's requirements in most instances. But money will be needed to retain the services of attorneys and consulting engineers. Land for a transmitter and tower site must be purchased. Deposits have to be made on equipment; the latter is required by the FCC at the time the application is filed, since the application must include a full description of the transmitting equipment to be used. Lease arrangements for studio space will have to be negotiated. Newspaper advertisements must be purchased to notify the public of your intentions to build a broadcast facility. In the preliminary stages money will be spent for secretarial help, telephone, and travel. Do not underestimate the time that will be consumed in traveling to and from Washington, D.C. for consultation with attorneys, engineers, and appearances before the FCC.

These are but a few of the necessary expenditures prior to the construction permit grant. Once the construction permit is received, much larger expenditures will be required. In addition to the construction costs of buildings and the erection of the tower or towers, the balance due on your transmitting equipment will have to be paid (or arrangements made for its payment). Furniture, office equipment, supplies, and especially studio broadcast equipment, will now have to be purchased. A staff will have to be assembled, trained, and retained on payroll in order that operations can commence in an orderly and professional manner once the license is approved and granted. This in turn means additional capital outlays for insurance, payroll taxes, telephone, light, heat, fuel, travel, and a myriad of other items—all before any income is received.

Although some attorneys, engineering firms, and equipment manufacturers do not require or expect payment in full at time of contractural agreements, all will insist upon some down payment, many times as high as 50%, on costs and fees. Some of the expenditure for the transmitter site can be forestalled by paying "option fees," but the full purchase price will have to be paid before construction begins. Just as equipment can be purchased on the installment plan so can land by means of mortgage arrangements. Studio space can also be leased by "option" with rentals to begin at the time occupancy takes place.

Once the station goes on the air, additional operating capital in large sums must be available. The station will be doing business, and on the books may be showing a profit, but accounts receivable will mount and mount. Broadcast station operators find that they are extending credit for periods in excess of six to nine months. Advertising, like any service, is not a tangible item. Too many retailers, especially those in small markets, do not realize how necessary and important advertising is to their business. And it's surprising how many clients and potential sponsors think that the "air" doesn't cost money and that broadcasters are subsidized or endowed with unlimited funds. On the other hand, creditors who hold the broadcaster in the same regard insist on being paid. Utility companies expect prompt payment for electricity and telephone service. The Internal Revenue Service expects regular remittance of payroll withholding and taxes. Employees must surely be paid. Newswire services, a must item for any broadcaster, many times insist on payment in advance. Licensing organizations such as ASCAP, BMI, and Sesac also insist on prompt payments.

A fairly good rule of thumb to use in estimating settlement of accounts receivable calls for 30% of the billing to be received within 60 days from the date of billing, an additional 30% within 150 days from date of billing, and the balance will be spread out over a period of nine months. The above formula, and an estimate of the monthly expenditures and cash required, should give the operator a fairly good idea of the amount of capital he needs for operating expenses.

At the time an applicant files for his license he must estimate the cost of construction, the operating costs for the first year, and the anticipated revenue. In practically every instance the applicant will state that his anticipated revenue will equal or exceed his first year's operating costs. There is a popular saying that "in marriage the first year is the hardest." Do not be nonplussed to discover that the first year of operating a radio station is a nightmare. And in many cases, not only the first year but the second and third years as well. I know of small market operators who estimate an amount of $35,000 to $50,000 over and above the expected cash revenue as the bare minimum to finance their operation during its first year.

### Selecting An Attorney

The selection of an attorney or attorneys is entirely a personal matter, but it is suggested that two be selected: One for matters dealing with state and local agencies, the other to prosecute the application before the FCC. The attorney who will advise, counsel, and deal in state and local matters should have wide and varied experience in appearing before zoning boards and authorities. He must be a man who has had many successes in having variances to local zoning regulations granted.

Opposition to a transmitter building, or to the erection of a tower or towers, may come from many undreamed of sources. A radio station in Bridgeport, Connecticut, in seeking to increase its power from 1000 watts to 5000 watts, had permission from city authorities to create a park and picnic area in which to erect their towers on unused city-owned property. Strangely enough the membership of a yacht club, of all people, aroused sufficient dissent on the premise that the towers would destroy the beauty of the landscape that the city withdrew its permission. Many home owners who reside in areas adjacent to the proposed tower site object most strenuously on the grounds that the structure will present undo interference to their present radio and TV reception. They persist in such complaints even though they are protected by FCC regulations against such an occurrence. Amateur pilots and air field operators are generally in the forefront of the opposition, for they consider the erection of any high structure as a hazard to air navigation. These are but a few examples of the opposition an applicant may encounter even when the site is located in an area already zoned for this type of operation. One can imagine the problems that will crop up should the site be located in an area where a zoning variance must be granted.

Any lawyer who is a member in good standing of the Bar of the Supreme Court of the United States, or the highest court of any state, territory, or the District of Columbia, is permitted to practice before the FCC. It is my suggestion that in selecting a lawyer to represent you in prosecuting your application before the FCC that you choose an attorney or law firm which specializes in this practice. The many ramifications, the rules, regulations, and procedures, the laws and their interpretations are so varied that only one who devotes practically all his time to this field is adequately qualified to represent you. Many attorneys who practice before the FCC are former employees of the Commission and their first-hand knowledge of the FCC and its operations can save you not only time but money. This has become such a specialty that in Washington, D.C. there is a separate bar association comprised of communications lawyers who practice before the FCC.

Before embarking on what may prove to be a costly experience, anyone interested in establishing a radio station should first consult with an attorney familiar with the advantages and disadvantages, the hazards and the problems that exist and must be overcome. The obtaining of a license is a long, drawn-out affair; it is time consuming and can cost dearly, for if a license request is denied every dollar spent in this endeavor is gone and can only be chalked up to experience. Men have prosecuted their application before the FCC and the courts for years and years before final approval or rejection. I don't want to give the impression that all grants take an interminable amount of time. There are cases where grants have been made after a relatively short period; however, they are far too few—the exception rather than the rule. A qualified attorney who specializes in practicing before the FCC should be selected and his advice and counsel should be respected. No attorney can tell an applicant how long it will take for his request to be acted upon, nor can he foresee all the problems that may arise. There are no set fees for their services. Whether a fee is high or low is a relative term. In the long run it is the result that counts.


## Your Consulting Engineer

As it is important to have a qualified attorney so it is important to have a qualified consulting engineer. It is the consulting engineer who will assist you in finding a frequency for which a grant may be obtained. Like the attorney he will have first-hand knowledge of all proceedings before the FCC— which frequencies are in litigation or unavailable, for example. He, too, can save you a great deal of time, trouble, effort and money. In addition he can be of great value in recommending specific types of equipment, during planning and construction, and the engineering personnel your station will need. If no frequency can be found for the area of your choice he may be able to advise you of available frequencies in other areas.

The same care one exercises in choosing an attorney should be employed in the selection of a consulting engineer. He should be qualified to practice before the FCC. The engineering staff of the Commission know these men, their excellence, and their modes of operation. As a group they are highly specialized and in great demand. As in the case of attorneys there is no set fee for their service. Fees are generally set according to an estimate of the time involved. Your attorney can advise and recommend a competent and qualified consulting engineer. In prosecuting your case the attorney and the consulting engineer will be working as a team. It is not a rare occasion to find an attorney recommending a consulting engineer and being fully aware that they are on opposite sides in another proceeding before the FCC. Their integrity, both the attorney and the consulting engineer, is above reproach.

## Operating In "The Public Interest"

Assuming that one has adequate financing (available or obtainable), the next step is where to locate a station. The FCC requires that an applicant show that the public interest, convenience, and necessity will be served through the operation under the proposed assignment; that there will be no overlapping of signals as prohibited by FCC regulations; and that the new station will not cause objectionable interference to existing stations. The last two items are the concern of the consulting engineer, and we will discuss this in more detail later. The first item is the all important one: The FCC requires the operator to structure his programming in such a manner that it is in the public interest. The Commission has neither defined nor stated at any time the percentage of a radio station's programming that should be devoted to a particular area of interest. The Commission is aware of the fact that there can be variations between communities.

## The Frequency Search

Many people who seek to enter the broadcast field first hire a consulting engineer to determine if there are any frequencies available in a general area. Then, if a specific community looks good, they proceed to undertake an economic survey to determine if it would be financially advisable to try establishing a station in that particular area. Some of these are the "investors" who are in the profession strictly for monetary gain. Others, and in the main, are men who have had some success with operating radio facilities. Both groups know that to begin an economic survey as a first step in any area too often results in disappointment, for frequencies are too few and certainly never readily available. But, let us suppose that you have selected in area, and after the economic survey you feel that it is economically feasible to establish a facility in the area.

Your consulting engineer now begins his survey to determine if a frequency is available for the market you selected. He will scientifically survey the entire spectrum for an AM frequency that might work. (For FM operations the FCC has already allocated various channels to specific areas.) Using his expertise the engineer will determine the primary service area, the secondary service area and the intermittent service area. He will compute the strength of all signals now giving any type of service to the area, no matter where they originate. He knows that the FCC gives priority when granting licenses to those applicants who offer a primary service to an area. His work will be meticulously performed. He will leave no room for error. In his survey to determine a frequency, the consultant will indicate a general area in the community where the transmitter should be located. Once the exact location of the transmitter site is established the engineer begins further tests. He must make almost a step-by-step study of the proposed signal in every direction. He will have to indicate any interference your signal will cause to existing stations, no matter where they are located, even though none of these stations has a signal reaching your selected area. Existing services must not experience interference by any new service. The engineer also will have to indicate population densities and the signal strength those areas will receive.

## The Transmitter Site

As indicated above the selection of a transmitter site is all important. The primary objectives should be to adequately serve the population center in which the studio is located and to give maximum coverage to the adjacent areas; to cause and experience a minimum of interference to other stations; to cause and experience minimum interference from other stations; and, where the towers are to be erected, to present a minimum hazard to aircraft and airfield operations. In addition the proposed station must provide a minimum signal of 25 to 50 mv/m (millivolts per meter) over business or factory areas; a minimum field intensity signal of 5 to 10 mv/m over the most distant residential section of the city or town where the studio is located; must insure that signal absorption is minimal for any obtainable sites in the area; and, that the population within the 1 mv/m contour does not exceed 1.0% of the population within the 25 mv/m contour.

Most engineers will advise their clients that the ideal transmitter locations are marshy areas and salt water bogs, or an area where the soil is damp most of the time, from which one has a clear view of the entire population center and where tall buildings in the business section of the city cast a minimal shadow across residential areas. The type of land described above is usually lying fallow and unused. It is land least desired by commerce or industry and would generally command the lowest real estate price. In purchasing such property, or in employing an agent for such a purchase, may I caution you not to divulge the proposed use you intend to make of the property. Cost-wise the reason for such caution is obvious. Unwanted and unusable land suddenly becomes very valuable when it is known a buyer exists. (Other reasons for this caution will become apparent when we discuss the possibility of competing applications.) You should also realize that this type of land is not easily resellable, that you may have to hold it for a considerable period of time, and that you face more of a possibility of having your request for a license denied rather than granted. Every effort should be made to reserve the land by employing the business tactic of long-term options, along with a previously agreed upon selling price.

## The Studio Location

The same "option" procedure should be employed when seeking a studio location. Many radio station operators, especially those in small markets, build their studios at the transmitter site. This type of combined operation has both advantages and disadvantages. Some of the advantages are:

1.  Lower overall construction cost.

2.  Savings in rent for studio space or outlay of capital for a comparable acquisition.

3.  Reduced maintenance costs.

4.  Reduced operating costs.

5.  Smaller equipment requirements.

6.  Fewer employees are needed to operate the facility.

7.  The complete operation is at one location.

Some of the disadvantages are:

1. Not readily accessible to the public, performers, and personnel.

2. Noise and other technical problems due to the presence of the transmitter.

3. Separate facilities should be rented for the sales and commercial staff causing:
   a. additional telephone expense.
   b. delay in mail distribution.
   c. delay in inter-office communications.
   d. supervision problems.

4. Loss of prestige and advertising value of a studio not located in the "core" of the community.

Of course you may decide that your sales and commercial staff should also be located at the transmitter site, which eliminates number (3) above; however, every operator sooner or later discovers that his sales staff must have an office in the "core" of the community. Most of your listeners, as high as 95% of them, will never visit your radio station. As far as they are concerned you could be broadcasting from a barn or a garage. The only thing they are interested in is the programming you provide and the quality of the signal they receive. They will be totally disinterested in the amount of space you have, the number of people you employ, the type of equipment you use, and whether or not you are making money. In fact, don't be surprised to learn that most of them think that the federal government subsidizes you.

You as an owner must decide for yourself whether or not to have a combined facility (studio and transmitter under one roof) or to build separate facilities. If you do not plan on operating a combined facility the following suggestions may prove helpful. Wherever feasible the studio and business office should be located in the heart of the business area. This makes it easier for the retailer and businessman to visit your sales staff and confer with your copy writers. Such a location also will prove to be a "time saver" for your salesmen in making contacts and the necessary service calls. At one time or another every resident of a community has occasion to visit or drive through the business area. Your "call letters" and frequency prominently displayed is a plus factor in promoting your station. Performers and program participants will not be reluctant when asked to appear and it will tend to increase the amount of "live programming" you will be able to produce. Personnel will have more time available on their lunch hours for shopping purposes, and nothing makes a sponsor feel more grateful for his relationship with a station than to have that station's personnel shop at his establishment. The radio station's personalities are given more opportunities for exposure and to be seen "in the flesh," not merely as a voice emanating from a box.

Broadcast equipment manufacturers can supply you with dozens of studio layouts. The consulting engineer is your

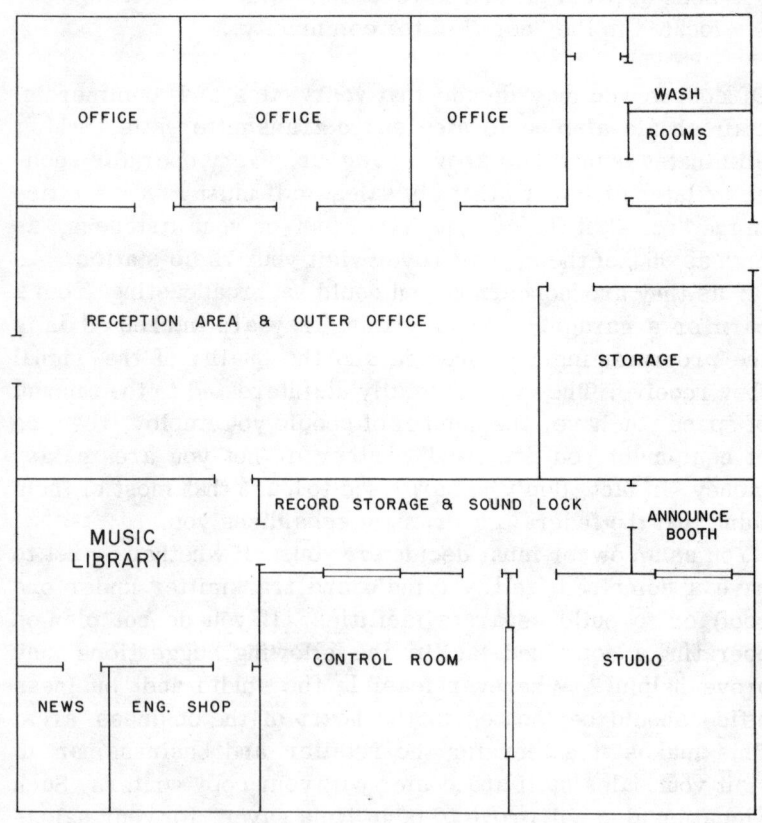

**Ideal small-station studio and transmitter facilities layout.**

best advisor in this matter. We have found an ideal layout for a combined studio and business office similar to that shown here. It allows ample working space for supervisory personnel, personalities, clerical staff, sales staff, engineering, news department, library, and production facilities. The two studios, though they seem small, should prove more than adequate. The day of big audience - participation shows, requiring large studios, is past. Seldom will you find the need for studio space to accommodate large groups of spectators. Should such space be required you will find it more economical to rent space as needed, rather than spend large sums on building such studios that are used only on rare occasions. Hotel ballrooms, school auditoriums, church social halls, or gymnasiums will more than serve the purpose, are usually readily available and will accommodate more spectators than any studio you would want to build. In studio design, above all else don't cut corners when it comes to soundproofing or "deadening." Remember, the listener wants and expects the best sounding signal possible and if you don't give it to him, the mere flick of the dial will bring him another station.

It is important to remember that the FCC regulations makes it mandatory that a station's main studio be located in the area that the station is licensed to serve. This area will be listed and clearly defined on both the construction permit and license. This does not, however, preclude the establishment of broadcast studios elsewhere. Such remote studios are permitted by FCC regulations. In cases where such studios are established FCC rules and regulations require that at least 66 2/3% of a station's local program time must be broadcast from the main studio. I must emphasize 66 2/3% of its local program time. This should not be computed on the basis of the number of programs broadcast. It must be computed on the total number of hours and minutes devoted to broadcasting. Should a station be affiliated with a network then the computation is 66 2/3% of the non-network or local program time.

# CHAPTER 10

# Application to Operation

After having selected an area or community, retained attorneys and engineers, found a frequency, and located your transmitter site, you must now undertake the necessary steps to apply for a "construction permit."

## Personal Qualifications

All applicants for a "construction permit" must be citizens of the United States. Such permits are denied to any corporation or group in which any officer or director is an alien. It will also be denied to any corporation if one-fifth or more of its capital stock is owned or controlled by any foreign interest. All applicants must be legally, technically, and financially qualified at the time of filing. Any qualified citizen or group may apply for a construction permit by following the procedure as prescribed in the Communication's Act of 1934. There have been some amendments to the Act, but basically, the applicant has to show the following:

1. That the proposed assignment will tend to effect a fair, efficient, and equitable distribution of radio service among the several states and communities. In respect to this you have to list the signals of all stations that can be heard in the area which you wish to serve, and be sure to indicate if these signals are weak or distorted. Also, if applicable, indicate whether or not there is a full-time service in the community. Remember, the FCC will give priority to your application if your facility will provide a primary or first full-time service to an area.

2. That there is no overlapping of signals as prohibited by present FCC engineering regulations. This has to be carefully documented in minute detail by your consulting engineer.

3. That the establishment of your facility will not cause objectionable interference to existing stations. Again, this will have to be carefully documented by your consultant. The FCC will not allow a new facility, even if it will bring a first-time primary service to an area, to cause any interference with stations now operating or authorized to begin construction. The FCC will allow some interference, of course, but it must not be "objectionable" as defined in the regulations. Where there is any interference caused to existing stations, not only will the Commission engineering staff object to the issuance of a permit, but you as an applicant will find yourself involved in litigation before the FCC with these stations.

4. That you (or your group) are financially qualified. You will have to present a statement of your financial status, listing all your assets, liabilities, and borrowing potentials. Such a financial statement will be required from each and every member or potential stockholder, should the applicant be a group or corporation. It must be remembered that the FCC requires applicants to indicate their financial ability to operate the new facility for at least the first year, regardless of anticipated income.

5. That you are legally qualified. Not only must you (or all officers and directors in the case of a group or corporation) be a citizen of the United States, but you must also show that everyone connected with the operation of the business entity is of good moral character and possesses other qualifications sufficient to provide a satisfactory public service. In making this presentation an applicant should list his membership in business, church, fraternal, civic, welfare, and social groups. Emphasis should be placed on those areas where he has served as an officer or member of the board of directors. It is also advisable to list any works which have been published, as well as all awards or citations received. Many applicants attach letters of character reference from prominent personalities both in and out of the broadcast field.

6. That the technical equipment, the transmitter location, and other phases of the proposed operation comply with FCC regulations. Here again your consulting engineer's verification is needed. He will have to indicate full compliance with the separate regulations and full compliance with the requirements of good engineering practices as established by the FCC.

7. That the facility sought is not in violation in any way with the rules and regulations of the FCC and existing international agreements. In order to prevent chaos and to establish an orderly broadcasting system, the FCC has promulgated certain rules and regulations which divide the frequency spectrum and establish classes of stations and limits power. To further these objectives the United States is a party to treaties (ratified by the U.S. Senate) with other nations, notably Canada and Mexico. Under these treaties certain frequencies are allocated to each country; however, U.S. stations may operate these frequencies under certain conditions. The frequencies involved are referred to as "U.S. clears," "Mexican clears," and "Canadian clears." A complete listing of all such frequencies is readily available from the FCC.

8. That the application meets certain population standards. We discussed this problem in the preceding chapter concerning the selection of a transmitter site. Your consulting engineer can document this part of your presentation.

9. That the public interest, convenience, and necessity will be served by the proposed operation, should the permit be granted. As part of this presentation the applicant must present a full program outline for a complete or typical week of operation, clearly showing the percentage of time that will be devoted to each program category. Very careful attention should be given to this part of the application to insure complete accuracy. At the time a station applies for renewal of its license, which at the present time is every three years, the FCC will carefully compare the station's programming performance to its promises when the application was filed. It also will be of great assistance to present letters of recommendation from the leaders of the political, business, church, civic, and social welfare communities. Wherever possible these letters should indicate the areas in which you will be

providing a community service now lacking or where improvement is needed.

In the preparation of your application for a construction permit the two most important people are your consulting engineer and your attorney who will prosecute your claim before the FCC. Take their advice and suggestions seriously. I cannot stress too strongly their competency and honesty. Their knowledge and ability will save you time and money.

## "Public Notice"

At the time you file your application for a construction permit, it becomes necessary under the law that you give "public notice" of such action; that you advertise such action in a newspaper regularly serving the area in which you desire to locate your facility. If your application is for a facility in an area in which you already have a station (for an FM station where you now have an AM station, or vice versa) you must also advertise this action on your present facility, in addition to the newspaper advertisement. The FCC also requires that you maintain a reference file for public inspection.

Many people active in other businesses cannot understand the reasons for this requirement. They feel that it too often opens a "pandora's box" of trouble and travail for the applicant. The main purpose of the FCC in establishing this requirement is to insure that those interested in entering an objection to your application will be given sufficient notice and opportunity to take such action. It precludes any conjecture concerning secrecy or favoritism. It not only provides ample notice to those who might desire to object but also allows ample opportunity to those who might seek to contest your application by applying for a license in the same area even if the frequency is different. The reasoning behind the latter requirement is the Commission's responsibility to see that only the most competent and most capable applicants receive licenses so that the best possible service is provided any given area.

Just as the FCC requires that all applicants give "public notice" at the time they file their request for a construction permit, the law also requires the FCC to advise the public of the receipt of such applications. In fact, the FCC makes such announcements at least twice. The first public announcement through official channels occurs at the time the application is received, and it is officially announced again when the application is formally accepted for filing purposes. The FCC will not and cannot under the law make any further announcements or take any further action on the application until at least thirty days has elapsed from the time they notify the public that the application has been formally accepted for filing. At some time after the 30-day waiting period, the FCC will announce a "cut-off" date, which means that after midnight of the announced date the FCC will not accept any competing applications. This procedure makes it possible for any interested party anywhere in the country to present any objections or for anyone interested to compete for the right to erect the facility. It also aims towards the orderly processing of all applications without undue delay.

Inasmuch as anyone or any group may file a competing application until midnight of the cut-off date this places an added burden upon the original applicant. He must be on the alert constantly for objections and new applications. In most cases competing applications will not be filed until the last minute. The fact that you are the first to file for a facility will have little bearing on the final decision as to who receives the license, for the final decision of the FCC will be based on competency and ability in the interest of the community. Many people feel this is unfair to the first applicant because he is the one who discovered the area and the frequency. He has spent considerable time and money in preparing his application; he has advertised his action and made his files available for public inspection. Of course, all competitors have to follow the same procedures; however, they do have the advantage that they can file their application at the last minute without the fear that others will file any competing applications. Also, once it is known that a specific frequency will work in a given area, any number of competitive applications can be filed on it, often reducing by a large amount a consultant's fee for a frequency search. Therefore, the possibility of competing applications should encourage an interested party and his advisors to be extremely thorough in preparing the case.

## Your Application Is Processed

If no competing applications or objections are filed, you can look forward to receiving your construction permit without appearing before the Commission or any of its committees or staff. This will not take place overnight, though, because all applications are given a number and placed on a processing "calendar." Competing applications, though given a later number, move up the calendar with the original application so that no additional delay in caused to the first applicant.

If objections or competing applications are filed, you should be prepared for a long period of delay, usually requiring that you, your consulting engineer, and your attorney appear before various FCC bureaus. Every phase of each application is carefully scrutinized and examined. After each FCC bureau or department has completed its studies and made recommendations, all applications are assigned to a "hearing examiner" who will hold as many sessions as he deems necessary before making a decision. During these hearings it is not uncommon for FCC bureau or department personnel to appear and make opposition to any application under consideration. At these hearings all applicants are given every opportunity to present their case, indicate their opposition to other applications, and to cross examine any and all who appear.

After all considerations and hearings, a final decision is made and a construction permit issued. Where there are no objections or competing applications, and where the grant was made without a hearing, the law provides a "cooling off" period during which petitions may be filed for reconsideration of the grant. Such a petition must be filed within 30 days from the date of the grant; however, anyone filing such a petition must show good cause why objections were not filed prior to the grant. It also is not rare, in cases where there were competing applicants, to have appeals taken even after an exhausting series of hearings. Some of these appeals have been taken to the highest federal courts.

## Beginning Construction

Should you be fortunate and obtain a construction permit you must, by regulation, begin the construction of your facility within 60 days. You must plan your construction in such a manner that the facility is completed within six months of the time you start. You actually have a total of eight months to complete construction of the facility from the date the FCC reaches a decision and awards the grant. If for any valid reason you cannot begin construction within two months of the date of the grant, or complete it within the allotted time, you may apply to the Commission for an extension. Such requests when made for valid reasons are usually granted. Under no circumstances should any construction be undertaken prior to the receipt of the grant, regardless of how insignificant it may seem. There have been cases where construction permits have been withdrawn because the applicant began some construction before the construction permit was issued. I know of one case where the applicant, who had no objection or competing application on file, had to vacate his construction permit because he began construction activity before receiving his grant. Figuring that he had no opposition and that the grant was a certainty, and trying to beat the weather, he constructed the concrete pilings for his tower. A competing station already on the air in the same city, learned of the prior construction and complained to the FCC. The Commission then took the entire grant under review and consideration. Only after a long delay, and great additional expense, did the Commission rule that there were extenuating circumstances for the applicant's action and reinstated the grant.

Another word of caution. Never, never, under any circumstances make any "deals," financial or otherwise, prior to obtaining your grant without first consulting with your attorney. Most of these so-called "deals" must be reported to the FCC. Failure to do so can result in the revocation of any grant or license issued. Many times competing applicants, in order to save time and money and to expedite action on their appli-

254

cations, will merge their interests or one of the parties will withdraw his application. Everything pertaining to such action, no matter what the consideration, must be reported to the Commission. In fact, no application can be withdrawn without permission from the FCC. Once an application is filed the Commission must be kept advised of any and all matters pertaining to the application.

Simultaneous with the construction start, the applicant should apply for "call" letters. Stations east of the Mississippi River generally have call letters beginning with the letter W, and stations west of the Mississippi River have call letters beginning with the letter K. Your call letters are your identification and the letters of your choice will be granted if they are not now assigned to another facility or if no valid opposition is made to the FCC. This is strictly a matter of personal choice. Some station owners use their initials or those of a family member. Station WLIZ, Bridgeport, Connecticut, reflects one of the owner's wives names, Elizabeth. Radio Station WNAB in the same city was not "named" after the National Association of Broadcasters. It so happened that its owner, Harold Thomas, dropped into a luncheonette for some coffee and cookies. When he saw the initials NAB on the box of cookies and considered the promotion that had gone into this product he decided to apply for this identification. Most call letters indicate the state, region, or community in which the station is located. At the time your call letters are requested it is mandatory under the regulations that you notify every station within your signal area of the request and to indicate compliance with the rule by filing a copy of the notification with the Commission. The FCC will make available, upon request, an alphabetical listing by call letters of all licensed commercial broadcasting facilities.

## Equipment and Program Tests

When you have completed construction you must apply for permission to conduct equipment tests—a request practically never denied. There are specific rules to be observed in making these tests. They must be conducted by an engineer

(1st class radiotelephone licensee), preferably under the supervision of your consulting engineer, during specific periods of time. Inasmuch as your consulting engineer will be involved in this operation he will be in the best position to advise you concerning the rules and regulations. He will have to indicate that the equipment is performing according to the statements made in the engineering report at the time you filed for your construction permit.

It must be remembered that this is only an equipment test, not a program test. Program tests are permitted after equipment tests have been satisfactorily completed and you have filed for the station license.

At the time you file for your license (after equipment tests), you must show compliance with all the terms, conditions, and obligations as you set forth in your original application for your construction permit. You should receive permission to conduct program tests and the station license without difficulty, unless some new cause or circumstance requiring further action has been brought to the attention of the FCC.

## BUYING OR SELLING A STATION

Certain procedures are necessary when one seeks to sell or purchase an existing radio station. Application must be made to the FCC by both the seller and the buyer, seeking permission to transfer control from one party to another. In his application the buyer has to indicate to the Commission practically everything discussed so far. In addition, the buyer and the seller have to disclose full and complete details, financial and otherwise, pertaining to the transaction. They both have to comply with the regulations pertaining to public notification and maintain a file for public inspection.

The prospective purchaser must be cognizant of the FCC regulations which forbid him, while the application is pending, from influencing the programming of the station; nor may he, as the buyer, provide any supervision over personnel or operation of the facility until the transfer is approved.